CURFEW TO CURFEW

CURFEW TO CURFEW

S.R. Arun

Commonwealth

Curfew to Curfew

First Published : 2006

ISBN 81-311-0098-7

Published by :

Ajay Verma
For COMMONWEALTH PUBLISHERS
4831/24, Prahlad Street,
Ansari Road, Darya Ganj,
New Delhi - 110002
Ph. : 23272541, 23257835
Fax : 91- 011- 23257835
e-mail : campusbooks@hotmail.com

Typesetting by :

Arjun Computers
Delhi - 110051

Printed at :
Roshan Offset Printers
Delhi

DEDICATED

TO

RIOT VICTIMS

T. V. RAJESWAR
Governor, Uttar Pradesh

Raj Bhawan
Lucknow - 227 132

सत्यमेव जयते

FOREWORD

The State of Uttar Pradesh offers training ground for administrative and police officers due to its multifarious and peculiar conditions. The State has been witnessing communal and caste riots apart from sensitive issues like Ayodhya. The State has the largest population having geographical and cultural diversities and is therefore, prone to sensitive law and order situations.

Sri S.R. Arun, during his three and half decades of service as an I.P. S. officer, had an opportunity to deal with such situations in various capacities including that of Director General of Police of the State. His account of various law and order situations of the State gives a peep into the basic causes and direction to control them.

The book deals with various riots having genesis in labour agitation, agrarian demands, the agitation for separate "Hill State", communal and caste conflicts. The author gives detailed experiences of Curfew-like situations. Innocent and peace loving people suffer in such situations and therefore, these situations are best avoided in managing law and order problems unless it is imperative to clamp them.

The book offers an empirical study of law and order situations and I trust that it will be of use for the administrative and police officers, political leaders and others who are interested in the subject.

2/1/05

(T.V RAJESWAR)

Preface

It was the year 1959 and I was studying in the D.A.V. College, Kanpur. As a young boy doing my B.A., I had a circle of friends who really looked forward to walking across the road to the famous Green Park Stadium, which was a regular venue for international cricket matches. We, often, went to the stadium to sit on its luxuriant lawns and study for hours. Another option for similar 'outdoor activity' was the Nanarao Park.

Without much of a warning, one day our college closed down and there were not classes but the hostellers stayed back. The policemen had allegedly raped a woman named Satia, in police chowki Badshahi Naka a part of Collectorgunj police station. The people had come out on the streets to protest against this leading to some violence and imposition of curfew. On one of those idle evenings, some friends and I were strolling down to the Nanarao Park when an elderly gentleman stopped us and advised not to go any further as that area had been placed under curfew. Innocently we tried to reason with him that we had nothing to do with any dispute and we were casual walkers to the park. He must have been a patient man because he smiled at us and tried to explain to us, what curfew meant and, what its breach could lead to. Little did my friends or I understand the legal sense of the term 'curfew' but now fully educated about the repercusssions of our act, we quickly turned back.

My education about curfew and its implications really began when I entered the Indian Police Service, some years later.

The last decade of the twentieth century witnessed communal flare-ups on an unprecedented scale. The Ram Janmabhoomi agitation led by the Vishwa Hindu Parishad and supported by the Bharitya Janata Party reached its crescendo in the early years of this decade. The society had already begun to polarise on communal and caste-lines and in many towns and villages communities were snarling at each other.

In 1990, I was posted as the Inspector General of Police, Kanpur Zone. The area of responsibility included communally sensitive cities like Aligarh, Kanpur, Agra, Mathura and, Firozabad. As the agitation turned on its heat, all these cities began to boil. I recall those months as the most challenging ones in my professional life. As Aligarh became tense, curfew had to be clamped and I had to rush from Kanpur and camp there to supervise the situation. The condition had barely improved, when I got instructions from the D.G.P. to rush back to Kanpur as the city required my presence more. I started immediately and drove out of the curfew-ridden city. We were able to cover the distance in a little over four hours and as we drove into Kanpur, it's streets already looked like Aligarh's. From one curfew ridden city to another, my journey through riotous situations continued.

As Additional Director General of Police (Law and Order), U.P. just a few years later, I found myself holding fort at the holy city of Varanasi, which had seen an outbreak of caste riots. On one of those evenings, I received a call from the D.G.P. to rush to Kanpur, which was also by that time under curfew following the murder of a Dalit B.J.P. leader called *Kala Bachcha.* As if caste and religion were not enough fuel for these spiralling fires, the demand for the creation for a separate state of *Uttarakhand* began to take a violent turn. The largest cities in the hills-Dehradun and Nainital, were the most volatile. The police found itself in the extremely tough task of containing demonstrations, which soon became *Uttaranchal* had to be placed under curfew as the agitation boiled over it's top.

Indeed those were difficult times and as a senior police officer, I often found myself rushing from one curfew ridden situation to another. From 'Curfew to Curfew' I learnt the most important lessons of my life-both professional and personal. How the innocent people are used as canon fodder by the interested sections. It was always such poor people who lost their invaluable lives while, the brains behind stepped over them to gain new heights. How oldest of friends were consumed by mindless frenzy and ended up destroying each other's worlds. It also taught me lessons of human greatness. How seemingly ordinary people can muster enormous courage to defend their neighbours from the assault of their own brethren. This work is an effort to share these lessons with you.

I will feel amply rewarded, if this attempt of mine becomes of any use to readers in general and agencies engaged in handling of law and order, police officers, magistrates, politicians, social scientists, media and research scholars in particular.

I am thankful to my wife Shashi for helping me in preparing the manuscript and also for refreshing my memory here and there about various incidents which were in her knowledge. Sri Vijai Nath Singh, retired D.I.G., the then C.O. City Meerut during 1968 communal riots, has provided me several inputs, for which I am thankful to him. How can I forget to thank, Late Sri S.K. Mukerji the then I.G.P. Meerut Zone and Sri V.K. Gupta, the then S.P. City Meerut and Presently I.G.P./Assistant to D.G.P. U.P. , who were there in Meerut during serious communal riots of 1987, for helping me a lot by providing useful narrations of various incidents. I am grateful to Sri S.K. Chandra, retired D.I.G. and the then S.S.P. Moradabad, who took lot of pains in going through some of the pages of the manuscript and made very positive contributions, particularly about the B.K.U. agitation of 1988. Many erstwhile colleagues, whose names are difficult to be mentioned here, have been of great help to me as they have provided very useful inputs. My special thanks to Sri K.L. Gupta, my next-door neighbour and retired D.G.P., U.P. who went through the manuscript very carefully and made useful contributions.

Photographs of 1977 Shia-Sunni riots, then given to me by Verma Photographer, Krishna Nagar, Lucknow and Ramesh Studio, Quandari Bazar, Lucknow have been of great help and they have been displayed at appropriate places. I thankfully acknowledge their help. Sri Man Mohan Sharma, a renowned Photo Journalist of Lucknow, who had covered several incidents all over U.P., has very kindly provided me several coloured photographs, some of which have been made use of. I thankfully acknowledge his valuable contribution. I profusely thank every body for their very valuable contributions.

I am highly grateful to my relative and name sake Dr. Shri Ram Bakshi, Ph.D., D. Litt., another of several useful books, particularly about History, for going through the entire manuscript very meticulously and making it possible to present it in this shape.

I am highly indebted to HE The Governor of U.P., Sri T.V. Rajeswar for agreeing to my request for writing the *Foreword*. He has been the top police officer of the country and has a vast experience in dealing with the various problems regarding police intervention. Sri Rajeswar is a very erudite and scholarly person, who has taken great pains in going through the manuscript before writing the *Foreword*. I express my respectful thanks to him.

I gratefully acknowledge the role of my publishers Commonwealth Publishers' particularly Sri Ajay Verma and his team for presenting this book.

S.R. Arun

Abbreviations

A

A.C.	Air Conditioned / Assistant Commandant
Addl.S.P.	Additional Superintendent of Police
A.D.M.	Additional District Magistrate
A.I.R.	All India Radio
A.I.T.U.C.	All India Trade Union Congress
A.S.P.	Assistant Superintendent of Police

B

B.J.P.	Bhartiya Janta Party
B.K.U.	Bhartiya Kisan Union
B.M.	Babri Masjid
B.M.A.C.	Babri Masjid Action Committee
Bn.	Battalion
B.P.R.D.	Bureau of Police Research and Development
B.S.P.	Bahujan Samaj Party

C

C.C.	Company Commander
C.I.D.	Criminal Investigation Department
C.M.	Chief Minister
C.O.	Circle Officer
Coy.	Company

C.P.M.F.	Central Para Military Forces
C.P.T.C.	Central Police Training College
Cr.P.C.	Criminal Procedure Code
C.R.P.F.	Central Reserve Police Force

D

D.G.C.	District Government Counsel
D.G.P.	Director General of Police
D.I.G.	Deputy Inspector General of Police
D.I.R.	Defence of India Rules
D.J.	District Judge
D.M.	District Magistrate
Dy. S.P.	Deputy Superintendent of Police

E

E.O.W.	Economic Offences Wing

G

Govt.	Government

H

H.Qrs.	Head Quarters

I

I.A.S.	Indian Administrative Service
I.G.P.	Inspector General of Police
I.P.C.	Indian Penal Code
I.P.S.	Indian Police Service
I.P.	Indian Police/Imperial Police

K

K.G.M.C.	King George's Medical College

L

L.I.U.	Local Intelligence Unit

M

M.L.A.	Member Legislative Assembly

M.P.	Member of Parliament
M.Q.M.	Muttahida Quami Movement
	N
N.H.	National Highway
	O
O.B.Cs	Other Backward Castes
O.P.	Out Post
	P
P.A.C.	Pradeshik Armed Constabulary
P.C.S.	Provincial Civil Service
P.M.	Prime Minister
P.S.	Police Station
P.T.C.	Police Training College
	R
R.A.F.	Rapid Action Force
R.J.B.	Ram Janam Bhoomi
	S
S.D.M.	Sub Divisional Magistrate
S.I.	Sub Inspector
S.P.-C.B.-C.I.D.	Superintendent of Police-Crime Branch-Criminal Investigation Department
S.P. City	Superintendent of Police
S.S.P.	Senior Superintendent of Police
S.V.D.	Sanyukt Vidhayak Dal
S.C.s	Scheduled Castes
STs	Scheduled Tribes
	U
U.K.D.	Uttarakhand Kranti Dal
U.P.	Uttar Pradesh
	V
V.H.P.	Vishwa Hindu Parishad

List of Photographs and Maps

CHAPTER - 10

CHAPTER - 14

Contents

1

About Curfew

Many of us do not know precisely as to what does the curfew mean. The dictionary meaning of curfew is "the ringing of a bell at fixed evening hours after which inhabitants are not allowed to stir abroad". 'Curfew order' means an official order not to come out of the house after the sun set. Curfew has not been defined in legal terminology but its expression is understood very well by the citizens. Legally speaking curfew is a direction issued by the competent magistrate under section 144 of the Criminal Procedure Code.

Chapter X of the Criminal Procedure Code 1973 deals with "Maintenance of public order and Tranquility". While part 'A' relates to 'unlawful assemblies', part 'B' deals with 'public nuisance', part 'C ' with 'urgent cases of nuisance or apprehended danger' and part 'D' with 'disputes as to immovable property'. Under part 'C' is Section 144 which relates to 'power to issue order in urgent cases of nuisance or apprehended danger'. In cases where there is sufficient ground for proceeding under this section and immediate or speedy remedy is desirable the District Magistrate, the Sub-Divisional Magistrate or any other Executive Magistrate specially empowered by the State Government in this behalf, may, by a written order stating the material facts of the case and served in the prescribed manner 'direct any person to abstain from a certain act or to take certain order with respect to certain property in his possession or under his management, if such Magistrate considers that such direction is likely to prevent, or tends to prevent, obstruction, annoyance or injury to any person lawfully employed, or danger to human life, health or safety, or a disturbance of the public tranquility, or a riot, or an affray. An order can be passed *ex-parte* in cases of emergency or where the circumstances do not permit of the serving of the notice on the person against whom the order is directed. An order under this section may be directed against a particular individual, or to a person residing in a particular place or area, or to the public generally when frequenting or visiting a particular place or area. Such order remains in force for two months unless withdrawn earlier or extended by the State Government by a notification for such further period not exceeding six months.

Curfew is usually directed to public to remain indoors with a view to control the riotous situations. Breach of the order under this section is punishable under Section 188 IPC. Usually curfew is clamped on serious breach of peace but pre-emptive curfew can also be imposed if the situation so demands. A foreign research scholar asked me recently as to what is undeclared curfew. In law there is nothing like undeclared curfew. At times Magistrates and police officers, with a view to avoid panic and publicity, in order to control the worsening situation for the time being in a particular area/segment, tell the people to remain indoors which creates curfew like situation and as soon as the things normalise, the usual life is restored.

Janta Curfew

Certain parties give call for public curfew on a given day and time to oppose the policies of the ruling party or the ruling party presses for mobilising public opinion in their favour. In such situations the administration and the local authorities want the normal life to continue but those giving such call of '*Janta Curfew*' come out in streets to appeal and often intimidate the people to remain indoors and to keep their shops and business establishments closed. This kind of curfew has no legal sanctity and is often not endorsed by the general public.

Area under Curfew

Stone Pelting Crowd

Police Chasing the Crowd

Deserted Vegetable Market

Burnt Shops

Fire Fighting

Removing Patient to Hospital

Area under Curfew

Quick Bath During Curfew

Curfew Bound Locality

2

Modinagar Labour Riots – 1967

In February, 1967, immediately on completion of the general elections to the Lok Sabha and U.P. Vidhan Sabha, I was promoted from the post of ASP Bareilly and posted as Additional Superintendent of Police Meerut on my first promotion to senior scale of the IPS after having put in about three-and -half years of service . The District Meerut used to have 35 Police Stations including 6 P.S.s of Meerut city under the charge of a Deputy Superintendent of Police known as C.O.City whose work was directly supervised by the S.S.P. Remaining 29 P.S.s fell in rural area of which I was the supervisory officer subject to overall control, command and guidance of the Senior Superintendent of Police. There were 7 Tehsils namely (1) Meerut Sadar, (2) Mawana, (3) Sardhana, (4) Baghpat, (5) Ghaziabad, (6) Hapur and (7) Garhmukteshwar. Ghaziabad had a resident Sub Divisional Magistrate generally an IAS officer and a Deputy Superintendent of Police of sufficient seniority. This C.O. used to supervise the work of (1) Sahibabad, (2) Ghaziabad Kotwali, (3)Sihanigate, (4) Muradnagar and (5) Mussoori Police Stations under the control of the Addl.S.P., whereas Modinagar Police Station of this Tehsil was directly supervised by the Additional S.P. The Meerut District has now been truncated into four districts namely (1) Meerut, (2) Baghpat, (3) Ghaziabad and (4) Gautambudh Nagar (NOIDA).

Modinagar is situated on Delhi-Haridwar highway, about 25 KMs north of Ghaziabad and about 20 KMs south of Meerut.

Modinagar, mainly an industrial town, was having various Modi Group of industries and sizable population of factory workers. On either side of this road were residential areas including labour colonies. Modi's residence and police station Modinagar were also situated on the main road towards Delhi. There was no road diversion on the highway, hence any road blockade used to cause serious traffic problems.

All the factories used to have labour trouble, but Modi Spinning and Weaving Mills, popularly known as *'Kapra Mill'* (Established in 1946 and commissioned in 1949) having about 9,000 workers, was always in focus due to agitations launched by the leftist trade union *'Karmchari Union'*. From August, 1967 onwards the labour movement started intensifying and there were periodical calls for agitation in this factory, but the district administration avoided confrontation and asked the Labour Department to sort out the problems.

Murder Exploited

In September, 1967, *'dharna and gherao'* agitations continued and labour union leaders also sat on hunger strike for several days. Sardar Satnam Singh, one of the trade union activist who also used to sit on *dharna*, was found murdered on the morning of October 5, 1967, in his labour quarter and quite a few thousand workers collected there demanding immediate arrest of Modis as according to them they were the murderers. The Inspector in-charge Police Station Modinagar, who had come for court evidence to Meerut got this news there on telephone from his P.S. and immediately informed me personally about this case that morning. We immediately left for the scene of occurrence in my Fargo Pickup. On reaching the locality we were stopped by the crowd saying that we were all men of Modis as we used their diaries, pens etc. which they gave us as gifts. I brought out my diary and pen and waived it to the crowd telling them that none of the items were gifted to me either by Modis or any body else and they were supplied to me by my office. We were allowed to reach the labour quarter where the dead body was lying but we were prevented from entering it as the crowd demanded that Modis be first arrested and produced before the crowd. We tried to persuade the crowd to see reason and allow us to go inside so that we could examine the scene of occurrence and start further action. On this the crowd started demanding that police dogs be summoned before we enter the quarter. I asked them as to how many persons had been inside the quarter since this morning. I was told that several persons from the crowd have been inside. I told them that police dogs are to be given smell from the object supposedly touched by the culprit or footprints left by the suspect. Since several persons had been inside, there was possibility that the dog might pickup the smell of any body who had visited the place after the occurrence and in that case they will have to allow the police to pick up that person as possible culprit of this murder. The crowd was not prepared for this kind of reaction from us. After great persuasion we were allowed to go inside. The quarter had two rooms, a verandah, a kitchen and a toilet. Several persons including wife of the deceased with a small son were sitting and weeping in the verandah. We consoled them and told that the real culprits will not be spared by the police. On close examination we found that two cots were lying in one room. The dead body was lying on a comparatively inferior bedding whereas the cot with better bedding was vacant but it wore wrinkles, indicating that some guest was there with him as he (deceased) might have offered better hospitality to him. We, on enquiry, were told that the deceased was seen in the company of another *Sardar* (Sikh) at a *pan* (betel) shop near his residence that evening and he had returned there after witnessing *Ramlila*. On further probe we learnt that the father-in-law of the deceased was a *granthi* (priest) in a *Gurudwara* at Muradnagar and Satnam's wife was there that night and was brought to Modinagar on getting the information of this murder. A *Sardar* (Sikh) boy who, was seen in the company of Satnam Singh that evening was also residing in Muradnagar. A Sub Inspector went to Muradnagar, which is a few kilometers away from there, and returned about an hour later with that Sardar, who was still bearing the blood-stained clothes. He confessed of having committed this murder as he was in love with the wife of the deceased, who had sent him that evening to Modinagar to finish her husband so that thereafter they could enjoy themselves and marry in due course. Though, we solved this murder and avoided confrontation for the time being but the labour unrest kept on increasing and the mill owners declared lockout in December, 1967.

Location of the Mill

The Modi Spinning and Weaving Mills was located on Delhi – Meerut road on the west and its main gate opened right

Modi Mill

on the road. Towards east were the residential colonies, a park, some open plots and few buildings under construction, towards south the highway having shops on both the sides and the residential colonies, towards north the highway and a wide *nullah* (drain) with a wide culvert and residential areas. There was lot of space on the three sides for the crowd to collect but towards west of the road, there was hardly any space except the pavement and the high wall of the factory. The highway was very busy and the only traffic lifeline, hence it could not be closed. There was lot of space inside the factory which had four units, namely, A, B,C and D.

Tension Mounted and Lock out Declared

However during the month of October the trouble continued and the management and the labour union used to have their bouts of disputes. Prohibitory orders under section 144 Cr.P.C. were issued in November. For a few weeks the workers continued with their agitation and the tension kept on increasing gradually.

The strike notice was given by the union to stop work from 19th December. Even the conciliatory efforts of the Labour Department officials could not solve the problem. On December 26, the workers stopped working in all the four units of the *Kapra Mill* which continued on 27th also. The management declared the lockout on 27th but the workers refused to leave the factory. The next shift also was there and got ready to enter and join the striking fellow workers. This created very tense moments but we could succeed in persuading the strikers to leave the factory premises late in the night. The trade union leaders started demanding that the management including essential services staff should also not be allowed to function as the lockout meant total stoppage of all the work and complete shut down of the factory, whereas the Management and the Labour Department explained that under lockout rules the essential services were exempted. This became the major rallying point for the striking workers and the trade union leaders exhorted that either nobody or everybody goes inside the Mill. The call, for stopping the entry of the essential services staff and the management on December 29, was given and hectic preparations started.

Administrative Preparations

I and my counterpart Magistrate Sri B.D. Gupta, PCS, Additional District Magistrate (Executive) Meerut, S.D.M. Ghaziabad Sri A.P. Singh (IAS-1964), other functionaries of the Tehsil, the Police Station and the Labour Department used to meet often to discuss matters with the management and the Trade Union leaders so that the situation could be defused and amicable solution found. Sri S.P. Watal the District Magistrate and Sri R.D. Pandey the Senior Superintendent of Police were fully briefed and kept informed by us. Both of them were seasoned and mature officials who commanded lot of respect and co-operation of the public and the subordinates. They used to give us valuable and useful tips about handling of this problem. Whereas I and Sri A.P. Singh were very young and raw, Sri B.D. Gupta was a dedicated, experienced, and fine officer .Sri Sardar Hussain Inspector in-charge was again a fine specimen of a police officer. Taken together we formed a good team combining experience, youth and dedication. Our seniors reposed full faith in us. As the appointed date of confrontation started approaching, we also made preparations to meet the unforeseen complex situations and called for extra manpower and resources. I refreshed myself about the rules and the riot control drill, which was taught to us during training at Central Police Training College Mount Abu (Rajasthan) in 1964 and Police Training College Moradabad (U.P.) in 1965.

The "D" Day

Finally the talks failed with the workers and the management and our efforts for amicable solution did not fructify. While the management was to carry on with the maintenance of essential services, the workers threw the challenge that they will stop the essential services and the management staff from entering the factory on the morning of December 29, 1967.Our job was to see that the law and order was not disturbed and the peace was maintained . The police and the PAC were deployed at strategic places and heavy deployment was also made on the road in front of the Mill for the dual purpose of the show of force and also as striking reserve.

On the fateful winter cloudy morning I along with ADM Sri Gupta reached Modinagar, whereas Sri A.P. Singh joined us from Ghaziabad. We went around the town and the likely places of trouble, took stock of the latest situation and also checked the police arrangements. Finally we stationed ourselves on the road near the main gate of the factory where PAC and policemen were also kept in reserve. Till then the police were not provided with the mobile wireless sets and therefore, the means of communication available to us were the nearest telephone at the factory gate and the runners on cycles/motor cycles. Police Station Modinagar was about one kilometer away from there which had a telephone. Meanwhile the workers had started collecting in groups on all the sides who were told to disperse. As we were waiting, we saw few essential services staff walking on the road from the southern side towards the main gate who were stopped by the workers telling them that they should go back as the lockout was total and they will not be allowed to proceed further. When they insisted to proceed they were abused, manhandled and beaten. The police intervened, arrested some of them and made them sit in a truck to be taken to police station. On this the crowd, which had started swelling by then, resisted and did not allow the truck to proceed further and the truck had to be reversed to the spot where we were waiting. We managed to get Sri S.P. Watal, the D.M. on phone at Meerut from the factory gate and apprised him of the grim situation. He instructed us to handle it as best as we could. The S.S.P. could not be immediately contacted but the D.M. told us that he will inform him. Before we could react the crowd started marching menacingly ahead demanding that their fellow workers be freed. The brickbatting on us had also started and the slogan shouting crowd came closer to the truck and succeeded in taking away the arrested persons who too had jumped and disappeared in the crowd. The police and the PAC continued to struggle as the brickbatting, throwing of bamboo sticks and the iron rods etc. picked up from the nearby construction sites, was intensified by the rioters. We gave repeated warnings but the crowd did not budge. The ADM ordered the use of tear gas which was thrown and fired but did not have much effect as the wind direction was unfavourable. The *lathi* (cane) charge after repeated warnings also had no effect.

Several police and PAC men got serious injuries. Sri Surendra Sharma Company Commander PAC was hit on the nose by an iron rod thrown by the rioters and that caused serious bleeding and cut of the nostril. As I was busy in handling the situation, some body threw an iron rod at me but I was not aware of that. Before it could hit me directly on the head, the PAC truck driver saw it and he gave me a push to one side which saved me from getting severe injury but in the process he got injured. The crowd also fired few shots, perhaps from the country made weapons. We kept on giving repeated warnings but the crowd did not disperse as a result we had to resort to firing. When a few shots were fired and a section of the crowd started dispersing, but the crowd in other directions kept on rioting causing injuries. A few more rounds had to be fired which left one dead on the spot and some injured, who were taken to hospitals by the rioters and also by the police and four of them died bringing total deaths to five. Besides several policemen, PAC *Jawans* (soldiers), Magistrates received injuries, who were subsequently taken to hospitals for treatment. I also received serious injuries in my hands, legs and feet but did not immediately feel them as I remained much engaged in tackling the difficult situation as I was the senior most police officer present on the spot.

About half an hour later Sri R.N. Mehrotra Dy. S.P. arrived with additional manpower and resources from Meerut. D.M. Sri

Watal and S.S.P. Sri Pandey also arrived. They enquired about the latest situation and took control of further arrangements. Sri Pandey took me inside the factory and made me sit on the lawns as he saw me exhausted. He told my driver, who was there, to take off my shoes. He kept on telling me that we should not worry as he would take care of us all. A few minutes later, I started feeling severe pain in my body particularly in the right elbow and the left ankle. I could not put on my shoes as the foot had swellen by then. He sent me to District Hospital Meerut, though I insisted on staying back, as my presence was needed more at the spot. My family members, particularly my mother and wife were waiting with anxiety when I reached the hospital. I can imagine the plight of the family members of other injured, both workers and security personnel.

Curfew Clamped

The curfew was clamped which was later on lifted as soon as the situation came under control.

Traffic Stopped

Seeing the crowd and the ongoing situation, the traffic had stopped a few meters away. The traffic was also stopped near P.S. Modinagar. Subsequently it was cleared and diverted via longer route on Hapur road.

The Media

There was no important newspaper either from Meerut or Ghaziabad, and Delhi used to cover western U.P. All India Radio was there but Television coverage had not come up. Videotapes were unknown. Delhi media had rushed for coverage. The District Magistrate briefed the press and also issued the press statement regarding the whole incident.

Visits by Politicians

It was SVD (Sanyukt Vidhayak Dal) Government in U.P. with Chaudhary Charan Singh as Chief Minister. Sri Prabhu Narain Singh, a socialist, was the Labour Minister. Several politicians including the veteran leftist labour leader Mr. S.A. Dange visited Modinagar and the injured in the District Hospital. None of them thought it fit to see the injured police and PAC men. When Sri Prabhu Narain Singh was taking the round of the District

Hospital, I was expecting him to come to me also, as he was a member of the Cabinet and I had also sustained fractures and the Doctors had apprised him about my presence there. Perhaps we were considered as the anti-labour people. It was indeed both sad and demoralising for the Administration.

The Judicial Enquiry

The U.P. Government ordered a judicial enquiry into this incident. I was discharged from the hospital after ten days but my foot was still troubling. One evening Sri R.D. Pandey took me to Modinagar so that I could give him spot briefing. On way he kept on assuring me that, as we had acted in good faith and with sincerity towards duty nothing was likely to go against us but our preparations should be very thorough and nearest to the truth. I briefed him in detail at the site and he gave me very useful practical tips.

Sri Prem Prakash, the District Judge Muzaffarnagar was appointed as the enquiry judge, who was asked to submit his report in six months. He was a short statured person but a thorough professional. He later on became the Law Secretary and the Legal Rememberencer U.P. and subsequently rose to Judgeship of Allahabad High Court. Sri Data Ram Singhal, the District Government Counsel (Criminal), Meerut , who was really the learned counsel defended the District Administration. Sri R.K. Garg, the Supreme Court Advocate, and a committed communist comrade, represented the workers. All of us had to work very hard as the Enquiry Judge was not only very thorough but also fully committed to the time schedule of six months. He held sittings in Meerut and Muzaffarnagar. Sri S.A. Dange, Vice President of the World Federation of the Trade Unions and the General Secretary of the AITUC (All India Trade Union Congress) besides other local *'Karamchari Union'* leaders appeared on behalf of the workers, Sri K.N. Modi , Vice Chairman and Director Managing Agents, Modi Spinning and Weaving Mills appeared for the management, Sri S.P. Watal, D.M. and Sri B.D. Gupta represented the District Administration, whereas I and Inspector Sardar Husain were the star witnesses for the District Police. At the arguments stage, Sri Kanhaiya Lal Mishra, legal luminary and Advocate General U.P. was to appear. Initially he was reluctant to come as the Advocate General did not appear in a Court below the High Court. With lot of persuasion and repeated requests he agreed to appear. I and Sri B.D. Gupta went to Allahabad to brief him but he could not find time for us. He asked us to come to Allahabad again and accompany him in the same train. He used to get briefing in the running train. I fell ill and could not go to Allahabad but Sri Gupta had gone who accompanied him in the train and briefed him there. Sri Mishra finally argued our case for four days. The Enquiry Report was given within six months. Since we were not called upon to explain subsequently, we thought that our actions were found justified.

Though, we stood exonerated, I always felt sorry for those who lost their lives. I really do not know as to what ought to have been done to avoid the loss of precious human lives, particularly of the poor workers who were the bread-earners for their families.

3

Firozabad Communal Riots

Firozabad was part of District Agra till 1989. It is situated on Moghul Road, National Highway No. 2 and on Delhi- Kolkatta Railway route. This was created as new district on 5-2-1989, after carving out certain areas from Districts Agra and Mainpuri. Firozabad is the district head quarter. Tundla and Shikohabad are the other important towns. Firozabad is famous for glass works particularly for chandeliers and bangles. Bangles are worn by females of all ages, girls, married women and widows, of course the colours and designs change for each category, particularly widows. Good quality bangles are worn by married women and that is why it is also called *'Suhag Nagri'*. It supplies bangles to most of the places in India particularly in northern India. Shikohabad is also known for glass works. Tundla is important Railway Junction on Delhi-Howrah route. River Yamuna flows towards south of these towns and certain areas falling in the belt of this river have ravines where dacoits have been finding shelter and the belt was known for kidnappings for ransom, serious murders and dacoities. Outlaws calling themselves as *'Bagis'* (rebels) have been committing such crimes after forming formidable dacoit gangs.

According to year 2001 census Firozabad City has population of 5,10,800 out of which 48% are Hindus and others and 52% are Muslims. It has sizeable population of Jains, who are mainly engaged in trade and commerce and many of them thrive on Muslim workforce. Both the communities are engaged in glass works and have been living peacefully except when they were provoked and passions aroused on communal lines by calls and counter-calls on certain issues, necessarily not being local ones. Firozabad had been communally sensitive place, where riots took place in years 1936, 1947, 1962, 1972, 1992 and 1993. In 1990 on call for *'Kar Seva'*, there was lot of tension and curfew was clamped to pre-empt the serious riots.

I was Commandant XII Battalion PAC Fatehpur which was raised in June, 1971 and I had the privilege of being the founder Commandant of this Unit. We remained deployed at Bangaldesh borders in West Bengal for Refugee duties from June, 1971 to January 1972 at the time of 1971 Indo-Pak war. On repatriation our Bn. was located at Fatehpur (between Kanpur and Allahabad) where we were provided some old and dilapidated buildings vacated by local Judiciary. Our *Jawans* lived in tents and some of the senior officers lived in makeshift buildings. For us duty at borders was difficult and nobody was allowed to keep the family. Jawans could not be provided family accommodation and some of them hired private houses in Fatehpur town. Life was difficult here also but our morale remained high.

One evening of June 16, 1972, I returned to my residence after a round of my Battalion, and playing badminton. Around 9 P.M. I received a phone call from Mr. A.K. Dass I.P., I.G.P. (U.P. Police Chief). He told me that Firozabad had serious riots that day and I must reach Firozabad at the earliest for law and order duty there. He also permitted me to take jeep with a guard. I quickly got ready and called for the PAC guard and we left Fatehpur by road same evening. By the time we reached Kannauj, all of us were feeling sleepy, we halted at a Petrol Pump for some rest. I stretched myself on the seat of the jeep, while driver and Jawans lied down on ground. Then there used to be no motels or road side *'dhabas'* with cots for rest as they are available now. After about one hour's rest we left and reached Firozabad around 5 a.m.

On way to Kotwali Firozabad we found the city under curfew and roads littered with brickbats. I went to Police Station Kotwali Firozabad and reported for duty. On enquiry as to what had happened, I was told that on Friday, June 16, after *Namaz* at *Jama Masjid* the agitated Muslim crowd went berserk and indulged in rioting, arson and attack on policemen. This happened in protest against the 'Aligarh Muslim University Bill' brought by Government of India. Muslims kept their shops closed, hoisted black flags on their buildings, and wore black arm-bands while going for Friday prayers. About 4,000 Muslims offered Namaz and while they were dispersing, some of them got violent, raised objectionable slogans, attacked policemen on duty, set the *Poorab* (Eastern) police outpost on fire and looted belongings of the staff there. At other places also, incidents of arson, loot and attack took place and police had to resort to use of force including firing to disperse the rioters.

I was told that no place was readily available for our stay. Officers from other places also started coming. Little later we were taken to Jain *Dharamshala*, in the campus of famous Jain temple, where rooms were made available for our stay. I had carried my kitchen box and the orderly, who cooked food for me but subsequently a common kitchen was run and all the officers who had come from outside were eating there only. The system proved very useful and we gladly paid the mess bill.

After getting ready on 17th morning I went to PWD Inspection House to call on the senior officers. There I met Sri Onkar Sharma, S.S.P. Agra, Sri Pratap Singh DM Agra, Sri Shiv Swarup DIG Police, Agra Range and Sri R.S. Jauhari Divisional Commissioner Agra. They briefed me about the incidents that had taken place and the duty that I was required to perform. Sri Shiv Swarup, a very experienced, competent, witty and man of unimpeachable integrity, was my S.S.P. Meerut in 1967 and had a liking for me as I had worked under him as Additional Superintendent of Police Meerut. He told me that forces are reporting from various places and they need to be utilised properly under proper supervision and control, so that riots are controlled as early as possible. Sri Jauhari was very experienced, intelligent and professionally competent officer, who used to give me very practical tips. For Sri Onkar Sharma, it could be said that" *Sir mundate hi oley pade*"(Rain of hailstorm soon after head shave off) as he was posted to this District only a few weeks ago. Sri Pratap Singh D.M. was polite, very considerate to every body but was a hard task master.

As I had some experience of Meerut communal riots of 1968, I decided to familiarise myself of the places and the local problems including role of local police, who initially handled the riots on the first day. I along with local guide went around the city to see the topography, *mohallas*, particularly the predominantly Hindu and Muslim localities and also the mixed areas which needed greater attention. I saw the places where incidents of rioting, loot, arson and damage to religious places, particularly mosques and temples, killings, attack on police personnel and also police firing had taken place. As the day progressed information started pouring in about incidents that were taking place in several localities. It was time to react immediately and all the senior officers, police and Magistrates had a very tough time. That day incidents of 3 murders and 7 arsons were reported some of which had occurred on the previous night of 16/17-6-1972.

The orders in writing about duties etc. of the police force, PAC and the outside officers were not available till then as things had happened all of a sudden. I being the second senior most police officer after Sri Onkar Sharma, was given the task of drafting the orders on behalf of S.S.P.. After getting free from the day's hectic work, I sat at Kotwali with the local Inspector and the Deputy Superintendent of Police, who assisted me in drafting the orders. I went to Inspection House next morning with the draft, which was seen and approved by the senior officers there. Sri Onkar Sharma signed them and the same were circulated to all concerned. The duties were distributed shift wise so that forces and supervisory officers could get time for food and rest.

Things started coming under control but stray incidents of arson, attack and murders continued during next two nights. Regular briefing meetings of officers (Magistrates/ Police/ PAC / Fire Brigade/local civic services etc.) before the change of morning and evening shifts, were held where DM and S.S.P. used to take stock of the situation of the twelve hourly shift and necessary instructions about *'do's'* and *'don'ts'* for the next shift were given. Civic problems about sanitation, distribution of rations in curfew bound areas, treatment of the sick and injured etc. was taken care of by the local administration. Curfew used to be relaxed in phases, till the situation normalised. The traffic on national highway being very heavy, could not be stopped or diverted on any other route and had to go on the recently constructed bypass road, which passed through outskirts of the city. There were a very few houses towards northern side of this road but it needed constant patrolling and vigil so that no untoward incident took place with traffic, particularly truck drivers. Delhi-Howrah railway line and Firozabad railway station were paid adequate attention. *Mohallas* across the railway line were also affected and regular attention was paid to that area. I had also to visit Makkhanpur area where some tension arose between glass factory workers. The adjoining areas and outskirts of Firozabad were given attention as people coming and going were likely to be affected. To check likely fall out at other places, particularly Agra City, DM/S.S.P. had to concentrate there also and I was required to hold the fort in their absence.

Local administration started holding Peace Committee meetings with persons of both the communities. Administration also started removing the riot-hit scars, particularly brickbats, burnt items and repair of damaged religious places etc. Muslims complained against police high-handedness and indiscriminate use of force particularly firing on Muslim crowds. Whereas they also wore grudge against Hindus for arson and destruction of their mosques, and failure of police to protect them, Hindus too complained of avoidable Muslim aggression. Regular efforts helped in restoration of normalcy.

Sri Kamla Pati Tripathi, the Chief Minister, U.P. visited this town and went around the riot-hit areas. His interaction with local people, particularly Muslims and announcement of repair of damaged places at Government cost, had a great healing touch. He left by train from Tundla for Lucknow in first class as there were no AC coaches then and I was deputed to escort and see him off there. His visit to Firozabad went a long way in restoration of early normalcy.

Coming to lighter part of our stay there, those of us, who were not on duty, used to have our lunch and dinner together. Lot of experience sharing and cutting of jokes used to take place. Sri R.S. Tolia, Assistant Commandant of 24th Bn. PAC Moradabad. an elderly, witty and humorous person, used to make us laugh by narrating his experiences in funny ways. He was very strict in his duties. Sri Radhey Shyam, Assistant Superintendent of Police Agra, who also stayed with us, took care of our welfare including messing and also used to provoke Sri Tolia, for coming out with humorous stories. On the whole it was a nice experience for a young officer like me. I left for my

Unit at Fatehpur after about a fortnight's duty. Incidentally no person of my PAC Bn. was deployed there.

Sri R.S. Jauhari, IAS, the then Divisional Commissioner Agra, is presently living in Lucknow. Though my association with him started at Firozabad only, he has been very nice to me thereafter. Whenever we meet, he never forgets to talk of these riots

I was Inspector General of Police of Kanpur Zone in 1990-91 and Firozabad also fell in my jurisdiction. The Vishwa Hindu Parishad call for *'Kar Seva'* at Ayodhya in October, 1990, created communal tension every where and I had to visit all the sensitive places of my Zone. Whatever I had known of this place earlier, I passed on my experiences to local officers. I must say that they took lot of pains in maintaining peace at that point of time, though many cities and towns were put under curfew and Firozabad was no exception.

After demolition of disputed structure at Ayodhya on December 6, 1992 by the *Kar Sevaks*, like several places in India, Firozabad too had riots which took a very heavy toll of lives and property. At that time I was posted as Inspector General of Police, Economic Offences Wing, CID Lucknow and had nothing to do with the maintenance of law and order but I used to observe the happenings with concern. Since 1992, this place has been free from riots and people are living in peace. I wish that peace prevails for ever.

4

Lucknow Shia-Sunni Sectarian Problem and Solution (1888 – 1998)

Lucknow City is situated on either side of river Gomti and has played a significent role in various fields. It was capital of Shia rulers of *Avadh* and subsequently of the British regime and is presently the capital of Uttar Pradesh. Lucknow played crucial role during the war of India's independence. It has been an important seat of learning and has institutions like Lucknow University, King George's Medical College (now University), which has produced renowned doctors, Bhatkhande College of Dance and Music, Da-ul-Muballighin, world famous Dar-ul-Uloom-Nadwa-tul-Ulema (Nadwa), and Shia institution 'Sultan-ul-Madaris'. Lucknow has given several literary figures like, Sauda, Mir Taqi Mir, Mirza Dabir, Mir Anis, Nasikh Lukhnawi, Pandit Brij Narain Chakbast and Daya Shankar Nasim in Urdu and Hindi writers like Bhagwati Charan Varma, Yash Pal, Amrit Lal Nagar, Shri Lal Shukla and K.P. Saksena (Satirist) etc. In Islamic theology, Maulana Abul Hasan Ali Nadwi fondly remembered as Ali Mian (Sunni) and Maulana Kalbe Abid (Shia) were international figures. 'Lucknow Gharana' of dance is very popular and famous dancers Birjoo Maharaj and Ahmad Jan Thirkua were known world over. Who does not know Beghum Akhtar, the queen of Ghazals and film maker Muzaffar Ali, producer of several hit films on art and culture of his city

Lucknow. Clothes having work of *Kaamdani, Zardozi and Chikankari* (embroidery) are very popular and they provide lot of job opportunities, particularly to Muslim ladies and girls. Lucknow has been electing Sri Atal Bihari Vajpayee, former Prime Minister, as Member Lok Sabha.

Lucknow city is known for *Ganga-Jamuni Tehzib* (composite culture) and traditions of *Nafasat* (elegance), *Nazakat* (delicate), *'Pahle Aap' 'Pahle Aap'*(After You- After You). That is why on arrival at Lucknow Railway Station one is greeted by the words; *'Muskaraeye ki Aap Lucknow mein hain'* (Smile that you are in Lucknow). Shias remained the rulers of Avadh with Faizabad as Capital which was subsequently shifted to Lucknow. Sunnis, though in majority, were the subjects as were the other communities. The Hindu-Muslim amity and friendship was cited as example for other places. Despite all this the two sects have

Lucknow Railway Station

differed on certain matters and they had not been seeing eye to eye with each other. There are certain things which differentiate them from each other like dresses. Whereas Shia Maulanas would usually wear sherwani (a kind of coat), black gowns and put on black/white turbans (*pagris*), Sunni Maulanas would wear green, blue or white turbans with *achakan/sherwani*. During mourning period from Moharram to Chehallum, Shias would wear black clothes. Common Sunnis would generally wear *lungis* (long cloth) but Shias would not do so at all. Sunnis wear *pyjamas* (trousers) which should not touch the ankles but there is no such requirement for Shias. Sunnis generally keep flowing beard but Shias keep trimmed beard which could be seen from 40 steps. While offering Namaz Sunnis keep their hands folded keeping them near navels whereas Shias keep their hands hanging downwards. For performing marriages usually presence of two *maulvies* (priests) and exceptionally of one is required in Shias, but in case of Sunnis only one *maulvy* is needed and even if one is not present, ritual could be performed by any one who knows basics of Islam. While teasing each other, Shias raise one finger, signifying their faith in one caliph only namely Hazrat Ali - Ibne-Abitalib also known as Hazrat Ali Murtaza, whereas Sunnis raise four fingers, indicating that they believe in all the four caliphs namely Hazrat Abu Bakr Siddiq, Hazrat Umar Farooq, Hazrat Usman Ghani and Hazrat Ali Murtaza. All this is done during local sectarian tensions only. Slaughtering of animals and selling meat is mainly the profession of Sunni butchers called *Qasais/ Chikwas* and Shias also buy it from them.

In 1977, of the total 3 lakh Muslim population of this city, about 75% were the Sunnis, called *'Ahle Sunnat'* and 25% Shias known as *'Ahle Shias'*. There are sizable pockets of each of the two sects in the old City, situated close to each other, where they often clashed, particularly between 18th of *Ramzan* to 21st of *Ramzan* (Martrydom of Hazrat Ali) and then from 1st of Moharram to 12th of Rabi-ul-Awwal (Barabafat-Birth Day of Prophet Mohammad). Local administration had to remain very alert and on tenterhooks during this period of about six months and D.M./S.S.P. also spent most of their time in Kotwali Chowk, personally supervising the law and order arrangements. It would be better to know the background of the sectarian problem of Lucknow, so that we could properly appreciate the discussions and references made in the following pages.

The Faith

I neither intend to hurt any body's susceptibilities nor do I know much about the origin of Islam, yet I am trying to mention few points, which were projected from time to time, by the leaders of the two sects, before the administration. In 567 A.D. Mohammad (PBH) was born as a posthumous child of Abdullah in Mecca (Arabia). In 607 A.D. He attained priesthood and started preaching that all human beings were equal and there was only one God i.e. *Allah*; but tribesmen of Mecca planned to kill Him as they did not endorse his preachings. *Allah* directed Him to leave Mecca, following which He migrated to Madina and new Islamic calendar *'Hijra'*, started with his *Hijrat* (migration) to Madina. In historical perspective, the Shia-Sunni dispute started with the issue of rightful successors (*Khilafat or caliphate*) to Prophet Hazrat Mohammad after his death. Sunnis regard all the four caliphs, namely (1) Hazrat Abu Bakr Siddiq (632 A.D.), (2) Hazrat Umar Farooq (634 A.D.), (3) Hazrat Usman Ghani (644 A.D.) and (4) Hazrat Ali (656 A.D.), as rightful successors, whereas, Shias regard Hazrat Ali (first cousin of Prophet Mohammad and husband of Fatima, youngest daughter of the Prophet) as only successor to Prophet and feel that three others were usurpers. As Moawia, son of Abu Sufian, Governor of Syria, did not accept Hazrat Ali as caliph, he fought battle with him. Hazrat Ali, while offering morning prayers at 4 a.m. at Kufa mosque, was attacked on 19th of *Ramzan*, who subsequently died on 21st of Ramzan at 4 a.m. and Yazid son of Moawia usurped power. Hazrat Hussain, grand son of Prophet Mohammad, was invited to visit Kufa, and while he, along with his 72 male companions, besides women and children, some of whom were aged only 6 months including Hazrat Asghar, was on his way; they were intercepted by the army of Yazid and a battle was fought at Karbala. where even food and water was denied. Whereas, Sunnis hold *'Madeh-e-Sahaba'* congregations in praise of all the four caliphs, Shias refrain from *'Madeh'* and they at the same time deprecate and denounce Yazid, the Governor of Syria, before whom Zanabe Zainab (sister of Hazrat Imam Hussain) was produced in chains after massacre of Hazrat Imam Hussain and his companions. Most of the Sunnis observe Moharram to commemorate the event of war between Yazid and Imam Hussain (son of Hazrat Ali) at Karbala in 680 A.D. symbolising victory of truth over evil, because they believe that *"qatle Hussain asal mein marge Yazid Hai; Islam zinda hota hai har Karbala ke bad"* (martyrdom of Hussain is in fact the death of Yazid; Islam emerges alive after every Karbala). During Moharram, Shias commemorate the martyrdom of Hazrat Imam Hussain and his family at Karbala, as the cruelest and saddest historical event.

Lucknow Followers

All the festivals of Muslims, both of Shias and Sunnis are celebrated according to dates of lunar calendar except *Nauroz* (similar to Holi), which is celebrated on 21st of March each year by Shias. Whereas the sighting of the new moon is announced by the Maulana of Firangi Mahal for the Sunnis, the same is done by the *'Chand Committee'* consisting of important Shia Maulanas. In old city Shias took out hundreds of processions spread over few weeks in a year which were managed by various *Anjumans* (Committee). On sighting of the new moon every month *'Nauchandi'* processions were taken out on *Jumerat* (Thursday), *Juma* (Friday) and *Hafta* (Saturday) which used to pass through the densely populated Sunni mohallas, particularly Patanala and 'Pul Ghulam Hussain' where names of all the four *Caliphs* were written on the mosques which caused irritation to Shias. Some times to tease the Sunnis, the Shias would raise objectionable slogans, referred by some of them as *'tabarra'* in a manner that the last words of the verse would end at the gates of the two mosques which would hurt the feelings of Sunni community and invite their retaliation resulting into serious sectarian riots. Shias use closed campuses of their *Imambaras* (religious places) for observing *matam* (mourning) etc. and Asfi Imambara, popularly known as Bara Imambara, the historical building which attracts lot of tourists, had been used for mass Shia congregations particularly for Friday prayers (*Juma Namaz*) including Namaz of last Friday of Ramzan, *Id* and other important occasions. Sunnis observe mass prayers of last Friday of Ramzan, (*Jumat-ul-vida*) at Tile-wali-Masjid situated on the right bank of river Gomti and opposite to Bara Imambara. Mass Id-prayers are held at the Idgah Aishbagh, and other mosques. *Milad Sharifs* (Religious discourses) are held mostly in nights at various places but during first fortnight of Moharram they are held at the famous 'Hata Shaukat Ali'. Shia processions of *Alam, Taboot and Tazias* were taken out from various mohallas to famous Talkatora Karbala passing through Victoria street. On Bara-Wafat day Sunnis, individually as well as under *Anjumans*, used to pass through Shia localities with their wrapped flags and form a procession outside the city limits, where they used to unfurl '*chariyari*' (Four Companions) flags and marched in a procession to a place called '*Kala Pahad*', under rural police station Kakori. Shia mourning ends on eighth of *Rabi-ul-Awwal* with the taking out of '*Chup Tazia*, (silent Tazia) procession where they do not recite any verses and march silently. Thereafter on twelfth of *Rabi-ul-Awwal* comes Bara Wafat, the main festival of Sunnis and Shias used to create problems for them so that they could not celebrate it on grand scale with gaiety.

Islamic months in order of sequence are (1) Moharram, (2) Safar, (3) Rabi-ul-Awwal, (4) Rabi-us-Sani, (5) Jamadi-ul-Awwal, (6) Jamadi-ul-Sani, (7) Rajab, (8) Shaban, (9) Ramzan, (10) Shawwal, (11) Ziquad and (12) Zilhijja.

Important occasions for the two sects, from law and order angle, which start with Ramzan and end with 12th of Rabi-ul-Awwal are arranged in Table 3.1 :

FIRST PHASE (1888 – 1909)

Beginning of the Dispute

In 1888 Shias in their Azans introduced "*Khalifat-ahu bila fasl*" [*Khalipha Bila Fasla*] meaning thereby that after Prophet, Hazrat Ali was the Caliph without gap. Sunnis filed suits against this innovation and the court held that it was praise by Shias just as '*Madh-e-Sahaba*' was by Sunnis. Sunnis started inscribing names of four caliphs on the four corners of their Tazias as also on accompanying banners and started reciting '*Madh-e-Sahaba*' instead of *Mersias* (elegy).

In 1905 Shias opposed the effort of Sunnis to organise *Mela* (fair) at Talkatora Karbala during Moharram following which some restrictions were imposed by the Deputy Commissioner, Lucknow. In 1906 Sunnis took out '*Madh-e-Sahaba*' procession led by Maulana Abdul Shakur, which was retaliated by Shias with the '*Tabarra*'. In 1907 this dispute worsened which led to appointment of '*Piggot Committee*' in 1908. On the recommendations of this Committee, U.P. Government accepted that Sunnis had the right to express at suitable times and at

Table 3.1

Islamic Month	*Date & Time*	*Activity*	*Venue/ Route*
Ramzan	19th (After morning namaz) of Shias	Taking out of Alam, taboot procession (Green wala–taboot	Qazmain to Patanala area via Pul Ghulam Husain, Akbari Gate and Victoria Street
Ramzan	21st Morning	Procession of Hasan Mirza's Taboot of Shias	Qazmain to Talkatora Karbala via Victoria Street
Ramzan	Last Friday1 P.M.	Shia Namaz	Bara Imambara
Ramzan	Last Friday1-30 P.M.	Sunni Namaz	Tile wali Masjid
Moharram	1st (For Shias)	Shahi Zari Procession	Bara Imamabara to Chhota Imamabara
Moharram	7th (For Shias)	Mehandi ka Julus	Bara Imamabara to Chhota Imamabara
Moharram	8th (For Shias)	Daria wala Julus (Procession of river)	Jinnaton wali Masjid near Gomti River to Patanala via Shahmina Road
Moharram	9th (For Shias)	Procession	Najim Sahab ka Imambara to Dargah Hazrat Abbas
Moharram	10th (Ashra) (For Shias and for a section of Sunnis)	Whole day	Tazia Processions and some carry them individually also
Moharram	10th (Ashra) (For Shias)	Evening-Shame Gariban (Evening of the poor)	Imambara Guframab and other Imambaras

Contd. Table (3.1)

Safar	20th	Chehallum	Shia Processions
Shaban	14th/15th Evening and night	Shab-e-barat	Sunnis do fireworks, visit graves, light candles and recite Fateha
Shaban	15th before sunrise	Birth Day of 12th Prophet, Imam Mehandi of Shias	Shias write petitions (*Arzis*) praying for fulfilment of their wishes, wrap in wet flour and throw in River Gomti
Rabi-ul-Awwal	8th (Last day of mourning For Shias)	Chup Tazia	Shias take out silent procession
Rabi-ul-Awwal	12th (Wara Bafat)	Birth Day of Prophet Mohammad	After reaching an accord, Sunnis take out huge procession from Aminabad to Idgah Aishbagh
Zilhijja	10th	Id-ul-Azha (Bakra-Id)	Both the sects offer special prayers and sacrifice animals.
March	21st	Nauroz	Shias rejoice and throw colours on each other as Hindus do during Holi Festival

suitable places the distinctive doctrine of their faith viz. *'Madh-e-Sahaba'* with the restriction that they should not convert a Tazia procession into a *'Madh-e-Sahaba'*; it was not possible for the Government to issue a proclamation banning recitation of *'Madh-e-Sahaba'* at all times as demanded by Shias in connection with Ashra, Chehellum, and 21st. of Ramzan along with or on the route of any *Alam* (banners commemorative of the battle of Karbala), *Tazia, Taboots* (replicas of the coffins of the martyrs) or other Moharram processions or in the hearing of Shias; apart from these days the question of public recitation of *'Madh-e-Sahba'* be left to the operation of ordinary law. *Tabarra* was restrained because it was not mere assertion of the belief of Shias that Ali is immediate successor to prophet but because it pronounces imprecations on the first three Caliphs which cannot evidently be done without hurting the religious feelings of Sunnis. In 1909 Mr. Radice, the Deputy Commissioner of Lucknow issued a proclamation banning recitation of *'Madh-e-Sahaba'* by Sunnis only on 3 days viz. Ashra, Chehallum and 21st of Ramzan and on other days *'Madh-e-Sahaba'* could be recited publicly on obtaining a license under law.

SECOND PHASE (1937 – 1940)

In 1937 both the sects tried to take out processions and courted arrests followed by a Sunni memorandum to the Governor to resolve the dispute. In April 1937, a committee was appointed consisting of Justice J.J.M. Allsop, Judge of the High Court Allahabad, and H.S. Ross Senior Deputy Commissioner as member and they re-affirmed the views of the Piggot Committee. It observed that the right of Sunnis to recite *'Madh-e-Sahaba'* in public or private was not disputed but the method and circumstances in which it had been sought to make such recitation in Lucknow were in dispute. It was prohibited for ensuring public tranquility and to maintain the balance of public convenience. On 30-3-1939 a statement was issued which read,

> "Government hereby announce that the Sunnis will in any circumstances be given the opportunity of reciting *'Madh-e-Sahaba'* at a public meeting and in a procession every year on Barawafat Day subject to the condition that time, place and route, there of shall be fixed by the District Authorities."

Shias resented this and courted arrests in thousands creating serious law and order situations for six months and Army had to be called out to assist the civil authorities. In 1940 police had to open fire resulting in deaths of eight Shias and two Sunnis. Maulana Abul Kalam Azad, Congress President, appealed to Sunnis to abandon *'Madh-e-Sahaba'* which had no religious significance. On Barawafat in 1941 *'Madh-e-Sahaba'* processions were banned but in 1942 Sunnis defied the ban orders, courted arrests resulting in violence, police firing and killing of three Sunnis. In 1944 important Shia-Sunni leaders were externed under Defence of India Rules (D.I.R.) but the matter remained unresolved from 1945 to 1968 despite official efforts, prohibitory orders and prolonged litigations.

THIRD PHASE (1969 – 1977)

Political Considerations

Congress governments remained in power both in U.P. and Delhi till 1967. Mr. Syed Ali Zaheer (Shia) and Sri Mahavir Prasad Srivastava, both representing Lucknow city in U.P. Assembly, remained Ministers. Sunnis, though, supporters of Congress Party, did not feel happy with them as they felt that both of them were siding with Shias. In 1967 U.P. Assembly elections, two Sunnis namely Sri Syed Saghir Husain and Mr. Zain-ul-Abdin, though, unsuccessfully contested from Lucknow West against Mr. Syed Ali Zaheer and Lucknow Central, against Sri Mahavir Prasad Srivastava respectively, they made inroads in some of the Sunni votes and ensured the defeat of the two ministers. In 1974 Smt. Swarup Kumari Buxi, local Congress MLA, was member of the 'Reconciliation Committee' which recommended that only 25 persons of Shia Community, while taking out processions, would pass through Pul Ghulam Husain, the congested Sunni area. Sunni leaders say that the then Jan Sangh Party also supported Shias and in 1974 while a procession was to pass from Pul Ghulam Husain, Sri Nanaji Deshmukh, a prominent Jan Sangh and Hindu leader was present there along with his supporters.

Dispute Intensified

During Moharram in 1969 a pamphlet entitled "*Ahle Karrar Se Appeal*" was circulated by one Altaf Husain Secretary "*Idara-E-Tanzeem-Lashkare-Hussain*" appealing to Shias to wear green caps to symbolise unity and publicly recite *Tabarra* if Sunnis recited *'Madh-e-Sahaba'* publicly. Sunnis resented circulation of this pamphlet and formation of *'Tabarra Volunteer Force'*. On 26-5-1969 *'Chup Tazia'* procession was brick-batted by Sunnis in Mahmoodnagar which resulted into serious riots leaving six dead and 148 injured, including 67 policemen. 43 shops and 104 houses were burnt. Leaders of both the communities were arrested and lodged in Lucknow jail which brought the two communities to the talking table. They were brought straight from the jail to Chief Minister's Residence, where they signed an accord and were released following which they had their dinner hosted by the Chief Minister and then sent to their homes. Efforts and also the stiff attitude of the then Chief Minister U.P. Sri Chandra Bhanu Gupta, who also belonged to Lucknow, led to this mutual agreement. The salient features of this agreement were that Shias would take out Alam processions but would not recite Tabarra in public and would praise Prophet and Imams in Milads without offending Sunni sentiments; Sunnis in their *Milads* would continue to praise teachings of Prophet without hurting Shia sentiments and no new *Milads, Alams, Majlises* and processions etc. would be introduced for either community.

In 1974 when Shia Chehullum procession was passing through Patanala on agreed route with adequate police protection, Shias recited Tabarra which resulted in serious exchange of brickbatting, stabbings, arson etc. by both the sects necessitating police firing resulting in 8 deaths and 84 injured, including 15 police men. An accord was again signed by both the sides in the presence of Chief Minister Sri H.N. Bahugana on August 28, 1974. A joint committee consisting of two senior I.A.S. officers namely Mr. Athar Hussain (Sunni) and Sri Ghulam Hussain (Shia) was formed but it could not give any amicable solution acceptable to both the sects.

About a fortnight before the Lok Sabha Elections, 1977 serious sectarian riots broke out. On *Barawafat Day* (3-3-1977) Sunnis took out a procession carrying *Charyari Flags*, with names of all 4 Caliphs written, to which Shias resented and serious riots broke out leaving 2 dead and 35 injured. On 24-3-1977 on the occasion of *Nauchandi*, Shias retaliated by taking out *Alam* processions on which Sunnis reacted which led to serious rioting, arson, stabbings etc. claiming 3 dead and 14 injured following which ban was imposed on all the processions of both the sects. Shias courted arrests at various places in July and August demanding that they be allowed to take out their customary processions.

'Luck'-'now'

I remained posted as Superintendent of Police, Intelligence Department, U.P. Lucknow for two years from August, 1975 to August, 1977. I handled the desk of labour and the non-communist and non-communal political parties. The work distribution was such that one desk officer would not know much about the other desk. Frankly speaking, I did not know much about Lucknow and its sectarian problem. On August 9, 1977, I took over as Senior Superintendent of Police Lucknow and remained on this post till March, 1980. Immediately after taking over I called on several senior officers and those who knew the intricate problem of this City, wished me all the best, telling that it was 'Luck'-'now'. I did not realise the implications of these good wishes immediately but got the taste of the intricate law and order situation in next few days which arose out of the ban already imposed on customary Shia processions including the processions of the martyrdom of Hazrat Ali which were scheduled for forthcoming 18th, 19th, 20th and 21st days of Ramzan. Sri Ram Chandra Takru, I.A.S., was the Collector and the District Magistrate of Lucknow, who had been handling this problem for about two years since his posting on 10-10-1975. The other two officers directly responsible for maintenance of law and order in city were Sri Mangla Prasad Misra, Additional District Magistrate City, posted since 1-3-1976 and Sri Uma Shankar Bajpai, Superintendent of Police City, posted since 1-7-1976 carried immense experience and they very well knew the people and the city topography. I was the only new officer as my immediate predecessor Dr. Girish Bihari was shifted within 11 days of his tenure and his predecessor Sri Balbir Singh Bedi had been there for about 15 months with a break of few weeks when he was sent to western U.P. on special assignment for Lok Sabha Elections 1977 and in his absence Sri H.D. Pillai S.P.C.I.D, who had earlier been Bedi's predecessor as S.S.P, was put on this hot saddle.

Holy month of Ramzan commenced in the second fortnight of August, i.e. after a week of my taking over in the District. Talks were held by us at various levels to find some amicable solution but nothing concrete came out. Customary Shia processions of martyrdom of Hazrat Ali were not allowed to be taken out which created lot of tension in the old city. Shias again courted arrests at various places on September 3, 4 and 5, 1977 which flared up the situation. On 21st of Ramzan (the night of 5/6 -9-1977) most important customary procession of Taboot of Hasan Mirza aught to have been taken out from Rauz-e-Nazaf under police circle Saadat Ganj but was not permitted. Shias *Majlis* attended by several thousand persons was going on within the precincts of nearby Dargah Hazrat Abbas where around 2.30 A.M. the crowd got restless and was about to come out to attack the nearby Sunni localities. I was informed on phone at my residence by a prominent Shia leader on condition of anonymity, (now I disclose his name with his permission as Maulana Hamid-ul-Hasan) saying that to him lives of the people were more important than the processions and he sincerely urged me to rush sufficient force to Dargah within minutes as there was possibility of heavy loss of lives and property. After assuring him of immediate action, I contacted Control Room Chowk and got the officers and PAC in reserve rushed to the area. I woke up Sri Takru, went to his residence which was on way to Chowk area and along with him reached the place within minutes. By that time few Sunni houses in Wazirbagh area had been set on fire. We immediately imposed curfew and brought the situation under control before the day broke. Precautions continued for several days. *Shri Krishna Janamashtami*, Hindu Festival, also fell during those curfew days when temples were decorated but devotees could not go out because of curfew. Both Sunnis and Shias of Wazirbagh area would tell us that as the dispute was between them only why should the security forces prevent Hindus from visiting the temples and *Jhankies* as there was no risk either to or from them. Though we appreciated their sentiments, but could not differentiate between people falling in the curfew bound areas. Namaz of last Friday of *Ramzan* was performed on 9-9-1977 by both the sects amidst tension as Shias wore black arm bands and hoisted black flags, whereas Sunnis displayed red flags. On 16-9-1977 *'Id-ul-Fitr'* was celebrated with enthusiasm by Sunnis but Shias did not celebrate it saying that they were still in mourning as *taboots* signifying dead bodies were still lying. Curfew, which was clamped on 6-9-1977, continued till 18-9-1977 with periodical relaxations in phases in different localities. This period witnessed several cases of stabbings, arson etc. In Wazirbagh area, two women, one Sunni and another Shia of a Shia husband, had gone to fetch grass from nearby field. The miscreants killed Sunni wife and spared the other, as she belonged to their faith.

Prime Minister's Intervention

After *Id*, Shias started approaching various authorities to allow their banned processions particularly the *Alams* and *Taboots* of Hazrat Ali saying that till their taboots, symbolising dead bodies, are disposed off, no function of happiness like marriages etc. could take place in their community as they would continue to be in state of mourning. There were Governments of Janta Party, both at the Centre with Sri Morarji Desai as Prime Minister and in U.P. with Sri Ram Naresh Yadav as Chief Minister. Muslims in general and Sunnis in particular had voted for this newly formed Party which returned to power after complete rout of Congress party following the 'Emergency 'rule of Indira Gandhi from June, 1975 to February, 1977. Immediately after *Id*, Prime Minister Desai came to Lucknow on his first official visit, and besides meeting many delegations also met Shia delegation which apprised him of the situation saying that since they were a minority of Muslim community, their traditional processions were not being allowed as Sunnis,who were in majority and solid vote bank of Janta Party, were illegally opposing it. He was subsequently briefed separately by the Chief Minister and the concerned senior officers about the long drawn dispute and the serious efforts made recently to resolve the problem after *Id* and was told that if without mutual agreement, the processions of either community are taken out, there was possibility of major riot resulting into heavy loss of lives and property. The Prime Minister did not feel convinced and soon on return to New Delhi, he sent back his Secretary Mr. V. Shankar to Lucknow to study the local sectarian problem, then prevailing situation and report to him. He spent a couple of days studying the situation and went back to report to Prime Minister. Immediately after his return to New Delhi, came the decision that the processions of the martyrdom of Hazrat Ali, which could not be taken out earlier, be allowed. Several meetings and rounds of talks with the leaders of the two sects were held at various levels including the Chief Minister, where the current situation and the possible outcome of the taking out of the processions were discussed in detail. Senior officers including Chief Secretary Sri Kripa Narain, IGP (then police chief) Sri Lal Singh Verma, who had himself been S.S.P. Lucknow for about 3 years, Home Secretary Sri S.B. Sharan ,U.P. Intelligence Chief Sri S.C.Dikshit, Divisional Commissioner Mr. V. D. Vyas, Range D.I.G. Sri R.N. Gupta, District team of Sri R.C.Takru D.M. and myself met separately in several rounds and all of us jointly felt that processions could not be taken out without serious trouble and blood shed. The Chief Minister was also kept fully apprised, who too was convinced. Though, Delhi was kept fully informed about the prevailing situation, U.P. government was firmly told that the decision to allow the processions was irrevocable. Though, law and order is a State subject, State Government could not say 'no' as their own Party was in power at the Centre. We were asked to make the best possible arrangements for taking out these processions.

Processions Despite Acute Tension

The information about allowing the Shia processions which could not be taken out during last *Ramzan* spread like wild fire in old city generating lot of sectarian tension, reactions and counter reactions from both the sects. Sunnis in their meeting held at *'Teele Wali Masjid'* on 26-9-1977 decided to keep their shops closed the next day, mentioning that it was an act of peaceful protest against the delay in conceding to their demand for *'Madh-e-Sahaba'* processions. Sunnis closed their shops on September 27 and also did *'chiragan'* (illumination) on their mosques etc. on the night of 27 /28-9-1977. This kind of illumination on large scale was usually done on the occasion of Barawafat to express happiness and joy on the birthday of Prophet Mohammad but the night of 27/28-9-1977 was not the occasion to do so as it was not the date of Barawafat. Shias got busy in making preparations to take out their processions immediately on getting the green signal from the District Administration. Several rounds of talks were held by the district administration with the leaders of the two communities to elicit their co-operation so that Shia processions could be taken out peacefully. Sunni leaders assured that they would try their best for maintenance of peace but also warned that *'Ahle-Sunnat'*, were highly agitated on this unilateral decision in favour of Shias.

Shia leaders agreed to abide by the directions of the district administration about date, timings sequence and routes of the processions which were to be communicated later as it was not in the interest of law and order to do so in advance in view of the prevailing volatile and tense situation.

Administrative Preparations

The police arrangements made for the holy month of *Ramzan* were already continuing and further additional elaborate arrangements were planned for these processions. The old city was divided into seven sectors and each sector was put under the charge of one Magistrate and one D.S.P./A.S.P. in two shifts of day and night. Extra police force and PAC was summoned and deployed as pickets at sensitive and strategic spots and also provided to various officers and Police Stations as striking reserves. Tear gas and rubber bullet squads, fire fighting units etc. were also mobilised. Besides the City Control Room at Qaiserbagh, Chowk Control Room (specially established for this problem) was also augmented and put under the charge of a D.S.P. and a Magistrate in day and night shifts from 8 A.M. to 8 P.M. and 8 P.M. to 8 A.M. In all, 31 Companies of PAC (till then CPMF-Central Para Military Forces were usually not provided to States), additional District Police drawn from the rural areas and the Police Lines, 16 DSPs/ASPs, 16 Magistrates etc. were deployed from 26-9-1977. Whereas, the detailed and elaborate orders about police and PAC were issued by S.P. City Sri Uma Shankar Bajpayi, the deployment orders for Magistrates were issued by A.D.M. City Sri Mangla Prasad Misra. Joint briefing meetings of Magistrates, police officers including PAC, Fire Units, Local Intelligence Unit (LIU) and civic authorities were held every morning and evening before the change of shifts at Control Room Chowk, which were addressed by the A.D.M. City/SP City, D.M. Sri Takroo and myself. In these meetings, officers of the shifts to be relieved used to brief about the happenings during their shift, lessons drawn and precautions to be taken by the relieving teams. LIU officers used to brief us separately in advance and we did not make them speak in the meetings in order to maintain secrecy. After these meetings Sector Magistrates/Police Officers used to brief the contingents of their areas about precautions to be taken and certain *'Dos'* and *'Don'ts'* while PAC officers also briefed their troops. In these meetings administrative problems and other matters requiring immediate attention were sorted out then and there and this practice proved very useful.

The Taking out of Processions

In the evening briefing meeting on 27-9-1977, all the officers were told that the day shift duties will report back at 2 A.M. on 28-9-1977 so that resources get doubled while processions were actually taken out. The actual timings of the processions were decided very late in the evening by us in consultation with a couple of prominent Shia leaders so that immediate reaction of Sunnis could be minimised and Shia congregations in huge numbers could be avoided. It was decided that, the most important and prestigious *Taboot* of Hasan Mirza from Najaf be taken out first. Though this procession was about 200 years old, it came to be known as *Hasan Mirza's Taboo* as one Hasan Mirza who came to Lucknow from Calcutta around 1869 (about 108 years ago in1977), had undertaken the responsibility of taking it out on grand scale as was done in Matia Burj Calcutta. Some other processions of Kashmiri-Mohalla were to join at appointed places before passing the most sensitive Sunni area of Pul Ghulam Hussain where the number of processionists was to be reduced to 25 only as per agreements of 1969 and 1974 and remaining persons were to return back from there. Around midnight of 27/28-9-1977 it was decided to start taking out the processions from 4 A.M. on low key, so that they did not attract much of attention and also to avoid the possible reaction from the Sunni community.

While A.D.M. City/SP City mostly remained mobile, I and Sri Takru also took round of the routes and localities from where the processions were to pass. As vehicles could not pass through narrow and dingy lanes, we had to march on foot along with our reserve contingent, and our boots made lot of noise in otherwise silent night. We noticed that Sunnis too were awoke and ready to belligerently face and react to any situation. After ensuring that duties of both the shifts were in position, we gave the green signal to concerned Shia leaders and the police parties that processions in groups be taken out from 4 A.M. The first batch passed through Pul Ghulam Hussain around 4-30 A.M. where brickbatting was done from Sunni houses. It was life time experience for me as I was seeing these processions for the first time. Shia men, women and children gathered en-route, wept bitterly and kissed the *taboots* with reverence. Passing through sensitive localities of Victoria Street and Bazar Khala, we could safely reach them Karbala Talkatora for burial before the dawn In the meantime another batch of processions was taken out towards Patanala on Victoria Street, which too was brickbatted at several places, but was taken care of by the team of A.D.M. (Executive) Sri Suk Deo Prasad Tripathi and SP (Rural) Sri G.K. Shukla. Next batch of processions going towards Nakhas around 7 A.M. while passing through Mahmoodnagar, Abdul Aziz Road and Akbari Gate were very heavily brickbatted from Sunni houses. Some Shia boys also brickbatted in retaliation but they were immediately stopped by the police from doing so. By the time this procession reached Billochpura near Tudiaganj on Victoria Street, they were accosted by thousands of Sunnis who attacked the procession/*Taboots*, set fire to Shia shops and houses, burnt a transformer, fired gunshots, stabbed persons resulting in injuries and deaths. Police, burst tear gas shells, lathi (cane) charged, fired rubber bullets which did not have much impact on this determined crowd and they had ultimately to resort to firing. With great difficulty this volatile crowd could be dispersed. Shias ran for safety leaving behind *Taboots* which were later removed to other safer places. We immediately decided to clamp curfew in old city and D.M. Sri Takru informed of his decision on wireless set to Control Room, who in turn got the

Curfew at Billochpura

Curfew at Billochpura

Burnt Transformer

Burnt Shops

Burnt House

Burnt Houses

Fire Fighting

File Fighting

announcement done through police mobile vans and the vehicles of the sector officers.

Pitched Battle on Abdul Aziz Road

Sunni mobs came out on streets more or less simultaneously at several places in old city and indulged in rioting particularly in three areas of Nadan Mahal Road, Patanala and Abdul Aziz Road. Nadan Mahal Road witnessed burning of Prakash Cinema Hall, where A.D.M./SP City tackled the situation. In Patanala area heavy brickbatting was done where team of A.D.M. (E)/ SP(RA) and local sector officers had a very tough time in bringing the situation under control. On Abdul Aziz Road thousands of Sunnis came out with 'Charyari' flags creating serious law and order problem necessitating use of force by the police. D.M. and I constantly remained on round augmenting the help, wherever needed. At O.P. Patanala I saw a Home Guard hitting a *burqua* clad lady on head with lathi (cane) as a result she started bleeding. I admonished him and warned other policemen present to behave properly and got her safely escorted to her house.

We left for Akbari Gate area where situation became difficult to control, though two teams of experienced officers namely O.P. Sharma Addl. City Magistrate/Mahipat Singh Chauhan C.O. Chowk and R.C.Mani Tripathi Magistrate/A.B. Pandey Dy.S.P were tackling. On Abdul Azij Road starting from Akbari Gate to Tibia Dispensary and extending upto Bhola Nath Kuan, there were thousands of Sunnis trying to march in procession *(Madh-e-Sahaba)* towards Victoria Street with several *Charyari* flags. Neither there was any occasion for these processions nor permission was ever taken from the administration. The crowd had erected several barriers on this road putting rickshaws, carts, pipes and other material to check advancement of security personnel towards them. They were throwing brickbats, acid bottles etc. on police and also fired some gun shots at them, with the result some PAC and policemen had to take cover in verandahs. Near *Ek-minara Masjid* on Akbari Gate, very heavy showers of brickbats came like hailstorm from nearby Sunni houses hitting several security personnel and also D.M. Sri Takru on his thigh. All of us were putting on helmets which saved us from head injuries. I for the first time in my life, saw such hailstorm of brickbats coming from houses as men, women and children had indulged in it. Constable Jargham Husain (Shia), who knew the people and the topography very well, despite receiving personal injuries was of great help to us. Tear gas and Rubber Bullet firings had no effect on the mob on this road. In fact Rubber Bullets were used for the first time in the country, hence a team of experts from Bureau of Police Research and Development (BPR & D) of Govt. of India later came to Lucknow to get the feed-back and suggest improvement for future. It was absolutely essential to disperse this unruly mob as without that the situation could not be controlled and curfew enforced. Sri Takru knew the locality very well as he had spent his childhood with maternal grandparents in nearby *mohalla* Sarai Mali Khan. He suggested that while the officers there could continue to engage the crowd and deal with the situation, he and I could go to tackle the mob from behind. He took us to Chaupatian via Chowk, Khunkhun ji Road and Sarai Mali Khan. Seeing us near Bhola Nath Kuan with very heavy contingent of PAC, the police and PAC men felt greatly relieved as they were fighting for their lives. The crowd also got nervous as they did not expect any reinforcement from behind as they had already blocked the approach from Akbari Gate side. At this place we charged on the crowd with *lathis* and also used other force with the result the violent crowd got nervous and dispersed. This shows that the prior knowledge of the topography and the terrain of the officers goes a long way in handling the situations. With great difficulty we got the Abdul Aziz Road cleared after removing the barriers and pushing the crowds in lanes and houses. Curfew had already been clamped and its strict enforcement was ensured in *mohallas* situated on either side of this road, particularly Jhawai Tola. Following photographs will give some idea of the violent activities of the mob on Abdul Aziz Road and show the violent confrontation by the mob which made the movement of security forces very difficult.

Situation brought under Control

After ensuring that curfew had been enforced properly and the security forces were in command of the situation every where, we went to Chowk Control Room so that we could apprise the senior officers and the U.P. Government on telephone about the

SCENES ON ABDUL AZIZ ROAD

Road Blocks

Road Blocks

Road Blocks

Operation Clearance Near Chaupatian
(D.M. Sri Takru Supervising) Author was engaged in nearby areas

Operation Clearance

Dispersing Crowd in Jhawai Tola

happenings and the latest situation. We found that the Divisional Commissioner Sri V.D. Vyas and Range D.I.G. Sri R.N. Gupta were already there and were doing the needful to help us. D.I.G. Sri Gupta had already ordered for immediate movement of additional resources from other Districts of his Range and had requested the IGP (then U.P. Police Chief) for more PAC. In such a volatile and tense situation both these officers were of immense help to us and their actions and words of encouragement were great morale booster.

We soon went to K.G. Medical College and Balrampur Hospital (District Hospital) to see the injured and arrange for their proper treatment and also to guide the local police that other injured and relatives, who were stranded in curfew bound areas, be brought to hospitals for care.

Around 11.30 A.M. trouble erupted in *mohalla* Purana Nazaf Nibajganj when about 250-300 Sunni miscreants attacked Shia locality and indulged in looting, damaging and arson in their houses. Police and Magistrate immediately reached the scene and controlled the situation and Sri P.P.S. Sidhu (IPS-1975, Assistant Superintendent of Police) was earliest to reach. During Judicial Enquiry allegations were made by Sunnis that one young Sikh Police officer (Sidhu) fired without any provocation, on Sunnis, killing one person. On enquiry this allegation was found baseless.

In these incidents, 73 rubber bullets, 27 tear gas cells, 7 hand grenade cells, and 15 rounds of bullets were fired. On account of first day's incidents from the public side 13 persons died and 33 injured. 118 security personnel including PAC, District Police and Home Guards etc. were also injured, some of whom seriously. Curfew remained in force from 20-9-1977 to 10-10-1977 with relaxations in phases. Stray incidents of stabbings, arson, and attack on rival communities continued. The peculiar trend in all such riots always used to be that unless the figures of the dead of the two communities matched the incidents would not stop. The local public, over years got so much trained in being under curfew that they would be on roads immediately on declaration of the relaxation, purchase sufficient stocks and in such panic buying, shopkeepers and vendors would do brisk business in an hour or so during relaxation period and people would rush to their houses few minutes before the reinforcement of the curfew.

The last 15 minutes before clamping of curfew again needed utmost vigil as miscreants would stab the members of the rival sect and soon disappear by mixing in the crowd.

As a reaction to Lucknow incidents, the following day on 29-9-1977 there were serious Shia-Sunni riots in Kanpur City, which never had any history of such sectarian riots. The information system of these sects was so swift that while riots had started in Kanpur, we were informed by one of the local Sunni leaders about them, following which we took necessary precautions. The U.P. Govt. later ordered a Judicial Enquiry about riots of Kanpur and Lucknow.

As this matter was to come up for discussion in U.P. Assembly, which was already in session, the two Deputy Ministers of U.P. Govt. namely Sri Mukhtar Anees (Shia) and Sri Arif Mohammad Khan (Sunni) jointly took round of the affected areas during curfew relaxation period in the morning, as a goodwill exercise, before the matter came up for discussion in the Assembly. While I and Sri Takru were standing near Pul Ghulam Hussain, the most sensitive spot, the two Ministers also happened to be there. When all of us were discussing these incidents, a Shia lady, known as *'Gaddi wali'*, residing in a nearby house in front of Kashmiri Mohalla Chowki, who was coming on scooter with her husband, informed us that Sunnis have stabbed a Shia few yards away from the place where we were standing and had taken the injured in a narrow lane behind the Masjid (*Charyari*). Shias would call it coloured mosque as they refrain from using the word *Charyari*. The two Ministers immediately left the scene separately in their cars, telling us that we should deal with the situation. Of course we rushed to the spot, followed the trail of bloodstains, arrested the miscreants and rescued the injured and immediately clamped curfew in that locality. A little later we were told that Sri Arif Mohammad Khan had announced his resignation from the Government while the matter came up for discussion in the Assembly.

Visit and Peace march of Maulana Abdullah Bukhari

While the normalcy was yet to be restored in Lucknow, we learnt that Maulana Abdullah Bukhari (Sunni) of Jama Masjid Delhi, who was then close to the corridors of power, was coming to Lucknow on goodwill mission. Knowing the volatile situation, we briefed the state political leadership and urged that Maulana be persuaded not to come as his visit would not help in restoring peace. The higher political decision prevailed; Maulana came to Lucknow; held talks in which prominent leaders of either sect particularly Sunnis did not participate; visited Shia *Dargahs* and decided to take out 'Peace March' in the affected areas. We again approached the political masters, telling them that this exercise would be of no help as local Muslims, particularly Sunnis were against it. We were again overruled by the political leadership and directed to arrange for the 'Peace March' next morning. We decided that this march be first taken out in safer areas and if successful, could be tried elsewhere too. This march started on Aminabad-Rakabganj Road in Maulviganj area, predominantly having Sunni population with few Shias and we were also present to ensure peace during this 'Peace March'. They had hardly marched a few meters, when Sunnis in thousands came out shouting slogans against the march and the Maulana, making it almost impossible to proceed further. The march was abandoned in a huff and Maulana returned to his hotel. Here he insisted on immediate transfer of Sri Takru (D.M.) and refused to leave Lucknow till it was carried out. Next day Sri Takru was transferred as Special Secretary Home in U.P. Secretariat vice Sri Yogendra Narain, who took over as D.M.. Soon after this, the Maulana left for Delhi.

Settlement Attempts

A high level committee consisting of prominent Maulanas of both the communities from outside Lucknow, particularly from Hyderabad, Delhi and Bombay, but not Maulana Bukhari, was constituted by the U.P. Government, which held several sittings but could not find any amicable settlement and ultimately met the fate of earlier attempts.

The Judicial Enquiry

The U.P. Government appointed, Justice C.D. Parekh, a retired Judge of the Allahabad High Court, as a single member enquiry commission under the Commission of Enquiries Act 1952. The terms of reference were to hold an enquiry into the following matters of public importance :

(a) The incidents which took place in Lucknow City on September 28, 1977 involving acts of violence, arson, damage to property and injuries to public servants and others; and

(b) the use of force by the district authorities to control the situation and;

(a) The incidents which took place in Kanpur City on September 29,1977 involving acts of violence, arson, damage to property and injuries to public servants and others; and

(b) the use of force by the district authorities to control the situation.

The Commission was to enquire into and report in respect of the entire series of the said incidents with a view to:—

(1) ascertaining the facts regarding the incidents, and

(2) ascertaining the responsibility and the extent thereof relating to the said incidents including the handling of the situation by the authorities and the force used.

Under the Commission of Enquiries Act, the Commission is to evolve its own procedure. In this case the Commission directed that all the parties, individuals, organisations or institutions and the district authorities including police officers and officials shall file statements on affidavit giving gist of the statements which they intend to make.

Sri Prem Singh, Additional District Judge Ghazipur, and the Secretary of the Commission, issued the first notification dated 21-1-1978 inviting affidavits. The Counsel for administration was Sri T.N. Sinha, Deputy Government Advocate of U.P. Government, who after a few years was appointed as Judge of Allahabad High Court but unfortunately died on the morning of the day he was to take oath of office. Syed Ashraf Husain, aged about 65 years, Advocate, and a dedicated leader for Shia cause, appeared for Shias, who was duly supported by other Maulanas particularly, Kalbe Abid, Hamid-ul-Hasan, Ali Nasir Saeed Abaqati alias Agha Roohi, Syed Muzzaffar Husain Tahir Jarvali, Mirza Mohammad Athar, Mirza Mohammad Alim etc. Sunnis were represented by senior leader and Advocate Nazeer Ahmad aged about 65 years, Abdul Mannan, Advocate, Syed Saghir Husain, Maulana Abdul

Salam Faruqui, Haji Ghulam Hasnain amd Hasan Ahmad Siddiqui etc.

Before filing of the affidavits of the officers and staff of the district administration and the police, we along with Sri Takru and Mr. Sinha our Advocate, used to hold preparatory meetings in Police Lines, where we could work undisturbed, scrutinise all the relevant records, particularly the concerned files regarding promulgation of prohibitory orders, deployment and movement orders of forces and chronological sequence of events of the offices of D.M. and A.D.M.(City), S.S.P., SP City, District Police Control Room, City Police Control Room, Control Room Chowk, Fire Stations and Police Lines etc. Each one of us first prepared the draft affidavit based on one's memory and the concerning record; then exchanged them among ourselves with a view to read critically and make suggestions, then passed on to our counsel Mr. Sinha for giving it a final shape. After filing of affidavits of all the parties/persons, the Commission passed on copies of these affidavits to the concerned counsels. We prepared separate volumes in bound registers of the affidavits of the Administration/ Police, Shias and Sunnis, putting page numbers for easy reference and consultation, passed on one copy to each officer required to depose. This exercise was of immense help and even now after so many years it is still in my privileged possession as it helped me a lot in refreshing my memory subsequently when I dealt with this subject as IGP Lucknow Zone, Additional DGP Law and Order, U.P. and DGP U.P. and also in writing this chapter. The Commission, having its Head Quarters at Varanasi used to have sittings at Kanpur and Lucknow, work from 9 A.M. to 12.30 P.M. with half an hour's lunch break. This continued for about two and half years and the Commission gave its report to U.P. Government in about three years time, which was finally accepted by U.P. Government on 19-10-1982. Sri Takru happened to be Home Secretary then. The district administration came out unblemished in the findings which gave us a great relief.

Fourth Phase (1978 – 1997)

After unprecedented riots and ghastly incidents of September 1977, the U.P. Govt. left the matter to Lucknow district administration who were supposed to handle this problem and of course keep the Government informed. I and D.M. Sri Yogendra

Narain, in consultation with our team of officers decided that till the tempers cool down and conducive climate is created, it would not be safe to allow the processions of the two sects. Both of us, jointly and individually, established very smooth, cordial and friendly relations with the leaders of both the communities in particular and public in general. For about one year no processions were allowed as the ban used to be imposed under section 144 of the Criminal Procedure Code. However token protest arrests used to be offered.

In December, 1978, on the occasion of Moharram, Shias insisted to take out processions despite ban generating serious tension as Sunnis had opposed that. Preventive arrests of persons of both the sects were made. Shias gave a call that they would take out their processions on tenth of Moharram (11-12-1978) from early morning as per custom and tradition. The situation again became volatile and there was possibility of the repetition of the incidents of 28-9-1977. We kept on taking stock of the situation and kept the senior officers informed. Section 144 Cr. P.C. was already in force. In the evening briefing meeting of 10-12-1978 held at Control Room Chowk, it was projected that the situation could not be controlled unless curfew was imposed as Shias would come out in large numbers, who were likely to be forcibly stopped by Sunnis as was done on 28-9-1977 at Tudiaganj/ Billochpura. Fearing major riot and blood-shed, we came to the conclusion that it would be prudent to clamp curfew before the scheduled time of threatened processions. Till then pre-emptive curfew was never clamped and it was considered desirable to do so only after incidents had happened. Waiting for it was too risky. We decided to impose curfew well before the people woke up and came out on the roads. We informed senior officers at every level of our intention of doing so and got the green signal after due deliberations. The curfew was clamped from 01-30 AM on 11-12-1978 and people were taken by surprise in the morning. Shias defied curfew at few places and came out with *Alams* but were arrested after mild use of force at Patanala, Husainabad etc. 29 police personnel also received injuries. Curfew continued till 14-12-1978. Huge Shia crowd came out in Huainabad area on 11-12-1978, defying curfew. I (S.S.P.)) and Yogendra Narain (D.M.) rushed the to scene with two Coys of PAC. Some Jawans of the first Coy on seeing the advancing violent Shia mob with *Alams* in their hands, got little hesitant and did not react swiftly, which gave the impression to the crowd that we were getting demoralised, but the Jawans of the second Coy who followed the first Coy on debussing, pounced on the crowd, jawans making loud noises and charging with canes which demoralised the crowd which immediately dispersed and the situation was brought under control in that locality. On getting back to Chowk, I called the Coy Commander of the first Coy., admonished him for the momentary cowardice shown by his Jawans, gave him suitable instructions but told him that this very Coy would continue to be in my reserve. Thereafter they performed to our fullest satisfaction.

From 1979 onwards no processions were allowed but token arrests were offered by Shias on days of various customary processions. Shias used to meet in *Imambaras*, whereas Sunnis congregated at *Tile-wali-Masjid*, Idgah Aishbagh and other *Hatas* (campuses). Use of loudspeaker horns, except for *Azans* was prohibited but box type amplifiers could be used for local congregations like *majlis* and *milad* etc. This proved very useful in maintaining law and order and in noise pollution control. The public too did not oppose.

On important dates Shias would collect in Asafi Imambara, hold *majlis*, do *matam* and come out on road to court arrests, boarded the Govt. buses parked on road outside the gate (Roomi Darwaja), were taken to Police Lines and released later in the evening. While doing *matam* Shias recite verses beating their chests, and weeping bitterly. In 1979 on the occasion of tenth Moharram, Dy. S.P. Sri V.K. Tiwari, local C.O., who was having the exposure of this kind for the first time, was on duty near Bara Imambara. His duty was to supervise the courting of arrests by Shias and have them sent to Police Lines. As soon as Shias started coming out doing *matam*, Tiwari flashed frantic messages that D.M./S.S.P. should immediately rush to spot as Shias were getting restless and there was serious danger to peace. As we were sitting in nearby Chowk Control Room, we were at the spot within minutes, with extra force. Worried Tiwari apprised us that shouting and chest beating Shia crowd was coming out and were not listening to him. I told him that it was their traditional way of doing *matam* and it should not cause us any worry. On our enquiry Shias told us that court arrest programme was going on as agreed upon and there was no cause for worry. Shias were arrested, taken to Police Lines ground, seated on the steps of the stadium, water etc. was arranged and traditional food known as *Khichra* (rice and pulses) for the occasion was cooked by themselves and served. They were released in the evening and sent on buses to their areas. This became the usual exercise for future for the persons courting arrests.

Till 1977, on the night of 11th/12th Rabi-ul-Awwal, *Barawafat* (Birth Day of Prophet Mohammad) Sunnis used to hold the *'Mahfil-e-Milad'* at Aminuddaula Park, Aminabad, where about one lakh Sunnis would participate. They also used to do *'chiragan'* (illumination) on grand scale, on their buildings particularly mosques and beautiful huge gates temporarily erected for the occasion. Lot of people were attracted to see 'chirangan'. From 1978 onwards this was done on a low key as we had suggested to Sunnis that they should also not do any thing which may be objected to by Shias. Sunnis used to extend their cooperation on every occasion saying that so long the administration did not allow the processions of either community and the police dealt with both of them impartially, they would be able to keep their community (*Ahle Sunnat*) under control. This did not mean that elaborate police arrangements and adequate vigil were not maintained. Both the communities developed faith in our team, which came to be popularly known as *'Jodi'* of Yogendra Narain and Arun. Both of us jointly used to wish that we would try do a lot when we reach the top, i.e., I as U.P. Police Chief and he as Chief Secretary, for Lucknow in particular and U.P. in general.

In 1979, lot of tension was generated in the month of *Ramzan*. As Shia processions about the martyrdom of Hazrat Ali were not allowed. They decided not to celebrate *Id* and started agitation demanding that if their processions remained banned, then mass *Namaz* of Sunnis of last Friday at Tilewali mosque and of Id at *Idgah* Aishbagh should also not be allowed. As offering of mass *Namaz* had never been equated to any procession, there was no question of putting a ban.

For the last Friday of *Ramzan* for Shia *Namaz* (congregation of about forty thousand) the timings are 1 P.M. , which is offered at huge mosque within the fore walls and campus of Asfi Imambara, where as Sunni Namaz (congregation being over one

Roomi Gate, (Husainabad side)
Left of it is Tile-wali-Masjid (partly seen)
and Right of it is, Asfi Imambara with Mosque
(Not in Picture)

lakh) at Tilewali masjid, situated across the road of Asfi Imambara on the right bank of river Gomti is offered half an offer later at 1-30 P.M. in the mosque and on its open lawns. Advocate Ashraf Husain gave a call that Shias after offering last Friday *Namaz* would climb the ramparts of the Imambara facing the Tilewali mosque, and would recite *Tabarra* while Sunnis numbering over a lakh offer their *Namaz*.

This created a very explosive situation and our peace efforts to persuade Ashraf Husain to refrain from doing so did not bear fruits. We asked Sunni leaders to come forward to control their crowd, because if their *Namaz* is disturbed they would retaliate, and there was possibility of unprecedented bloodshed as the police force standing between the two crowds on the low lying road would not be able to control effectively. Sunni leaders assured us of their fullest cooperation saying that they would offer *Namaz* in their local mosques, to be held about an hour earlier to the main *Namaz*. Sri K.K. Misra, local M.L.A. of ruling Janta Party, who had very good rapport with the Sunnis also offered to be present. We made elaborate arrangements and stationed ourselves with very heavy reserves of police and PAC on the road, three to ten feet low, between the two shrines which were on higher planks, and use of force, particularly *lathi* charge was very difficult from that road. As decided, Sunni leaders came forward to be present on the fringe of their crowd towards road so that in case of need they could control their people from advancing towards Shia crowd on the ramparts of Bara Imambara. After their Namaz thousands of Shias climbed the ramparts and as soon as the Sunni Namaz began, they started shouting, perhaps '*Tabarra*' as nothing could be heard in the din.

Officers present at the Imambara gate did their best to control but could not do much because of the adverse topography. Within minutes the Sunni crowd felt disturbed, got up and started advancing towards the Imambara from where Shias were shouting, Sunni leaders came forward to pacify and control them saying that since their *Namaz* had ended peacefully, they should go back to their houses. Their voices could not be heard in loud shouts and we immediately offered a loudspeaker fitted police jeep, Sunni leaders while standing on its bonnet addressed their public. Police remained busy in persuading this crowd to listen to their leaders and leave for their homes as the *Namaz* had already ended peacefully. We thanked them for cooperation and left for supervising the peaceful dispersal of the crowds of both the sects till they safely reached their respective localities.

During my posting as S.S.P. Lucknow for about three years, I had to see and supervise the arrangements on every occasion. This gave me opportunity to know the people and their problems and finer aspects of the law and order situations, the mention of which has been made in the foregoing pages. I left the District with fullest satisfaction except that Shia-Sunni dispute remained unresolved and the ban imposed in 1977 continued for next twenty years. In whatever capacity and place I had remained posted, members of both the sects remembered me fondly and used to keep me informed about the sectarian happenings in Lucknow. After the transfer of Sri Yogendra Narain, they maintained similar relations with him and both of us used to derive satisfaction out of it.

After the demolition of the disputed structure at Ayodhya on December 6, 1992, several cities and towns including Lucknow were put under curfew. U.P. was put under President's rule with Mr. Moosa Raza as one of the Advisers. I was posted as IGP Lucknow Zone on the night of December 10, 1992 i.e. four days after the demolition and Lucknow also fell in my jurisdiction. One evening when Mr. Moosa Raza was on round of Lucknow city and I along with other officers were accompanying him, he noticed that where ever he went, people were greeting me very affectionately, upon which he enquired from me as to how is it that so many people were knowing me so well. Sri Ashok Priydarshi, the then District Magistrate apprised him about my earlier background. On my promotion and posting as Additional D.G.P., Law and order, U.P., I had to supervise the arrangements about this sectarian problem also. Once the situation was aggravated when few donkeys with names of certain caliphs written on them were found in the Kashmiri Mohalla locality. Police took them away and averted the ugly situation. What a way to disturb the peace?

Recourse to Courts

From time to time several persons and parties approached the Lucknow Bench of Allahabad High Court and the Supreme Court for grant of one relief or the other. In 1941, Shias of Jaunpur got a civil court decree to recite *Tabarra* on seven persons (Yazid, Umar-bin-Sa-ad, Hurmila, Shanoh, Shis, Shimr and Khuli) said to have been directly involved in murder of Imam Husain and this decree was upheld in first appeal before the Sessions' Judge. On appeal, the High Court (Mr. Justice Allsop and Mr. Justice Mullick) said "no court should exercise its power to give any declaration to the effect that any person or persons is or entitled to bring down curses upon others in public streets and highways. We express no opinion whether any particular form of recitation is or is not offensive to the feelings of the Sunnis, but we think it was quite wrong to include in the declaration a statement that the plaintiff (Shias) have a right to call down imprecations on the persons mentioned in the plaint. . . . It is equally clear that the law has placed the power in the hands of Magistrates or the police to license processions and interfere with them if they are likely to cause breach of public peace or in other way interfere with the welfare of the community "(A.I.R.-(32)1945, Allahabad-54). In Ashraf Hussain and others *Vs* State of U.P. and others (1982) the Supreme Court observed that "As it appeals to us that the matter is very sensitive involving not only the religious sentiments between the two sects of the Muslim community but the disputes between the two sects are potentially dangerous to disturb public tranquility, it will be only appropriate that if a proper representation is made by the appellants or other members of the Shia community to the State Government; such representation should be considered on its own merit by paying proper attention to the sensitive and emotive issues." Supreme Court in Syed Asural Husain and others *Vs* State of U.P. and others directed that the District Magistrate (Lucknow) after hearing both the sides may issue directions in strict compliance with the judgment of this Court in Ghulam Abbas *Vs* State of U.P. (1981). In 1993 one Ganga Singh, President Akhil Bhartiya Nehru Brigade, filed a writ petition in Lucknow Bench of High Court Allahabad praying for issuance of direction to parties concerned to manage and to allow taking out of processions of *Tazias* and *Alams* by persons having faith on Hazrat Imam Husain on the day of *Ashra* and *Chehallum* in each and every year. Mr. Justice H.N. Tilhari directed that the District Magistrate Lucknow will make effort to hold the meeting of representatives of the two sects at the earliest where effort shall be made to solve the matter before 1-7-1993. The meeting was held but no amicable solution could be found.

Final Phase

In 1997, Shias launched agitation for immediate restoration of their processions. They sat on indefinite *dharna* and started holding meetings. In the meantime two Shia boys committed self-immolation which added fuel to the fire. Sunnis taking serious notice of this wrote a protest letter to Chief Minister U.P. mentioning that they condemn the act of self immolation by Shias and urge that they should not create conditions which may vitiate peace and Shias should also agree to solving this problem of taking out of Sunni *'Madh-e-Sahaba'* processions and *Azadari* processions of Shias, under the supervision of the Government. Mr. Javed Murtaza, Advocate, President, Ali Congress (Shia) Lucknow, in his letter dated 14-06-1997 to U.P. Govt. mentioned that "The Shia community of Lucknow has raised its discontentment through various means from courting arrest to self immolation. The *dharna* at Dargah Hazrat Abbas is continuing for the last two months. During this period three

Shia youths namely, Yusuf Husain alias Bhopali, Mohd. Abbas alias Babbu and Ishrat Altaf alias Guddu have sacrificed their lives through self-immolation in protest against the continued ban on *Azadari* processions. Due to the impervious attitude of the Government and the District Administration the Shias have no option but to do or die. So the Shias of Lucknow have resolved to disregard the illegal and the unconstitutional prohibitions imposed by the District Administration and the date of 24-06-1997 has been set as deadline where after the Shias will take out their customary processions as has been the custom and tradition in the past. It will be open to the District Administration to let the Shias take out their processions peacefully or to shoot them or kill them or lathi charge them. We have resolved to live with dignity and honour."

Miss Mayawati of Bahujan Samaj Party (B.S.P.) with Bhartiya Janta Party (B.J.P.) as coalition partner, became the Chief Minister U.P. in the last week of March, 1997 and was also having the Home portfolio with her. I was appointed as the Director General of Police (D.G.P.) on May 3, 1997 and at that point of time Mr. Brijendra Sahai was the Chief Secretary, Sri P.L. Punia as the Principal Secretary to Chief Minister and Sri Harish Chandra Gupta as Principal Secretary, Home. Shias had started their agitation to mount pressure in view of the forthcoming '*Azadari*' period of *Moharram* and *Chehallum*. Several rounds of talks were held by the Chief Minister but no solution could be found. She issued an appeal on 22-6-1997 on the occasion of *Chehallum* saying that during past 20 years several Governments came to power but seeing the sensitivity of the problem, no Government could relax the ban imposed on the processions. This year Shias have come up with the demand that their Tazia processions be allowed. Sad incidents of self-immolation have also occurred. Seeing the problem in totality from legal and law and order point of view and its sensitive nature it would not be desirable and appropriate to lift the ban on *Tazias*. With a view to find amicable and acceptable solution the Government have formed a Committee of Principal Secretary Home and Director General of Police, which will consider all aspects, talk to all parties and concerned religious leaders, find unanimous solution and submit its report to Government in three months. In these circumstances she appealed to religious leaders and the public of both the communities to maintain peace and amity and help the Government and the Administration in maintenance of peace. She also assured that Government would act with all the sincerity to solve this problem. A notification dated 23-6-1997, regarding formation of this Committee was issued under the signatures of Chief Secretary Sri Brijendra Sahai.

I always felt sorry for the inevitable ban on processions but soon on becoming D.G.P., I started feeling that given a chance I would do my bit to resolve this complex problem. I as D.G.P., U.P. and Sri Harish Chandra Gupta as Principal Secretary, Home as joint members of this Committee started the work immediately. First few meetings with the leaders of the two sects were held in Chief Secretary's Committee Room. It was not convenient for the parties concerned to go to Secretariat without entry passes and other formalities, hence subsequent meetings were held in the Committee Room of the Office of the Divisional Commissioner Lucknow in which besides the leaders of both the sects, officers including the Divisional Commissioner, District Magistrate and his other Magistrates and police officers ranking from the Zonal I.G.P., Range D.I.G., S.S.P. and others used to be present to assist the Committee.

On the occasion of *Chehallum* on 26-6-1997, few disturbing incidents took place which adversely affected the law and order situation of Lucknow city. Several hundred Shias including prominent leaders were arrested and sent to jail. Few prominent leaders were transferred to District Jail Lalitpur, whereas others were lodged in Lucknow Jail. D.M. (J.S.Mishra) and S.S.P. (Rajni Kant Mishra) went to Lalitpur in state plane on 7-7-1997 to hold talks with the detained Shia Leaders, who after talks got a message faxed from Maulana Syed Kalbe Jawad Naquvi to the effect that sad incidents of 26-6-1997 occurred due to misunderstanding; Committee of two officers should start its work immediately in which religious leaders only should participate and Shias would not hold any demonstration etc. for the next three months till the work of this Committee continues. The detained Shia leaders were subsequently released and brought to Lucknow and other Shias detained in Lucknow Jail were also released. Postponement of the agitational programme by Shias created a conducive climate for talks by the Committee.

Consequent to the decision taken in the first sitting held in the night of 26/27-6-1997 of this Committee, D.M. Lucknow through his letter dated 28-6-1997 invited the parties concerned to file their written statements clearly indicating (1) main issues of this problem, (2) suggestions for settlement, (3) expectations from Government and Administration and (4) expectations from the other (rival) sect. Sunnis filed their written statement on the pad of 'Majlis Tahaffuz-e-Namoos-e-Sahaba', which was jointly signed by Mr./s (1) Maulana Abdul Aleem Farooqui (son of Maulana Abdul Salam, who had earlier actively participated in the movement and grand son of Maulana Abdul Shakoor who had started this agitation in 1905), (2) Saghir Husain, (3) Hasan Ahmad Siddiqui, (4) Haji Ghulam Hasnain, and (5) Fazle Alam, Advocate (President Sunni Youth Federation). Another statement of All India Mohammadi Mission (Sunni) was filed by its president Dr. Quamar Ali Minai "Sajjada" Dargah Shahmina, Lucknow but their claim was not subsequently entertained as they never had any locus-standi. Shias filed more than one statements, one by Sri Javed Murtaza, Advocate another by Sri M.M. Tahir, President, 'Edare Tanzeem-Ul-Millat' and the third one filed on the pad of Syed Kalbe Jawad Naquvi, Imam-e-Juma, and signed by (1) Maulana Dr. Syed Kalbe Sadiq (Vice- President All India Muslim Personal Law Board), (2) Maulana Syed Kalbe Jawad, (3) Maulana Agha Roohi, (4) Maulana Syed Hameed-Ul-Hasan, (5) Maulana Mirza Mohammad Athar, (6) Maulana Adibul Hindi and (7) Maulana Zahir Ahmad Iftkhari.

After several rounds of talks a unanimous resolution was drafted, by me in consultation with others, on 12-10-1997; its gist being that for the amicable and permanent settlement of the century old Shia- Sunni problem of Lucknow, both the parties with the help of the 'Two Member Committee' appointed by the Government have reached an agreement so that the continuing tension between the two sects comes to an end and they perform their religious functions peacefully without hurting the sentiments of the other sect and give an everlasting gift to their city of glorious culture and heritage making it an example before the world. It was agreed that to begin with Sunnis would take out their processions on 12th of Rabi-ul-Awwal and Shias would do so on 21st of *Ramzan,* 10th of Moharram, Chehallum and 8th of Rabi-ul-Awwal. Names of these processions would be given by the respective sects in consultation with the District

Administration. The routes, time and manner of processions would be decided by the District Administration in consultation with the representatives of both the sects. Both the sects would refrain from doing things which may hurt the sentiments of the other community and result in disturbance of peace. District Administration would continue to take necessary steps for maintaining law and order. This resolution had a very sobering effect and efforts continued for making it possible to take out processions during forthcoming *Ramzan*.

The sittings of the Committee continued and some visible solution had to be exhibited as holy month of *Ramzan* had started on first of January, 1998. In a meeting held on the night of January 17/18, 1998, an agreement was signed by the representatives of the two sects, R.P. Singh, D.M. and Arun Kumar, S.S.P., mentioning that to begin with Shias would take out a test and token procession on twenty first of *Ramzan* falling on 21st of January from karbala Puttan Shah near Bazar khala and Sunnis would take out their test and token procession on same date and time on Abdul Aziz Road. As the team of officers did not have the earlier experience of the routes and areas, they expected me to guide and I said the routes of the token processions were alright but adequate vigil be maintained. Maulana Syed Hamid-ul-Hasan, Jamia-e-Nazmia (Principal Nazmia Arabic College) in his note dated 19-1-1998 mentioned that this agreement of one day was neither victory nor defeat for anybody but was the victory of the peace and the efforts made in achieving it; every thing can be achieved by talks; and it will have everlasting effect like greenery in the desert.

There remained the problem of continuity in administration. Lucknow had 4 District Magistrates (1) J.S.Misra, (2) Arun Kumar Sinha, (3) Raj Pratap Singh,(4) Sada Kant) and 4 Senior Superintendents of Police (1) Rajni Kant Misra, (2) Subesh Kumar Singh, (3) Arun Kumar ,(4) O.P. Singh) from June 26, 1997 to 1998. Principal Secretary Home Sri H.C. Gupta was replaced by Sri Rajiv Ratan Shah in last week of September soon on Sri Kalyan Singh (B.J.P.) becoming the Chief Minister of U.P. D.I.G. Range Sri Kashmir Singh was replaced by Sri Arun Kumar Gupta. Sri Desh Dipak Varma remained the Divisional Commissioner. Sri R.S.Mathur became the Chief Secretary on 31-7-1997 on retirement of Sri Brijendra Sahay. I was the only continuing link.

There came the crucial date of twenty first of January and twenty first of *Ramzan* incidentally falling on the same day. Though sufficient preparations had been made, I was keeping my fingers crossed remembering 1977 incidents. Token processions of both the sects were taken out safely and peacefully and there was sense of achievement in both the sects, District Administration too heaved a sigh of relief, Chief Minister Sri Kalyan Singh and ruling B.J.P. claimed it to be their major success and I personally felt absolved of the guilt that ban on processions imposed since 1977, when I was S.S.P., had ultimately been lifted. We congratulated each other and Chief Minister Sri Kalyan Singh gave a real pat on my back. I for one received several calls from both the sects expressing gratefulness for the role played. Thereafter agreements were again signed regarding dates, number of processions and the routes. I was always missing Mr. Yogendra Narain. What a paradox, that the day I was transferred from the post of D.G.P, U.P., Sri Yogendra Narain took over as Chief Secretary U.P..

It is now six years since 1998. Processions are being taken out peacefully. Sunnis have named their procession as *'Madh-e-Sahaba procession'* which is taken out on Bara Wafat day from Aminabad to Idgah Aishbagh via Nadan Mahal Road, Victoria Street and Bazar Khala. Shias take out their *Azadari* processions on 9 main days. Peace prevails at present. Sunnis feel fully satisfied. Shias are partly satisfied as they are still insisting on the remaining processions but in their heart of hearts, are convinced about their achievement. I am not only satisfied but am very happy because this effort has not only brought peace but has avoided a lot of bloodshed which used to be witnessed year after year. My only wish and prayer is that 'History may not repeat itself' and Almighty May bestow His choicest blessings on Lucknow and the best wishes of 'Luck'-'now' given to me in 1977 by seniors, may prove lucky for every *'Lucknowite'* for ever.

Grateful acknowledgements of

1. Maulana Hamid-ul-Hasan, Principal Jamia-E-Nazmia Lucknow, Prominent Shia Leader and Shia Theologist for rendering help on theological aspects and the events.

2. Sunni leaders and Maulanas, who do not want to be named, for helping in providing background material and also the theological aspects.
3. Sri Shariq Alvi, UPPS (Retired) and Editor Azad Academy Journal for going through the manuscript and suggestions about religious matters.
4. Ms Varma Photographer, Krishna Nagar, Lucknow for very useful photographs.
5. Ramesh Studio, Quandhari Bazar, Lucknow for very useful photographs
6. Lucknow Magisterial and Police authorities for providing several inputs.

5

Meerut Communal Riots

Meerut, situated about sixty kilometers away from Delhi, has been the historical and most important seat in western Uttar Pradesh. District Meerut is situated between two holy rivers namely *Yamuna* on the west and *Ganga* on the north east. Hastinapur of *Mahabharat* fame and a Jain seat of pilgrimage is located in this district in north east near Ganga river. The land of the district is very fertile and it is known as grainery of U.P., main crops being wheat and sugarcane. Hindi similar to Haryanvi dialect is the local spoken language. People are known for hard work but are prone to revolt if things do not go the way they want. India's war of independence in 1857 started from Meerut Cantt. It is said that once Shravan Kumar, legendry devotee of his old and infirm parents, while taking them on his shoulders to Haridwar, lost his cool on reaching Meerut city, asked them to give remuneration for the services rendered, but after crossing Meerut became normal and asked for their forgiveness.

Population

According to 2001 census the population of Meerut district is around 30 lacs (15.44 lacs rural and 14.57 lacs urban) and of them about 16 lacs are Hindus, 12.80 lacs Muslims, 95,615 Sikhs, 16,185 Christians, and 7,236 others. Population of Meerut city is about 15 lacs of whom about 9 lacs are Hindus including over 2 lacs Scheduled Castes, and 6 lacs Muslims and about 1% population of Sikhs, Christians and others. People of District

Meerut are very friendly. In rural areas there are family ties among Hindus and Muslims majority of whom are Hindu converts, particularly in Jats, Mula Jats, Tyagis, Hindu and Muslim Gujars, Rajputs and Rangars.

Social and Economic Activities

Meerut has a distinct culture. People are very hard working including females who work labouriously in their fields. Food habits are simple but rich vegetarian food of milk, sugar and jaggery (Gur) preparations are common even in poor families. Social bonds are very strong.

Meerut City is known for its annual Nauchandi fair which is held after *Holi* festival and continues for about one month. Lot of business is transacted in this fair *cum* exhibition. This festival is known for entertainment and social harmony. Temple of Goddess Nauchandi and Mazar of Bale Mian situated in the precincts of the Mela Ground attract lot of devotees from both the communities.

Industries

Meerut has been one of the important cities of western U.P. There are several sugarcane factories in the District. A cooperative dairy on the outskirts of city has played an important

Nauchandi Devi Temple

Bale Mian Ki Mazar

Bale Mian Ki Mazar & Nauchandi Devi Temple (Side by side)

role in white revolution. Meerut city is famous for *Rewaris*, manufacture of sports goods, annual production touching Rs. 200 crores in the cottage industry sector, gold jewellary worth Rs.3 crores daily, scissors, handloom textiles which was the worst sufferer in 1987 riots and meat supplied to Delhi and several countries. The Modi Rubber factory had been playing very important role in manufacturing automobile tyres and tubes.

Several other small scale industries have also been playing very important role in the development and economy of this rich area.

History of Communal Riots

Meerut, a rich and affluent city, is also known for communal divide and disharmony. Since India's Independence in 1947, it has witnessed several serious communal riots, particularly in years 1961, 1968, 1973, 1982, 1987, 1990, 1991 and 1992. From very minor incidents to major emotive issues have been the cause for sparking off communal riots. As a reaction to violence in elections of Aligarh Muslim University in 1961, students of Meerut College took out a procession which was attacked near Jali Kothi (meaning burnt bungalow, gutted some times in past) a Muslim locality, necessitating imposition of curfew for 10 days from 6-10-1961 to 16-10-1961, which resulted in 18 deaths and 30 injured. In 1968 Meerut witnessed communal riots due to opposition by Hindu organisations of the visit of the then Chief Minister of Jammu and Kashmir Sheikh Abdullah. Curfew remained imposed for 8 days from 28-1-1968 to 4-2-1968. In all 12 persons lost their lives and 71 were injured. Detailed mention of these riots will follow in subsequent pages. On 11-12-1973 two Muslims and one Hindu accidentally collided in Mohalla Gudri Bazar and this insignificant incident resulted in serious communal riots in City in which 7 persons died and 66 received serious injuries and curfew remained imposed for 19 days from 11-12-1973 to 29-12-1973. In all 925 persons were arrested. In 1982 Meerut again witnessed serious communal riots, the immediate cause being detection of pig flesh in Jama Mosque in the night of September 2/3-1982, stabbing resulting into death of a Hindu priest Ram Bholey of Pipleshwar Mahadev Temple on 6-9-1982 which provoked the two communities resulting into armed confrontation. Curfew remained clamped for 22 days from 7-9-1982 to 29-9-1982. This riot left 18 dead and 72 injured. 992 persons were arrested to restore peace. A Judicial Enquiry, by Justice C.D. Parekh, retired Judge of Allahabad High Court, was conducted.

In 1986 Vishwa Hindu Parishad launched an agitation for unlocking of the gates of the disputed structure at Ayodhya. This created communal frenzy at various places not only in U.P. but else where too. On February 1, 1986 on court's orders the locks of the Ram Janam Bhumi at the disputed structure in Ayodhya were opened which generated tension at several places in U.P. as Muslims were opposed to this move. In Meerut on 14-2-1986 (Friday) Muslims observed 'protest day' by closing their shops, hoisted black flags on house tops, wore black arm bands and offered Friday *Namaz* in huge numbers while bearing black bands. Hindus retaliated by hoisting saffron flags on houses and shops, wore saffron bands on arms. After offering *Namaz* at Jama Masjid, a section was to go to Collectorate to hand over memorandum to the District Magistrate. Dispersing Muslim crowd raised objectionable slogans which was objected to by the Hindus of Sarafa Bazar. This led to brickbatting, arson, looting, stabbings etc. by both the communities which continued for several days. Serious riots broke out resulting into imposition of curfew from 28-2-1986 to 15-3-1986 (16 days). In these riots 9 persons lost their lives and 19 were injured. 16 police personnel were also injured. Due to arson one mosque, several shops and houses of both the communities were burnt resulting in very heavy economic losses. About 262 cases were registered by police and 824 persons were arrested. These riots left Meerut as a hyper sensitive place.

In early 1987, several programmes including *bandhs*, hoisting of flags etc. were observed by both the communities, which vitiated the peace and harmony of this City. Serious riots broke out on 14-4-1987 on the occasion of *'Shab-e-barat'* festival and curfew had to be imposed. After about a month unprecedented riots occurred which continued for about three months and curfew remained imposed in phases for several days. A detailed description of these riots will be given in subsequent pages.

On the occasion of Lok Sabha Elections of Meerut Constituency, on 20-5-1991, workers of Congress, Bhartiya Janta Party and Janta Dal clashed over alleged fake voting which resulted into serious communal riots in which 31 persons died, 58 injured and 1041 were arrested. Curfew continued from 20-5-1991 to 26-6-1991.

I had the occasion to be part of the teams which handled 1968 and 1987 riots. I am giving detailed description of these riots with a view to share my experiences.

MEERUT COMMUNAL RIOTS 1968

In 1967 Meerut was having population of about four lacs (57% Hindus, 42 % Muslims and remaining 1% Sikhs and others).

There were only six police stations in city area namely (1) Kotwali, (2) Delhi Gate, (3) Sadar Bazar, (4) Railway Road, (5) Civil Lines and (6) Lal Kurti (Cantonment). Work of these city police stations was supervised by the City Deputy Superintendent of Police (C.O. City) under the direct control of the Senior Superintendent of Police. Additional Superintendent of Police had nothing much to do with this circle. Sri Vijai Nath Singh a senior, seasoned and competent officer used to be the C.O.City in 1967–68. Sri Ram Dularey Pandey was the Senior Superintendent of Police.

I am giving the following version as told to me by Sri Vijai Nath Singh, as both of us are now living in the same colony in Lucknow after our retirements. Sher-e-Kashmir, Sheikh Mohammad Abdullah, the then Chief Minister of Jammu and Kashmir had been in controversy because he had been publicly saying that he was a Kashmiri first. This was being resented to by the Hindu organisations particularly *'Hindu Maha Sabha'* the *'Kashmir Bachao Morcha'*. *Jamait-ul-Ulema*, organisation of nationalist Muslims, led by Maulana Asad Madni were to hold a conference in Faiz-e-Am Inter College Meerut where Sheikh Mohammad Abdullah was also invited . The local Hindu leaders with the active support of the city M.L.A. Sri Mohan Lal Kapur, opposed this visit saying that Sheikh Abdullah should first declare that he was coming as Indian national and in case he did so he would be welcomed otherwise his visit will be vehemently opposed. In case he did not do so, he would not be allowed to enter Meerut. It is noteworthy that at that time Chaudhary Charan Singh was heading the S.V.D. (Sanyukt Vidhayak Dal) Government in U.P. and Jan Sangh was a ruling coalition partner. Chief Minister Chaudhary Charan Singh happened to be in Meerut city, his home district, a day before the proposed visit of Sheikh Abdullah and he addressed a press conference, where some persons from the media informed him that Meerut city was tense and there was likelihood of communal trouble due to the visit of Sheikh Abdullah that evening and that Hindu organisations had planned to take out a procession and stop Sheikh Abdullah's entry in Faiz-e-Am Inter College Meerut. The District officials present (the author was not present), told the Chief Minister that, although the situation was tense but they would handle it. Sri Mohan Lal Kapur, Jan Sangh, M.L.A., later on said that when the District Authorities cannot ban the entry of Sheikh

Abdullah, how could they stop their procession. Later the Chief Minister left for Delhi, giving necessary instructions to the D.M. and the S.S.P. Sri Ram Niwas Sharma, City Magistrate and Sri Vijai Nath Singh C.O. City were left to handle the situation as it was their duty to maintain the law and order in the city.

On 28-1-1968 afternoon *'Kashmir Bachao Morcha'* workers (about 200) collected at historical Bhainsali Ground (Shaheed Smarak-Martyrs' Memorial) where they held a meeting and started marching in a procession towards Faiz-e-Am Inter College, which was about 250 metres away from there on the main road towards Delhi. Police was also deployed to deal with the situation. The processionists started shouting slogans exhorting Sheikh Abdullah to announce that he was coming as Indian citizen before entering Meerut, else he should go back

Bhainsali Ground Martyrs' Memorial

Faiz-e-Am Inter College

(*Sheikh Abdullah vapas jao, ya apni nagrikta batao*). When this procession approached the gate of Faiz-e-Am Inter College near Income Tax Office, the Muslim crowd raised pro Abdullah slogans and attacked the procession causing injuries to many of them who ran helter skelter for safety. In this confusing situation Sheikh Abdullah, somehow reached the College around 7 P.M. The City Magistrate and the C.O. City, present on the spot continued to handle the situation and also told the City Control Room to inform the D.M and the S.S.P. about the deteriotating situation and to tell the Police Lines to rush some extra police force.

That evening I, along with my wife, was ready to go to some friend for a social call. Little before sun set I got a telephonic call from the City Control Room informing that Sri R.D. Pandey, S.S.P. had left for evening walk and could not be contacted and Sri S.P. Watal, D.M. was also not at his residence and his whereabouts were not immediately known to his camp office staff. I contacted Sri P.K. Mehrotra, Reserve Inspector and told him to immediately collect the maximum staff available in the Reserve Police Lines and dispatch them to Bhainsali Ground and also to send few police men at my residence who could accompany me. I tried to contact the S.S.P. and the D.M. on phone but could not get them. I got in touch with my counterpart magistrate A.D.M. (E.) Sri B.D. Gupta and requested him to reach my place, which was on way to the scene of trouble, at the earliest as we were required to reach Bhaisali Ground without losing time. Within minutes a few police men and A.D.M. arrived. I had also changed to winter working uniform. We proceeded to the trouble spot and on reaching the scene near Bhainsali Ground, we saw that the police force was dealing with the rowdies near Income Tax Office crossing. The furious crowd from the Faiz-e-Am College side was pelting stones and throwing burning rockets locally called (*khatangas*) on policemen and the processionists. Modinagar riots and firing, which had taken place barely a month back, were very fresh in our minds, so A.D.M. Sri Gupta and I discussed and decided that we will avoid police firing, lest both of us are branded as trigger happy officers. I briefed all the policemen on duty there and told them to exercise utmost restraint and to use force only when ordered by me. I asked the tear gas squad and the lathi (cane) party to remain with us and the armed party should, remain behind these parties and they will wield only that force which we ordered. As it was a chilly, cloudy and windy winter evening, it started getting dark little earlier. We were trained not to use tear gas after sunset and against the wind direction. Ignoring this, we decided to use as much tear gas as possible so that the crowd could be kept engaged and guessing whether it was firing. While lathi squad was dealing with the crowds in the nearby areas particularly, Jali Khothi locality, the tear gas squad was firing intermittently but heavily on the larger rowdy crowd towards the College. This way we could manage to push the crowds inside the College and the lanes of the locality. Those days walkie–talkie wireless sets were not available to the security forces and the Magistrates, hence we could not contact other officers particularly the City Magistrate / C.O. City and the D.M./S.S.P. and did not know as to what was happening in other areas and what the team of the city officers was doing.

I had a briefing from Sri Vijai Nath Singh while writing this article in September, 2001. He said that on that fateful evening, he and City Magistrate Sharma kept on dealing with the crowds of both the communities and while they were pushing the crowds in College and *mohalla* lanes, another Muslim crowd came out of the nearby *mohalla* Machhlian and attacked the persons who were coming out of the cinema hall after watching the evening show and were unaware of the outside happenings. This aggravated the situation and led to rumour mongering that Hindu ladies were manhandled and their breasts chopped. C.O.City Sri V.N. Singh, who was handling the situation, entered a shop to use telephone for asking extra reinforcement as the situation was getting worse but in the meantime the shopkeeper started downing his shutter fearing mob attack. As Singh was trapped inside, he rushed and blocked the shutter before it could be completely closed and somehow managed to come out. Counterpart City Magistrate Sharma lost contact with him as he got busy in some other disturbed area. Clashes between the two communities spread to other areas of the city, resulting in injuries, loot and arson in markets. The scant local police tackled the situation.

The meeting inside Faiz-e-Am College continued and the news of the ongoing incidents went inside the campus through the injured who narrated their own versions which infuriated the audience present, thereby causing more sensation and resentment and attacks on the police operating outside. Our team remained on the road and with great difficulty we could manage to disperse the crowd. In the mean time it started raining which helped us in early dispersal of the crowd from the College and also in the *mohallas*. The District Magistrate and the Senior Superintendent of Police reached Kotwali and took control of the situation and ensured further action at other places. Curfew was clamped and Sheikh Abdullah was safely sent back to Delhi under police escort.

Police Station Delhi Gate, which used to be an outpost of Kotwali Police Station till about two years (1964) ago had hardly any spare accommodation for starting a Riot Control Room. Because of its strategic location in the riot-hit area, a temporary control room was immediately opened with A.D.M.(E) and myself as overall in-charge. Our duties were to maintain record of the extra force and officers reporting for riot duties, dispatch them for duties in shifts and urgent calls, keep account of the incidents reported including dead and injured, patients admitted in various hospitals and their safety from crowds, arrange rescue of stranded persons particularly those coming from outside at railway and bus stations, arrange issuance of curfew passes, attend to distress calls and make suitable arrangements etc. Both of us remained busy there for several days, had our meals there only, slept together on a cot kept in the quarter of a head constable, used the toilet of that house and I reached my residence after seven days, though it was hardly a kilometer away.

Following morning of the first night of the riots, telephone calls started pouring in about dead bodies lying in gutters, injured waiting in houses for being taken to hospitals, shops and houses burnt and also panic calls about collection of crowds ready to attack on the other community. We kept on compiling the details and occasionally passed them on to the D.M./S.S.P. We were also informed that few dead bodies had been taken to the mortuary in Police Lines for *post-mortem* examination. A call from Delhi was that Sri Mohammad Yunus Salim, Deputy Minister, Home, Government of India (Congress) accompanied by Maulana Asad Madani, Congress M.P., was arriving to see the situation of the riot hit areas and they would go around to various places including the mortuary. We informed the D.M./S.S.P. who directed us to depute a Magistrate and a Deputy Superintendent of Police to accompany them and dissuade them from visiting the mortuary as it has never been the practice to take the V.I.P.s to mortuary. They insisted to go there and also desired that the A.D.M and the Additional S.P. should accompany them. As we were bogged down in the Control Room, and till that time there was no body else to take care of the situation, we requested them to excuse us but they kept on insisting. We briefed the D.M./S.S.P., who very reluctantly agreed to our accompanying them and also ask them to complete their visit soon, as our presence in the Control Room was essential. They went around the city in Muslim localities and then went to the mortuary despite our suggestion to the contrary. On way they insisted that we should tell them the exact number of dead bodies taken to mortuary and also the breakup of Hindus and Muslims. I informed them that the exact number is not known as dead bodies were still being recovered and taken there but till we left the Control Room the number reported was about half a dozen but the community wise break was not reported. On reaching we found fourteen bodies, smeared with mud, lying there which had been recovered from the gutters and but for three, rest were of the Muslims. Mr. Salim got infuriated and scolded us by telling that we were insisting on not taking them there so that they could not see the correct picture. Our plea that we did not hide any facts and some bodies had arrived there after we left the Control Room, could not convince him. I confess now after 31 years of this riot that we did not hide any information from the Deputy Minister but he took it to his heart and a year later when he visited Gonda, where I had joined as Superintendent of Police and went to call on him at the Inspection House, he immediately recognised me telling that I was the same person who was at Meerut during riots there.

Sri Vijai Nath Singh told me that rumours played a crucial role in these riots. On third day of the riots, a message received was that Muslims of *mohalla* Islamabad (predominantly Muslim locality) had attacked the Hindus of Bank Colony and immediate help be rushed before they are wiped out. He along with Sharma, City Magistrate and some force left for Bank Colony. On way they saw a few hundred panic stricken Muslims herded in a mosque. They got down and went to them to enquire about the situation. They told that they have collected in the mosque because Hindus from nearby Bank Colony have damaged and set on fire five mosques and they were to attack the Muslims of Islamabad, hence they have taken shelter in this mosque. They took two prominent Muslims to other mosques to show and convince them that no mosque had been attacked or damaged. This convinced them who on return told fellow Muslims in that mosque that it was all rumour and there was neither any attack on Muslims by Hindus nor was there any crowd collected in Bank Colony. This restored confidence in Muslims of Islamabad. Hindus of Bank Colony were also told the factual position and they too got convinced and confidence was restored in both the communities. This goes to show that the rumours, unless quickly contradicted, can aggravate the situation as people tend to believe them to be true.

Role of panic in such situations also plays a very important role as is evident from the following incidents. During round of the curfew bound areas Sri Vijai Nath Singh found a P.A.C. picket very panicky in a thickly populated Muslim *mohalla* under police station Railway Road, who feared attack from the locals. Sri Singh took the panicky picket commander, deep inside that locality and made him to see the things that Muslims were inside their houses. This exercise restored confidence in P.A.C. contingent who performed well thereafter in that locality. One Mr. Sharma, a prominent Jan Sangh worker and resident of a locality behind the Police Station Kotwali informed the police that there were noises of "*Maro Maro*"(Kill Kill) which was creating fear psychosis in the local Hindus. Police party went to that locality and they also heard the similar noise. As soon as they would reach the place from where the noise was coming there used to be complete silence in that curfew bound area. This continued for sometime but police party kept continuous watch and ultimately found a lunatic woman hiding nearby who used to make these noises at regular intervals causing panic in the locality. This action of police dispelled the feeling of insecurity in people of the locality.

Several other problems were also experienced. There was a problem of reaching the stranded passengers at railway and bus stations to different areas. Buses under police escort were run at regular intervals. Sick persons were to be taken to hospitals and the curfew passes had to be issued for them and the accompanying attendants. The office goers also asked for curfew passes but they were told to abstain and concerned offices were advised not to press for their attendance till the curfew was in force. Some persons particularly the local political workers also insisted for curfew passes but this was fraught with risk as such workers while contacting their supporters could foment further trouble. Press persons were also issued passes to cover the events. Educational institutions were closed. Curfew continued for several days and periodical relaxations were given in various localities in rotation. Police and P.A.C. had to work for long hours for several days and the problems of logistics were also taken care of.

Regular press briefings were not done but we used to brief the individual press representatives as and when they approached us in the Control Room. Till then there were no important newspapers published locally and most of the Delhi papers used to cover western U.P. Press briefings were also done at higher levels of the D.M/S.S.P., the Divisional Commissioner and the Range D.I.G of Police. Television and video coverage was unknown till then. But for All India Radio other electronic media was not in existence.

Chief Minister Chaudhary Charan Singh visited Meerut on third day of the riots, took stock of the situation, talked to local leaders, held a press briefing and instructed that the administration should handle it very firmly without caring for the political affiliations of the trouble makers. The then Additional Inspector General of Police C.I.D. Anand Swarup Gupta I.P., and number two police officer after the I.G.P. in U.P., visited Meerut, went around riot affected areas and gave suitable instructions to local officers. Mr. A.C. Ambwani, I.P.S., Range D.I.G. was always concerned and kept himself fully informed.

After about 34 years of these incidents, if we want to analyse as to what could have been done politically and otherwise, to avoid these riots, it could be seen that it was the beginning of the rule of different political party/parties Governments at the Centre and the State as there was Congress Government at the Centre and S.V.D. Government in U.P. As law and order is the State subject the State Government perhaps did not approach the Centre to persuade Sheikh Abdullah not to come to Meerut, who was visiting on the invitation of Jamait-ul-Ulema, a friendly organization of the Congress. Visit of the Union Deputy Minister for Home, Yunus Saleem could also have been avoided or deferred as the officers busy in controlling the riots and manning the Control Room had to accompany him. Timely action aught to have been initiated by the District Administration to ban the procession of 'Kashmir Bachao Morcha' and not to allow them to collect at Bhainsali Ground. Advance action for riot control should also have been taken to activate all officers to get ready for facing the expected law and order situation. Once the riots broke out, all out efforts were made to bring the things under control very quickly and efficiently.

COMMUNAL RIOTS OF 1987

Because of the opening of lock at Ram Janam Bhoomi/Babri Masjid complex at Ayodhya and various programmes of hardliners of both the communities in 1986, the communal atmosphere was already surcharged. 1987 was the year of serious disturbances for Meerut. On 1-2-1987 on the call for *'total bandh'* given by Muslims for Babri Masjid, Muslims kept their shops and establishments closed. Large number of Muslims from Meerut went to Delhi on 29-2-1987 to participate in a mammoth rally organised by 'Babri Masjid Action Committee'. As a counter measure Hindu organisations gave a call for *'Meerut Bandh'* which was again a complete success. Hindu activists, on a call, hoisted saffron flags on their houses, shops and other establishments; also used to beat gongs and *Thalis* (metal plates) from their housetops for fifteen minutes every evening for one week. Administration used to interfere, but these programmes and counter programmes increased the communal temperature of the City. The local administration used to organise peace committee meetings in different localities and *mohallas* but these efforts could not reduce the mounting communal frenzy. Syed Shahabuddin's programme of addressing a Muslim rally at Meerut on March 20, 1987 was banned by prohibiting his entry in Meerut. In the meantime famous Nauchandi fair started after Holi festival and it was hoped that as per experience of previous years, it would provide opportunities for business, cultural, social and other healthy activities and divert the attention of the local people. Unfortunately it did not happen this time.

On April 14, 1987, Nauchandi Mela was in full swing, which attracted huge traditional crowd from evening till late night. On this day fell the Muslim festival of Shab-e-barat, which used to be celebrated by doing lot of fire works in the evening. Ambedkar Jayanti (Birth Day of Dr. B.R. Ambedkar), also fell on this day, which was celebrated with enthusiasm by local scheduled castes. Strong police arrangements were made in Shohrab gate locality on Hapur Road, area adjacent to Nauchandi Mela and the traffic was also diverted to ensure smooth display of traditional fireworks by competing Muslim teams. A birthday party was being celebrated in the house of a Hindu in *mohalla* Lodhipura (Hindu locality) adjacent to Hashimpura (predominantly Muslim locality), which was not far off from the site of ongoing fireworks. Music being played on the loudspeaker in the birthday party was objected to by a few Muslim youths, who pelted stones, which was retaliated by the Hindus and this started a serious communal riot. It was rightly apprehended by the local authorities that if the riot spreads to Nauchandi fair, it would most likely result in extensive damage to human life and property, as about 2 lac innocent people whowere enjoying the fair, were unaware of these communal developments in the adjacent locality. Authorities could succeed temporarily in localising the law and order situation and saved the Mela from becoming the victim of communal frenzy. Incidents of arson gutted 54 shops in this area. The riot spread to other parts of the city and incidents of arson and stabbing took place in Delhi Gate area also, where passersby became the target of attack of the Muslim crowd.

On April 16, 1987 more incidents of arson and stabbing took place in the city resulting into imposition of curfew. In these riots 10 persons died, 23 were injured and 778 were arrested. Police had to resort to firing at two places. The monetary help was given to the next of kin of the dead, injured and to those whose property was damaged in arson. Curfew was lifted from 5 A.M. on April 28, as *Roza* (First of *Ramzan*) started on that morning. About two weeks passed off without any untoward incident.

I was posted as Deputy Inspector General of Police (Administration) at D.G.P., Head Quarters Lucknow, dealing with the desk of personnel management of all the Gazetted officers of U.P. Police and I.P.S. officers of U.P. cadre. Sri Ganeshwar Jha, (I.P.S. 1967) was Assistant to D.G.P. in the rank of D.I.G. He used to deal with various matters including law and order, intelligence reports and deployment of P.A.C. and other security forces. We very often discussed the matters of mutual interest and took each other's help. Sri Daya Shankar Bhatnagar (I.P.S.-1954) had taken over as D.G.P., U.P. in April. He was very strict in providing D.G. reserve P.A.C. Coys to Districts and expected the field officers to manage the law and order situations within the locally available resources so that P.A.C. Coys could be spared for intensive training. Any request for additional P.A.C. Coys was turned down sternly. Earlier the requests of field officers of the State were considered leniently resulting into excessive deployment at the cost of much needed in-service training. On 28-4-1987 there were 35 Coys (32 P.A.C. and 3 C.R.P.F.) deployed in Meerut. Despite repeated requests, on the grounds of prevailing communal tension and ongoing month of *Ramzan*, for extension of these Coys from S.S.P./Range D.I.G./Zonal I.G.P. Meerut, the thumb rule was applied and Coys of D.G.P. reserve were withdrawn, leaving behind only two P.A.C. Coys of the Range Reserve on 10-5-1987. This necessitated the withdrawal of Civil Police from rural areas for Meerut city resulting in depletion of resources in otherwise sensitive places (towns and big villages) falling under various Police Stations. Sri Ganeshwar Jha used to feel very uncomfortable as the papers used to pass through him and telephonic requests were also made to him. His verbal and written pleadings could not convince the boss.

On 16-5-1987, one Ajai Sharma (tenant) was shot dead by a Muslim landlord in *mohalla* Kainchiyan under Kotwali Police Station. It was explained as tenant-landlord dispute. Local authorities held Peace Committee meetings with a view to elicit public co-operation. On evening of May 18 one shop was burnt which escalated incidents of arson etc. and serious communal riots broke out which continued for over three months and curfew remained clamped from time to time from 18-5-87 to 7-9-1987. During this period several incidents of serious nature and varied dimensions took place. I had the occasion to see and deal with some of them and here I give the description as my colleagues and I, both seniors and juniors, perceived.

Serious riots broke out in the night of 18/19-5-1987. Around 9 P.M. in Suraj Kund area (Civil Lines) a kiosk (*khokha*) used for manufacture of carom boards, owned by a Hindu and given on rent to a Muslim was set on fire by unknown miscreants. A little later, timely arrival and intervention of police averted a serious incident of arson, when about 50 youngsters from *mohalla* Imliyan were brickbatting and were about to set a house on fire belonging to a Hindu (Mool Chand) in nearby Shahpir Gate locality. About a furlong away a shop 'Laxmi Confectionary' was looted, set on fire, owner Kulbhushan, aged 28 years, was stabbed by the mob from the Muslim *mohalla* Imliyan. Senior officers reached and controlled the situation and ordered the arrests. While arrests were being made (between 11 P.M. to 2 A.M.) by the police with the help of P.A.C., two P.A.C. constables with their rifles were dragged inside a lane by the crowd in *Mohalla* Hashimpura, P.S. Civil Lines. They were quickly rescued and one rifle recovered, while the other rifle was taken away by the miscreants. Muslim reaction of these arrests was manifested by provocative announcements. Loud speakers in the mosques were extensively used to arouse communal feelings and to give directions to the local Muslims by repeatedly chanting the phrases like *"Islam khatre mein hai"* (Islam is in danger). A Muslim crowd of about one thousand men, women and children was already on the road and housetops and they were indulging in brickbatting, arson and firing. Police firing was done to disperse the rioters. As a reaction to this, serious communal riots broke out in old Delhi and curfew was clamped there also. Thereafter authorities of Delhi Police and Meerut remained in constant touch with each other so that happenings of either city were known to each other for taking timely preventive action.

Next three days were the worst for Meerut as unprecedented incidents took place which not only engulfed the entire old city but also badly affected the new posh colonies which hitherto were known as the areas of cultured and gentle persons. On May 19 from 5 A.M. onwards, that is after the '*Sahari*' (meal before starting the fast), very serious Muslim reaction was seen everywhere in city particularly in old city. Police remained busy in tackling the situations which got aggravated due to equally strong reaction from Hindus. Army was called to assist the local administration which remained deployed for several days. Many lives were lost and hundreds received injuries. Loss of several crores of Rupees was suffered due to arson, loot, damage to property, the particularly in handloom factories, which were mainly owned by Hindus but had Muslim weavers from eastern U.P. and Bihar. Around 5 A.M. on 19-5-87, after the incidents of Imliyan, similar announcements were made from mosques of other localities exhorting Muslims to come out and react. Besides the localities on Hapur Road, in Islamabad, predominantly Muslim locality, Muslims came out in thousands from other areas and indulged in looting and arson damaging shops, houses, petrol pumps and buses etc. and they also used firearms. Crowds from Islamabad, Lakhipura and Ahmadnagar, besides firing from the weapons, also set on fire the shops, houses and factories particularly of handloom on outskirts of southern city in Pilokhari area. In east on Garh Road, crowds indulged in looting and burning of shops and houses. Road blocks and barriers were erected on Hapur and Pilokrari Roads to prevent police entry. One Dr. Prabhat Kumar, a young and promising medical practitioner was going on a call to Hapur. He was stopped on Hapur Road and his car set on fire by the Muslim mob, resulting in his death in the car itself. He left behind a baby son, young wife and father Dr. Har Pal Singh, Professor and head of the Department in local N.A.S. College. The students of N.A.S. College reacted violently and indulged in arson and loot of Muslim houses and shops in non-curfew areas of Sadar Bazar and Lalkurti. Dr. Prabhat Kumar was very popular in local Muslims, who, when came to know about his identity, felt very sorry on his loss. Later Professor Har Pal Singh, his father, forgetting the personal loss of his son, worked very hard for restoration of peace in the city. His young widow, a medico, also contributed in restoration of peace. They used to cite the example of their own irreparable loss telling the people that enough was enough and Meerut must return to normalcy.

On 19-5-1987 some other badly affected areas were Shorab Gate, Zaidi Farm, Khatta Road, Bhumia Pul, Rashidnagar, all predominantly Muslim localities, Tarapuri, Hindu locality and Shashtri Nagar (New Posh Colony). Curfew was imposed in areas of worst affected Police Stations (1) Kotwali, (2) Lisari Gate, (3) Delhi Gate, (4) Medical College and (5) Civil Lines (in few areas only). Army assistance was sought and columns deployed in worst affected and sensitive areas. Additional P.A.C. and C.R.P.F. Coys were also deployed. To augment the manpower and other resources Civil Police, Fire Brigades and senior officers were mobilised. Flag marches were undertaken, educational institutions closed, arms and ammunition shops sealed and preventive arrests made. Sensing the gravity of the situation Sri D.S. Bhatnagar, D.G.P. also airdashed to Meerut and returned a day later. There were Congress Governments in U.P. with Sri Bir Bahadur Singh as Chief Minister and at the Centre with Mr. Rajiv Gandhi as Prime Minister. During the same evening Chief Minister Bir Bahadur Singh, Mrs. Mohisina Kidwai, Union Minister for Urban Development and Member of Lok Sabha from Meerut and Union State Minister for Home Sri Rajesh Pilot arrived to take stock of the situation.

Next day on 20-5-1987 there was no improvement in the situation and several unpleasant incidents took place. Brickbatting and exchange of firing continued between Hindus and Muslims in *mohallas* Hashimpura and Laxminagar under P.S. Civil Lines, and Khatta Road in P.S. Lisarigate, resulting in serious damage to houses. In *mohallas* Mohammad Nagar, Zaidi Farm, Zakir Colony, Islamabad and Gola Kuan highly provocative slogans were raised on loudspeakers from mosques. Situations were tackled by the authorities with the help of police, P.A.C. and Army. Fire Brigade vehicles had the biggest handicap of non-availability of water supply as there were no fire hydrants and every time they had to go far away to Police Lines for refilling. Hindus reacted very strongly in predominantly Hindu areas and set fire to Muslim shops and houses in Sadar Bazar, Sotiganj,

Mawana Bus Stand, Prabhatnagar, Saket (a posh colony), Beghum Bridge (important business centre), Kutchery Chaupla (near Collectorate), P. L. Sharma Road and Shastri Nagar (another posh colony). Three Muslims were stabbed of whom one died. Near Jali Kothi under P.S. Delhi Gate Hindu shops were burnt by Muslims. Police and Fire Brigade units had a very tough time as almost the entire city was badly affected. There were rumours' galore all over. Muslims were being told that they were being maligned during *Ramjan* so that their festival of *Id* is spoilt. They were also telling each other that *Namaz* of last Friday on 22-5-87 be offered in local mosques instead of *Idgah*. Hindus felt that Muslims were attacking security forces, targeting Hindu property and moving in groups to commit violent incidents. It was also spread that a senior retired Police Officer from Muslim community (A.M. Shah-retired Additional I.G.P.) living in Civil Lines area, had also fired from his weapons. The communal atmosphere remained highly surcharged and panic stricken. Till this date, 24 persons had died and 34 injured. Another three Battalions of Army were called and deployed in most sensitive and worst affected areas of Hashimpura, Shohrabgate, Gola Kuan and Khairnagar.

On 21-5-1987 the riots spread to outskirts of Meerut city and rural areas. Incidents also took place in Sadar Bazar, Lalkurti, Kaseru kheda, Transport Nagar and Shastrinagar areas of city and Daurala, Kharkhoda and Kithore in rural belt. Two Pakistani nationals were also arrested while brickbatting and shouting slogans. Curfew was extended to the other affected areas in city. In Maliyana, adjoining area of western city, firing was exchanged between Hindus and Muslims during night but no deaths or injuries were reported.

On 22-5-1987 morning, when I was in office at Lucknow, D.G.P. Mr. Bhatnagar asked me to accompany him to Meerut that day. I asked him about my role there and the period for which I would be required to stay so that I could carry my uniform and other things accordingly. He told me that I will be required to co-ordinate on his behalf in providing extra resources etc., particularly in respect of manpower and equipment and I may be required to stay there for 2 to 3 days. I sat with Sri Ganeshwar Jha and took briefing from him. In the mean time my wife packed my things, whom I had sounded on phone about my programme.

Sri Bhatnagar, I and Sri Roshan Lal, Director U.P. Police Telecommunication left Amausi Airport, Lucknow in a small four seater plane of U.P. Govt. On way I felt uncomfortable and nausating during one and half hour journey to Hindon Airport Ghaziabad. Earlier I had travelled several times by air and once or twice in the same plane but I never got that kind of feeling. On landing I heaved a sigh of relief. From there we drove straight to Meerut and on reaching there we got busy with the work. Though, I had gone there prepared for three days, I could come to Lucknow after three months as I was posted there as Range D.I.G. and the law and order situations did not permit me to leave my jurisdiction.

Because of curfew and in order to avoid collection of huge crowds on May 22, last Friday of *Ramjan*, Muslims offered prayers in their local *mohalla* mosques and the traditional *Namaj* of *Juma-e-tulvida* could not be offered in Jama Masjid. Several incidents took place on this day also. A train was stopped by Hindu crowd at *mohalla* Nai Basti near Meerut City Railway Station, but timely arrival and firing by Police saved the situation from taking an ugly turn. Incidents of arson and loot took place in Kishan Pura, Begham Bagh, Rajban Bazar (Cantt) and Civil Lines (few stray incidents). Incidents of arson also took place outside the city in Partapur (outskirts of Meerut city), Sardhana (Tahsil H.Q.), Daurala (suburb), and Hastinapur (about 45 Km away). Search operations by Police and Army were launched in houses of *mohalla* Hashimpura where serious incidents had occurred on 18/19-5-1987 and rifles of P.A.C. *jawans* were snatched. One P.A.C. rifle was recovered. Loudspeakers were got removed from mosques and other religious places. Several Muslims were taken into custody and sent to Police Lines for further action. It was subsequently alleged that atrocities were committed by police and P.A.C. on these arrested persons, as in Police Lines they were locked in barracks, were denied water and other items with the result they felt difficulty in doing *Roza aftar* in the evening. In night they were taken out to parade ground where the new recruits were made to stand at two ends and these persons were asked to run from one end to the other and recruits while standing at their places used to beat them with *lathis*. They were later sent to Fatehgarh jail where some of them died. It was again alleged that they died because of the beatings in Police Lines

Meerut, while the other version was that they indulged in rioting in a jail necessitating use of force by the jail authorities which resulted in their deaths. It was again alleged that on that evening out of the persons arrested in Hashimpura, some were made to sit in P.A.C. trucks, taken away and killed. It was widely reported by the media as *'Hashimpura Kand'*

Hashimpura kand (Hashimpura Episode)

In late evening briefing meeting held on 22-5-1987 at Circuit House in which Executive/Civil, Police and Army officers were present, stock was taken of the day's happenings, the prevailing situation and the measures taken to handle the situation. I was also present along with the D.G.P. and that was my first exposure of these ongoing riots. Arrests and recoveries in Hashimpura were also discussed. Brigadier R.K. Singh, Sub Area Commander Meerut also gave the detailed account of the role played by his troops in handling these riots including Hashimpura. Nobody mentioned anything about adverse role played by the security forces. On early morning of June 23, in Circuit House, where I was also camping, some hush hush was going on about few residents of Hashimpura, who were injured but managed to reach Ghaziabad and were admitted in a hospital there. Nobody told me about this. Later in the morning the usual briefing meeting was held, where it transpired that the injured had told at Ghaziabad that after searches in Hashimpura that evening about 200-300 young Muslim boys were segregated from the rest, made to sit in P.A.C. trucks, driven away to Muradnagar on Delhi Road from where they went downstream on the canal road and then made them alight one by one, stand on the bank of the flowing deep canal, where they were shot at and thrown in the water. About 3 such injured could manage to cross to the other side, walked to national highway, caught the transport and reached Ghaziabad from where they informed Muslim leaders at Delhi and were admitted in hospital at Ghaziabad. Top Muslim leaders including Syed Sahabuddin reached Ghaziabad and took up their cause. Later few bodies were found in Hindon river in Delhi area on the border of Ghaziabad near 41st Bn. P.A.C. During next few days several bodies were recovered downstream in Ganga Canal in districts Ghaziabad and Bulandshahar. A platoon commander of 41st Bn. P.A.C. Ghaziabad was found responsible for these incidents, who had taken some of them to river Hindon flowing near his Bn. and got them shot and threw the bodies in the shallow river. He drove back to Meerut but did not inform the authorities so that the culprits could not be known. Criminal cases were registered and investigated by U.P., C.I.D., against police and P.A.C. and about one and half dozen of them were found guilty and charge sheeted after about eight years for facing trial before the court of law. These incidents shook many. Local Muslims got frightened but infuriated and started reacting violently with police and P.A.C., who too were scared of facing the Muslim crowds and always wanted to carry rifles so that they could save themselves. This episode raised several questions and called for strong remedial measures. Accusing fingers were raised on Army also because one Major Sharma, who belonged to that locality, was ill-treated by Muslims a few weeks earlier in riots.

'Maliyana Kand' (Maliyana Episode)

May 23rd also continued to witness incidents of arson, loot and stabbings. The worst happened in Maliyana, located adjacent to western part of the city. During day time Muslims of that village collected in a local grave yard, allegedly shouted slogans, which infuriated local Hindus, who collected to face that Muslim crowd. In the meantime a house was set on fire which aggravated the situation. Shots were also fired from the crowd. Several shops and houses of both the communities were gutted. Senior officers reached with reinforcements of Police and P.A.C. While dealing with the situation, firing was resorted to in which some Muslims were killed. In a nearby locality few bodies were found in a unused well. This incident in the name of *'Maliyana Kand'* received wide publicity against P.A.C. It was also said that these Muslims were preparing to leave for other villages to take refuge but Hindus mistook it as preparation against them and reacted in panic which forced the police to fire. Police also helped several Muslim families in shifting them safely to their relations in villages in rural areas.

The incidents of Hashimpura and Maliyana were very widely reported by the media. Credibility of not only local police and P.A.C. but also of the Civil Administration received a severe blow and the ruling Congress Govt. too had a very tough time.

'WE' and 'THEY'

Stray incidents continued to happen in various parts of the city till 27-5-1987. After about nine days curfew was relaxed on

26-5-1987 for about three hours in some areas and thereafter on other days in phases in other localities. The curfew caused untold miseries to people. Water supply was disrupted due to desertion of the staff from duties in localities of the rival communities. Essential supplies could not be arranged sufficiently. Children remained without milk. Even vegetables could not reach the city. Patients suffered for want of medicines, daily wage earners had to sleep without food, *Rozadars* suffered for want of essential items, and marriages had to be postponed. Because of fastings, Muslims felt the worst pinch. All this led to resentment against the local administration and security forces. Muslims continued to bear grudge and reacted at places by firing at police and P.A.C.. As Muslims were targeting them, Hindus developed sympathy for administration and security forces. This sharp reaction resulted in vertical division of the local population into 'WE' and 'THEY'.

The Police Control Room was functioning at PS Kotwali, almost in the centre of the walled city, a densely populated area and the roads leading to it were very narrow. Heavy vehicles had to pass through them and the parking was very difficult in and around Kotwali. Police and P.A.C. *Jawans* on reserve duty found shelter on the roof top and the scorching heat during day made their life miserable. As the entire area fell under curfew, people found it difficult to reach the authorities, who used to be there most of the time. Sardar Buta Singh, Union Home Minister, visited Meerut on 23-5-1987 and he also came to Control Room. His convoy was fired upon from Muslim houses but luckily no one was injured. Same afternoon, the local Station Commander, a Major General, took round of the curfew bound areas and the creaking sounds of the sirens of the vehicles of his convoy created lot of panic in the people, particularly the Muslims of the Kotwali area. He was later on apprised of this and thereafter the sounding of sirens and hooters was avoided by the authorities including Police and Army.

During curfew relaxations and in non-curfew areas politicians and other interested persons started visiting Meerut, meeting people of their respective communities and carried tales. Seven opposition members of Parliament visited Meerut on 25-5-1987 but they were not allowed to go to sensitive areas. Sri Ashok Singhal, General Secretary of Vishwa Hindu Parishad, accompanied by Swami Prabhu Dutt Bramchari visited on 27-5-1987.

Festival of *Id-ul-Fitre* fell on 28-5-1987. Curfew was relaxed for four hours in entire city from 7 A.M. to 11 A.M., so that Muslims could offer Namaz and celebrate Id. *Namaz* was offered in local mosques instead of *Idgah* and people could not go around to wish *Id Mubarak*. This did not help in easing tension but authorities could not take chance by relaxing curfew for longer duration.

The team of officers at the outbreak of riots was the same, which had handled earlier riots this year. The district level team was of Sri R.S. Kaushik as District Magistrate and Sri V.K.B. Nair as Senior Superintendent of Police, whereas at Divisional level Sri Ramesh Chandra was the Divisional Commissioner and Sri Nathoo Lal the Range Deputy Inspector General of Police. Sri S.K. Mukerji was the Zonal Inspector General of Police having jurisdiction over Meerut and Garhwal Ranges. Sri G.L. Sharma, who after his transfer had been awaiting posting orders at Chandigarh, was recalled to Meerut as Officer on Special Duty, Law and Order on 23-5-1987 and was subsequently posted as S.S.P. Sri T. George Joseph, I.A.S. officer in Super Time Scale, who had earlier remained D.M. Meerut was entrusted the job of rehabilitation of the riot victims and was subsequently made the D.M. as an exceptional case because this post was of the senior time scale of I.A.S. I continued to camp at Meerut and used to do the co-ordination work of providing required extra resources and manpower. Sri D.S. Bhatnagar, D.G.P., Sri Surendra Singh Chauhan, State Minister for Home U.P., Sri Gopi Nath Dikshit, Home Minister U.P., camped most of the time at Meerut or Delhi. Daily briefing meetings were also held in Circuit House, which were generally presided over by the Home Minister.

Prime Minister's Visit

After *Id* was over, a team of senior officers including D.G.P. Sri D.S. Bhatnagar (I accompanied him) Sri S.K. Mukerji, I.G.P. Meerut and Sri Ramesh Chandra Divisional Commissioner Meerut, was called to Delhi on 29-5-1987 where we met the Union Home Minister Sri Buta Singh and also went to Prime Minister's House for discussion. There we were told that Sri Rajiv Gandhi, Prime Minister will visit Meerut on 30-5-87. Sri Mani Shankar Aiyar, I.F.S., O.S.D. to prime minister had detailed briefing from us. The details of the visit could not be worked out as till then every thing was in the melting pot. We returned to Meerut same night and apprised the local officers to make preparations for the visit of the prime minister. There were only few hours at their disposal.

As the communal atmosphere of the city was emotionally surcharged and curfew could not be relaxed for longer duration and the P.M. wanted to visit the riot affected areas, the local authorities had very tough time in making preparations for the V.V.I.P. visit and at the same time ensure maintenance of law and order in surcharged conditions, as nothing wrong aught to have happened while the P.M. was in city. It was conveyed On 30-5-1987 morning that the P.M. would come by Helicopter, go around affected areas, meet the people at Circuit House and thereafter, will fly back to Delhi. Necessary preparations were made accordingly. Same after noon the P.M. landed at Army helipad, went around some affected areas including Maliana, which had been in news for atrocities on Muslims. While the P.M. was going from house to house in Maliana accompanied by Chief Minister Sri Vir Bahadur Singh, U.P. Home Minister Sri Gopi Nath Dikshit, other political dignitaries and the officers, Ms. Sarla Grewal, Secretary to Prime Minister was left behind as she found it difficult to walk briskly with the youthful Prime Minister. The senior officers and the security teams were accompanying the P.M. When I noticed that she was walking all alone, I introduced myself and started walking with her, as I was not doing any specific security or law and order duty. She asked me several questions including the uncomfortable question of the withdrawal of P.A.C. after the serious riots of April and I tried to convince her. She also made some unpleasant observations about the D.G.P., that were conveyed to her by the people. I had to keep quiet as she was commenting about my own boss. I, of course, apprised the D.G.P. about it, when I got a chance to do so.

At the Circuit House, the P.M. received several delegations and heard cross section of people who had come to see him. They conveyed their own feelings and also gave suggestions. He met the senior Civil, Police and Army authorities in a separate room and received briefings. While District authorities gave oral briefing, Army authorities did briefing with the help of a city map, which was well received. I contacted., Sri Mani Shankar Aiyar, who happened to be my batch mate of 1963, and enquired about further programme of the P.M. as arrangements had to be made in advance. He could not tell me the exact programme, but sounded that P.M. may go to curfew bound areas in Islamabad and other worst affected areas. I apprised the local authorities about this, who got uneasy because his visit meant physical risk to PM's security, create law and order problem as people would come out on streets despite curfew and also route arrangements from Meerut to Delhi for long road journey in night for which sufficient Police could not be mobilised at such a short notice. The Range D.I.G. and Zonal I.G.P., got busy in ensuring arrangements in Meerut and Ghaziabad districts as road journey was through both the Districts. District authorities of Meerut had no reaction time for preparations as visit to curfew bound areas was likely to come within next few minutes. Around sunset time the I.A.F. crew left as night flying with the V.V.I.P. was not safe. Whatever possible at few minutes notice had been done to take him to riot torn and curfew bound localities of the city. A few minutes later Sri Rajiv Gandhi came out from the Circuit House and met people who could not go inside and then asked to drive to curfew bound areas. He visited Islamabad, Pilokhadi, Bhumianpul (predominantly Muslim localities), Lisadigate (mixed locality, where one person was stabbed that very day), Brahmpuri (Hindu locality), etc. Despite curfew, people came out in large numbers, to apprise the P.M. about the situation and their woes and police had very tough time in controlling the unfrisked crowd in otherwise surcharged atmosphere. The mood of the local population was divided on communal lines and therefore, this manifestation was evident in their expressions also. Whereas, the minority community openly criticised the Civil and Police authorities, Hindus did not bear much grudge against the administration but did express unhappiness with various arrangements and thus the vertical divide was evident. The P.M. left late in the evening for Delhi and everybody entrusted with his security duties was concerned about his safe journey but heaved a sigh of relief on learning about his safe arrival at PM's house.

Transfers

Whatever might have transpired at political level but the shifting operations of the officers started immediately after the P.M.'s visit. Sri G.L. Sharma replaced Sri V.K.B. Nair as S.S.P.

on June 1, 1987. Sri R.S.Kaushik was replaced as District Magistrate by Sri T. George Joseph, who had earlier been a very popular District Magistrate of Meerut and was in Commissiner's scale. Sri B.K. Chaturvedi, an experienced officer of U.P. Police Service, who was completing fourth year as Superintendent of Police City Meerut was transferred and Sri Vijai Kumar Gupta young I.P. S. officer, Additional Superintendent of Police Lucknow, was flown in U.P. Govt. plane to take over the charge of City S.P. Sri M.A. Farooqui replaced the Additional District Magistrate City.

On June 1, D.G.P. Sri Bhatnagar, who had been camping at Meerut asked me to get ready to accompany him to Lucknow as he was to catch flight from Delhi. After lunch we left by road for Delhi, where he was summoned to attend a meeting with Chief Minister Sri Vir Bahadur Singh and Home Minister Sri Gopi Nath Dikshit at U.P. Niwas. While the D.G.P. attended the meeting inside the C.M.'s room, I waited outside. After about an hour the meeting was over and the decision was taken to post me as Deputy Inspector General of Police Meerut Range. Sri Bhatnagar came out and told me to go back to Meerut but did not tell me that I was being posted there. When I asked him as to how long will my presence be required there as I had been camping there to co-ordinate on his behalf, he avoided the straight reply and told that he would communicate it to me later from Lucknow. The D.G.P. left for Lucknow and I proceeded by road to Meerut.

After crossing Ghaziabad, a few kilometres away, I noticed that a scooter was lying on the road and some persons were surrounding somebody at the end of the road. I asked the driver to stop the car and find out as to what had happened. I also got down to talk to people. I saw that one man was lying badly injured in unconscious condition and his wife, who too was injured but was in a position to talk to, was crying but the onlookers did not extend any help. I asked the people to stay behind to take care of the scooter till the police arrived and I took the couple in my car so that I could hurriedly take them to Medical College Meerut. There was no wireless in that car, hence no message could be flashed to any police authority for immediate help. On way she told me that they lived in Ordnance Factory area Muradnagar where her husband was employed as an officer and there was a good Dispensary in the campus where they would receive first aid and treatment. I took them there as it was just a few minutes drive. The Medical Officer was summoned immediately, who examined him and started the treatment. While I was waiting to watch their condition, I was told that brother of the injured was a Medical Officer in District Hospital, Ghaziabad and if the situation so demanded they would take him there. I said that I was thinking of taking him to Medical College, Meerut for better and specialised treatment. The local Medical officer assured me that he would handle him safely and I could leave. I took their names and address and left. I stopped at Police Station Muradnagar, gave them the address telling that they should visit the scene, take care of the scooter and other legal formalities. On reaching Meerut I met the local officers and told them that I had been asked to camp there again. Sri Ramesh Chandra, Divisional Commissioner, gave a smile and told that I would be required to be there in another capacity as Range D.I.G. as had been conveyed to him by the Chief Secretary Sri Kalyankrishnan. I felt that D.G.P. Mr. Bhatnagar could have conveyed it to me at Delhi itself. As D.I.G. Administration I used to deal with this subject and I used to be in picture about postings and transfers of I.P.S./U.P.P.S. Officers but when it came to be my own transfer, the D.G.P. did not think it proper to tell me even after the decision had been taken and I was his trusted staff officer. In night at Circuit House I remained disturbed and kept on thinking as to how will I be able to help in normalising the situation when a section of local population had no faith on local police and P.A.C. and security forces too were scared of going in Muslim areas. On June 2, 1987 I took over from Sri Nathoo Lal. Sri D.S. Bhatnagar was replaced as D.G.P. by Sri Raj Nath Gupta. About a month later Sri Vijai Kumar Diwan replaced Sri Ramesh Chandra as Divisional Commissiner and after about three months Sri Vijai Sharma was posted as District Magistrate. Sri Satish Kumar Mukerji continued as I.G.P. Zone for next two years.

Incidents thereafter

No major untoward incident occurred till 27-6-1987 and situation was gradually returning to normal. People got to work whenever and wherever curfew was relaxed. Thereafter aggressive Hindu assertiveness became evident as several incidents particularly on the occasions of Hindu festivals took place which received wide publicity. Here we mention some of them.

Jagannath Rath Yatra

An innocuous but traditional annual *Rath Yatra*, similar to one taken out in Jagannathpuri (Orissa) on grand scale, was scheduled for June 29, 1987 in Sadar Bazar area. District Administration had asked the organisers to curtail the route keeping in mind the communal situation to which they readily agreed. Almost every thing was finalised but just before permitting them in writing the District Magistrate preferred to seek clearance from Government. The Home Secretary asked if there was a possibility of disturbance which D.M. could not rule out. Consequently permission was denied at the eleventh hour. This unexpected development made the organisers feel defeated and insulted. Hindus resented it vehemently and decided to take out the procession, come what may. Preventive arrests were made to which the Hindus resented and closed their shops. Some prominent Hindu leaders from Delhi also came to Meerut to press for this cause. Preparations started from both the sides i.e. the Hindus and the local administration. Hindus decided that their ladies instead of men would come out and pull the chariot of Lord Jagannath from the place where it was kept to destination, a local temple. The administration clamped curfew in Sadar Bazar area, so that people remained indoors and deployed Women C.R.P.F. Coy, so that they could deal with the women. On June 29 during day time, despite curfew and very heavy presence of Police, P.A.C., C.R.P.F. and Civil Administration, over a thousand Hindus came out defying curfew and while police was dealing with them the ladies pulled the chariot on the road, which was soon got pulled back to the place from where it had started. Force was used to disperse the crowd.

The administration heaved a sigh of relief as C.R.P.F. Women Coy, which was raised recently and was perhaps used for the first time in the country, dealt with sternly the women who came out to pull the chariot. Had they not been there, the male component might have been used to disperse these women rioters as the District Women Police was not available in sufficient numbers. Had they not been there, complaints of molestation and mal treatment of Hindu women might have been made. Over 60 rioters, but not the women, were arrested. Hindus decided to keep shops closed in various parts of the city till permission was granted for *Rath Yatra*. These incidents again raised the communal temperature in City. Hindus collected at Sidheshwar Mahadev Temple in Sadar Bazar to protest against the incidents of Rath Yatra, pelted stones on police, where upon force was used to disperse the crowd and some arrests were made. Same day one Satpal, a Hindu, was stabbed in *Mohalla* Dibainagar under Police Station Nauchandi, who later died in Medical College, where he was taken for treatment. On June 30, when a Hindu procession from Brahmpuri, was going towards Collectorate to court arrests, Muslim crowd in their locality in Valley Bazar area pelted stones. Incidents of arson, looting of shops, stabbings etc. took place in various other parts of the city. Police had to use force including firing in which some rioters were killed. Muslims closed their shops to resent the killings in police firing. Realising its mistake the District Administration ultimately allowed *Rath Yatra* which was taken out peacefully on 2-7-2001. This procession had unprecedented participation as compared to previous years. The overall situation continued to be tense. Stray incidents continued in city and rural areas for some more time despite the precautions by District Administration.

Kanvarias

When I was Addl. Superintendent of Police in 1967, a few thousand Hindus from rural areas used to carry holy Ganga water from Haridwar and offered at Shiva Temple at Pura

Devotees collecting *Ganga* water after Holy Dip at *Har-Ki-Pairi* , Haridwar

A child with Kanvar

Mahadev, situated on the banks of Hindon River under rural Police Station Binauli. No extra arrangements were required as local police managed the show. In July 1987 Sri T. George Joseph informed us that when he was District Magistrate, Kanvarias, who came in large numbers used to pose serious problems of

Kanvarias on Cycles

crowd control and law and order. As the entire area from Haridwar to Pura Mahadev, Meerut city and beyond towards Delhi and Bulandshahar fell under my jurisdiction, I studied the problem in detail and ordered the District Superintendents of Police to make suitable arrangements. Certain salient features could be of interest to readers, hence they are being mentioned here. In the month of Shravan, falling in July/August every year millions of Hindu devotees, from Haryana, Rajasthan and western U.P., go to Haridwar by trains, buses and other transport, collect holy water from river Ganga after having holy dip at *'Har ki Pairi'* and then march on foot for several days and nights, some of them non stop, for hundreds of kilometers to various destinations to offer the holy water in Shiva Temples of their choice on the day of Shravan Sivratri. The common faith is that by doing so the devotees would please God Shiva, who in return would bestow his choicest blessings and fulfill their wishes, called '*mannat*' or '*manauti*'. These devotees who carry holy water in 'Kanvar' hanging on shoulders, are called '*Kanvarias*'. Though they came from various places and did not know each other, yet they formed a fraternity and joined each other, whenever situation arose. Certain superstitions were also followed which created problems for the administration. Kanvarias would avoid passing under a 'Gular' tree and if per chance they passed any where

Ancient Shiva Temple At Pura Mahadev, Binauli Meerut

under it, they would blame the administration for that and insist that the concerned *Kanvaria* be taken back to Haridwar in a Govt. vehicle, so that he could start his journey again with a

Kali Paltan Temple Meerut Cantt

new '*Kanvar*'. Some of them would not like to be touched by anybody and if by chance somebody touched them, they would treat the '*Kanvar*' to have become impure and unworthy of carrying further for offering on Lord Shiva and would therefore, insist on being taken back to Haridwar for starting with a fresh '*Kanvar*'. Other *Kanvarias* would join them and make a common cause and create law and order problems. They would also create problems enroute in Muslim villages/localities and at times would destroy Muslim graves (*mazars*), and other religious structures. This again called for serious vigil. Road accidents resulting in deaths and injuries would also cause resentment in them. In this backdrop fell '*Shravan Shivratri*' of 1987 in the month of July when communal situation of Meerut and neighbouring areas was already surcharged .

News of '*Kanvarias*' gathering in unprecedented large numbers at Haridwar that year started pouring in. I alerted the Districts concerned to make suitable arrangements and also maintain adequate vigil. Devotees from Haryana went towards Ambala via Shaharanpur and there were no problems. Those bound for Rajasthan and certain other parts of Haryana, marched on National High way upto Meerut and then went either towards Delhi or Bulanshahar, Aligarh and Agra. Six Kanvarias, who had already walked over two hundred kilometres, and were bound for Dholpur (Rajasthan), were killed by a speeding truck while they were resting in night on G.T. road near Arnia (District Bulandshahar), a place between Khurja and Aligarh. As there were very few *Kanvarias* at that place, no law and order problem was created. I again issued instructions to Districts for adequate precautions and also to control over speeding of vehicles.

A few days before the actual Shiv Ratri day, *Kanvarias* started playing havoc with Muslims. A bearded Muslim travelling by a bus was attacked during day time, killed and partly burnt and left in a roadside field between Daurala and Meerut. The Sub Inspector incharge of P.S. Daurala prepared the inquest report and showed the body as unknown. The following day Zonal I.G.P. Mr. Mukerji, Commissioner Mr. V.K. Diwan and I left for Daurala to visit the scene of occurrence and to assess the situation. While we were in Cantt. area on main high way, we saw few *Kanvarias* setting fire to a truck driven by a Sikh. We could not save the truck as it was loaded with paper bundles which rapidly caught fire. However we could save the truck driver and the cleaner. Their alleged fault was that the truck was not being driven safely. Thousands of marching *Kanvarias* made a common cause and started creating scene. We some how pacified them and proceeded further informing the Control Room to rush Fire Brigade accompanied by police party. A little away from the tri-section of bypass, we saw the place where the Muslim bus passenger was killed and partly burnt. On reaching Police Station Daurala, I called for the papers including inquest report and the post-mortem report. I was told that the face of the deceased was burnt partially and a Passport having a photograph, was found on the person. The Sub Inspector had no answer as to why did he not bother to find out the identity of the deceased from the address given in Passport. I dispatched an accompanying Head Constable (Muslim) of my office and a constable of that Police Station on a motor cycle to the given address of a village in Baraut area. They were told by the villagers that an aged person of their village had gone to Shaharanpur and gave the address. On reaching Shaharanpur at given address, they showed the passport and the photograph, where they learnt that the person in whose name that passport was issued was actually alive and present. The aged man from that village of Baraut had left by bus for Delhi to arrange visa on that Passport. From the description it was established that actually that man was killed in that bus incident. Thus his relatives could know about his fate and could do the needful for the dead. I admonished the concerned staff and advised them to be more humane and professional. We also alerted the District authorities to exercise more vigil on road as well as in city as these rowdy *Kanvarias* could create many more problems.

It was mango season when this Yatra was on. Mango groves owned by rich Hindus and Muslims are taken on lease by Muslim *Kunjras* usually for two years as usually the mango crop remains lean in one year and bumper in the other. While this march of *Kanvarias* was on, a few days before the main day, some of them attacked Muslim *Kunjaras* of nearby groves on national highway after crossing Muzaffarnagar. This happened for two successive nights and the persons doing so were supposed to be *Kanvarias* from Meerut, who were already anguished due to the ongoing communal strife in their city. I and Sri V.K. Diwan Commissioner, decided to go to Muzaffarnagar to see things for ourselves and take suitable measures to prevent such happenings. Normally it was about one hour's drive to Muzaffarnagar from Meerut, but that day it took us over two hours.

Enroute we saw the devotees, men, old and young, women even from urban areas and children marching and chanting slogans of *'Bam Bam Bhole', 'Bhole Ki Jai'* etc. The double lane broad road was full of Kanvarias and vehicular traffic could hardly move on the tarred road. Business houses and factory owners had set up *'Kanvar Sewa Camps'* at various places right from Haridwar to Meerut and even beyond, where they were providing free tea and snacks, food, hot water, massaging etc. and place to rest. Devotees would usually pay for these services as they thought that getting free food etc. would not bring them the desired blessings of Lord Shiva. Such collections were generally diverted towards other purposes as those, who set up these camps would do it free out of feelings for their community and the service of *Kanvarias* was treated as service of God. We also noticed presence of Hindu activists in large numbers, who had divided the entire route in their zones, sectors, sub-sectors and beats. Those in beats would march along with the devotees as fellow *Kanvarias* and keep on indoctrinating and arousing their religious feelings on communal lines and carry on instructions with the help of other *Kanvarias*, who otherwise would not fall prey to them. The sub-sector people would ride the two wheelers and keep on patrolling their beats, remain in regular touch with beat fellows, tell them regarding rumours etc. and pass on regular instructions for execution. Those in sectors would move on trucks with loaded material to be used in case of need. Zonal people acted as think tank and did the planning for the entire journey. Seeing was believing because, had we not travelled, we could have never believed it. Sensing the mood of the lacs of marching people, we hurriedly completed our task at Muzaffarnagar and decided to return via Ramraj, Hastinapur and Mawana so that we could apprise the District Authorities of Meerut for immediate action before any thing serious went wrong. On this road we saw a few thousand *Kanvarias* but there was nothing abnormal. After crossing Mawana, we flashed message on wireless to Control Room Meerut to inform the D.M./S.S.P. to reach City Control Room at Kotwali, where we would like to talk to local officers. Within half an hour we were at Kotwali where officers had hurriedly arrived. We briefed them about the things that we saw and also told them that sensing the mood of the *Kanvarias*, most of whom were from Meerut, we could anticipate the worst to happen, both on highway and in Meerut city. Sri T. George Joseph, who had seen the things earlier, immediately agreed with our assessment but others were little surprised to hear us. These authorities were instructed to be on very high alert and do whatever, they could to avoid the worst to happen. They were also told to divert the traffic and not allow vehicles particularly the heavy ones to go on national highway.

The last batch of Kanvarias was on road between Muzaffarnagar and Meerut and the main rush was in the jurisdiction of District Meerut. On the night of July 21/22, a road side mosque was demolished by *Kanvarias* in village Walidpur by pushing a truck to the main wall but the local village Muslims, who were in sizable numbers, had to keep quite as the thousands of marching Kanvarias could do any thing because of their sheer presence in huge numbers. Next night of July 22/23, a few men posing as helpers of *Kanvarias* boarded a night bus near Daurala on some pretext as this bus was going from Delhi to Bijnor via Muzaffarnagar. When the bus crossed village Walidpur towards Sakoti Tanda, these persons, who had boarded this bus, identified the Muslim passengers, men having beards and women in burquas, made them alight and attacked them mercilessly killing 5 persons including three ladies and causing injuries to few others who were later admitted for treatment in various hospitals including Bijnor Medical College, Meerut and where the bus was taken by the driver and reported the incident there. Other fellow passengers could muster no courage to resist. This incident happened despite our briefing of the officers in the Control Room. It shook us all. People marching long distances to please Lord Shiva had no hesitation in brutally killing the innocent persons of the other faith. What an irony? One person killed was from Delhi and that sent shock waves there also as Old Delhi had also experienced the communal riots following the incidents of Meerut a few weeks earlier.

Main day of *Shiva Ratri* fell on July 24. A day earlier the atmosphere in Meerut city got very tense. Besides the incidents on the road, a Roadways bus going from Agra to Haridwar was attacked in city near Hapur bus stand by the *Kanvarias*. Near Islamia Degree College, one Ghulam Haider was stabbed, who was sent in precarious condition to Medical College for treatment. A Muslim youth of Abdullahpur, a village on outskirts of the

City was stabbed near District Jail and admitted in Medical College. Sensing the belligerent mood of the local *Kanvarias*, who were to do the *Jalabhishek* (offering the holy water) in Shiva Temples the next day, the Army was called again to assist the local administration as it was also Friday and Muslims were to offer mass *Namaz* in various mosques. Hindus turned out in large numbers for Jalabhishek in various temples including the main Kali Paltan Mandir in Cantt. near Sadar Bazar. Muslims too congregated in larger numbers for Friday prayers. The communal temperature rose very high and the situation remained tense and fragile.

After Shivaratri, incidents causing tension continued to happen. On 25-7-1987, the very next day of Shiv Ratri, Hindu crowd collected at P.S. Brahmpuri demanding release of arrested Hindus, got rowdy and the mob brickbatted very heavily on Policemen, forcing them to fire in self defence in which two persons were injured, who were rushed to hospitals for treatment. That day during relaxation of curfew, a Muslim fired at a Hindu in *Mohalla* Ahiran and the injured had to be shifted to hospital. On July 27, the two communities indulged in brickbatting on each other in riot-torn Pilokhari area. On call of *'Meerut Bandh'* on 30-7-1987 of Maulana Abdullah Bukhari of Delhi, to protest the bus killings, about 90% Muslim shops and establishments remained closed. Thereafter, the situation gradually started improving but the curfew continued in various areas, which was relaxed in phases on various days and was finally lifted on 7-9-1987, about three and half months of its imposition in last May.

In these unprecedented riots, 116 persons lost their lives,164 were injured, because of various incidents on several days, 28 Police personnel received serious injuries and 4495 persons were arrested.

Some Unforgettable Experiences

In May when serious riots started and curfew was suddenly imposed, a few trucks carrying meat to Delhi were left abandoned by the drivers as they had to flee for their lives. They remained standing there for more than a day with the result the meat got rotten, emanating foul smell which made life hell for the local people. Later on learning about it, these trucks were got removed.

On one afternoon when I and Sri V.K. Diwan were taking round on Delhi Road in city near trisection of Brahmpuri, we noticed a van parked on the road. On enquiry the passengers told us that they had returned from a marriage party along with the bride who too was sitting in the van and had been waiting there for about two hours as they got stranded due to curfew. We got them escorted to their house which was about 200 metres away. The security personnel on duty there did not allow them to move earlier as they had no authority to do so. Will that young bride ever forget that wait of the sultry afternoon?

Several marriages had to be postponed due to curfew in city. Will young couples, who were made to wait for weeks and months to get married, ever forget their nightmarish experience of Meerut? Why should mischief-mongers care for such sentiments?

Operation Normalisation

From the first week of June 1987, i.e. after about two weeks from the riots broke out and the situation could become some what stable, two pronged strategy was adopted for quickly normalising the situation. On one hand it was repeatedly hammered on police, P.A.C. and the civil administration to act impartially and not to give further cause of complaints, while on the other the communally surcharged atmosphere be normalised by adopting various methods including reconstruction and rehabilitation of the victims.

Rumours Galore

Rumours spread like wild fire right from day one, which kept on adding fuel to fire by the rumour mills which worked overtime. Worst incidents had occurred on 18/19-7-1987. A police jeep carrying a Deputy Superintendent of Police, Bulandshahar to Meerut for duty in night, ran over the crowd on Hapur Road killing a few Muslims. Muslims believed that police people were so reckless and biased that they would even drive on them, little caring for their safety. Perhaps this was the correct story, as the driver lost his nerves on facing the menacing crowd. This was one of the reasons for the anti-police announcements made from loudspeakers of mosques to confront the police. On the other, a rumour was spread in Hindu areas that Hindu ladies were taken out of houses on Hapur Road, stripped and their breasts chopped off. This made Hindus to retaliate against Muslims. Some of the senior police officers, who were coming for duty from Moradabad, and had stopped on road side tea shops, were practically made to believe by the story tellers that the atrocities committed on Hindu ladies were true. It was dispelled only when they arrived at the Circuit House and on verification were told, that nothing like that had happened. Such rumours flared up the frenzy in the population. Immediately there was no method to counter the rumours as announcements on loudspeakers fitted on vehicles, by police and magistrates would not be believed and some of the newspapers would even publish some such news which, though, incorrect was believed. Rumours galore continued for about two weeks. After discussions with media persons it was decided to publish a daily column captioned 'Today's Rumours–*Aaj Ki Afvaihen'* and it would be the duty of briefing officers, mostly D.M. and S.S.P., to collect the information before hand about the day's rumours and brief the media. This system worked very well in gradual restoration of normalcy.

Civil Defence Staff Utilised

Initially it took some time, during highly disturbed conditions, to mobilise the already existing Civil Defence machinery. Within a few days the volunteers (from both the communities) were on roads particularly during curfew relaxation periods. They would wear their uniforms and those without it would sport arms' bands and be on duty with whistles and canes. Locals used to obey them without hesitation while orders from security personnel at times were not taken in proper spirit. Fingers used to be raised on the impartiality of some of these volunteers but on the whole the system worked very well.

Peace Marches

Local prominent and respectable citizens came forward to do their bit in cooling down the tempers of the agitated citizens of both the communities. Master Sunder Lal, a respectable Freedom Fighter, Hakim Saif-ud-din, honorary Hakim to the President of India and widely respected gentle man, Professor Har Pal Singh, whose son Dr. Prabhat Kumar was killed in these riots, and several others would choose areas for themselves, where they would go during hours of curfew relaxation, for interacting with the people and requesting them to maintain peace. This exercise continued for several weeks and had some sobering effect. During

Shravan Shivratri period these efforts suffered a set back because of the unpleasant violent incidents but soon thereafter, they gathered momentum and helped a lot in bringing about the normalcy.

Meetings and Seminars Held

The District officials used to visit different localities on different days, where they would collect people of the area, talk to them with a view to finding out irritants and the local problems, then invite suggestions. Opinion making and confidence building exercises in different localities, followed by rehabilitation work, went a long way in winning the co-operation of the people of the two communities. Seminars were also held in educational institutions, where confidence building measures were discussed and solutions suggested and psyche of the participants including students was channelised in the right direction to end the feeling of 'We' and 'They'. The proceedings were widely covered in press. I held a meeting of the affected Muslims in my office. They were moved when I addressed their ladies as '*Khawateen*', which helped us to a great extent in winning their confidence and support. These exercises by the officers and the enlightened persons of society helped a lot in easing out tension and return of normalcy.

Return of the Migrants

Fear psychosis gripped many people. Several persons of both the communities, where ever they were in minority and found themselves insecure, left their houses and went to safer places of their friends and relatives. In posh Shastri Nagar colony the houses of two Muslims, a judge and an engineer were attacked by the crowd and they had to flee in a huff leaving behind their houses and property. Hindus from old city in Muslim pockets had to go to safer areas in Hindu localities. Hindu employees working in Islamabad area did not report for work fearing danger in that locality. Such persons were identified and approached to return to their old places and suitable Police/P.A.C./C.R.P.F. presence was ensured so see that nothing went wrong with them. Despite all this, several families dared not to return and sold their houses on lower rates and settled elsewhere. Muslims of Maliana were brought back from villages where they had gone. Several employees, particularly Muslims sought their transfers out of Meerut.

Relief Distribution

As curfew was clamped suddenly which continued for several days without any relaxation, people suffered great hardship for want of essential commodities of daily consumption particularly the milk. Subsequently supplies of milk, vegetables and rations etc. were arranged through Supply Department under police escort in various localities. As it was fasting month of *Ramzan*, Muslims faced greater difficulties. Army too started distributing rations particularly in areas where their troops were deployed. Around third week of May, while they were distributing wheat in a locality near Shastri Nagar during an afternoon, a Muslim lady accompanied by her children came to collect their shares. She brought her children so that she could get their share also. While she was returning and was a few steps away from the distribution point, she was stabbed and killed in a lane and her children became orphans. The poverty and helplessness of that woman was not sufficient for the killers to spare her even on humanitarian grounds. This incident moved the Army authorities also and thereafter they took adequate precautions and avoided this exercise which otherwise was meant for promoting their image.

During curfew relaxation periods and in non-curfew areas the relief distribution was done by the private parties in their respective communities. This sent the message in the two communities that their respective communities cared better for them rather than others including the Govt. machinery, though a lot was being done by the officials. A lesson to be drawn was that whosoever, wanted to give the relief material should have been asked to deposit it in a pool of the District administration and they in turn should have distributed it to needy people in different areas. This might have avoided the branding of the material coming from particular community for that community only and ought to have ensured that it went to anybody including the opposite community and that might have dissuaded the persons/parties to undertake this kind of work on communal considerations.

Losses, Assessments and Rehabilitation

Those, who suffered losses of lives, limbs and property, were given the opportunity of approaching the District authorities.

Revenue officials assisted by police authorities did the assessment of loss in each individual case and then compensation in cash was distributed to victims. A few shops and houses were also got reconstructed by the Govt. machinery. Sri T. George Joseph, who was in charge of the relief work, did an excellent job and in record time. Here I would like to mention an incident exposing an opportunist. A Muslim moneyed man, owner of Azad Market of old and delapidated building on Hapur Road near Nauchandi was getting nominal rent from the tenants. This market was completely gutted in riots and it was alleged that the influential owner himself got it burnt so that he could get rid of the old and poor tenants, majority of whom were Muslims. This market, having over 100 shops, was got reconstructed at Govt. cost and the old tenants were to be given possession. This was somehow, in my knowledge. One evening when I was waiting to see the Chief Minister at U.P. Niwas, New Delhi, I noticed a well dressed old Muslim sitting in the waiting room but I did not recognise him. A few minutes later when I went inside to have an audience with C.M. Sri Vir Bahadur Singh, he asked me as to why the Muslim gentleman waiting outside was being deprived of his claim over the reconstructed shops. I informed him that the ownership rights of that person were not being disturbed but he wanted that the reconstructed shops be handed over to him instead of the old poor tenants who were paying nominal rent, so that he could give them on higher rent to new persons. The C.M. got convinced and told me to ensure that only the real sufferers were benefitted. On return to Meerut I passed on the Chief Minister's instructions to Sri Joseph for suitable action. This story goes to say that some time the community feelings take the back seat when it comes to personal gains.

It took several months to rehabilitate the victims and crores of rupees were spent. The handloom industry could not recover fully and the worst sufferers were the Muslim weavers who came from eastern U.P. and Bihar and the factory owners, majority of whom were the Hindus. Any amount of monetary help to the poor for the loss of their bread earners could not heal the scars and wipe out the tears of their near and dear ones. The mischief mongers perhaps, had no repentance for the inhuman and barbaric acts, instead they boasted of such misdeeds.

Police Actions

The role of police was very important in ensuring the relief and rehabilitation of the affected persons. Besides accompanying the 'Relief Teams', the policemen from the city area played a key role in restoring the normalcy. Some of the measures taken could be enumerated as under.

Improving Behaviour and Performance

Hshimpura and Maliana episodes shook confidence of a section of the population in police and P.A.C. The majority community too did not feel very happy with their performance. Police and P.A.C. too apprehended attacks and reprisals in certain pockets and therefore, they did not feel safe on duty without arms. Civilian staff of various departments deployed for essential services like electricity and water supply would not be at places of duty unless police protection was provided. It was a major confidence building challenge. Police and P.A.C. personnel were collected in Police Lines before being dispatched for duty, where they were addressed by senior officers and told about the shortcomings of individual and group behaviour and then about certain 'Do's' and 'Don'ts'. On the job training by the supervisory officers was also arranged. Short term lectures to staff, while they were on rest and not on duty, were also arranged. Better man-management, supervision, leadership and accountability of the officers was also insisted upon. These steps went a long way in improving the performance and sagging morale of the District Police and P.A.C. personnel.

Registration and Investigation of Cases

Several problems arose about registration of cases with the police. Unless cases were registered with the police, they were not in a position to verify the deaths and injuries etc. and without such proof the compensation could not be paid. There were three categories of those killed, firstly where dead bodies were found, identified and post-mortem done; secondly where dead bodies were disposed of after post-mortem as unidentified and thirdly, where the dead bodies could not be found. Muslims used to take away the bodies of those who died in police firing and burried them quietly in their court-yards and later reported them as missing. Problems of jurisdiction of police stations also arose. During curfew, people could not go to lodge their FIR's, hence delays were there. Several persons continued to be missing and returned after several weeks. In such cases the relatives insisted on certificates of deaths to be issued so that they could get compensation but the police could not do so without proper enquiry/investigation. Hundreds of persons turned out at various police stations to lodge their F.I.Rs. but the local police in some cases avoided to register the cases. To overcome such difficulties, a counter was opened in the office of the Senior Superintendent of Police Meerut, where complainants could lodge their reports. A central team of investigating officers was formed to investigate riot cases, so that usual pleas of jurisdiction of police stations etc. could be avoided and the investigating officers could not say that they were otherwise busy with law and order duties, hence could not devote sufficient time to investigations. This exercise proved very effective and useful. In cases where dead bodies could not be found for long and that person failed to return and on police enquiries his whereabouts could not be found, affidavits were sought from their next of kin saying that they would refund the amount of compensation in case, the person for whom they claimed compensation, returned.

City Police Control Room

The City Control Room functioning from Kotwali experienced several problems during riot period. Kotwali was in old and congested area, where persons found it difficult to reach and hence could not communicate with senior officers, many of whom had to camp there only. There was insufficient parking place particularly for heavy trucks of security forces. There was no place except the roof where police and P.A.C. personnel on reserve duty could sit or rest during very hot summer days. The daily meetings were also held there for which there was no built up accommodation and open court-yard was used for this purpose where there used to be hardly any secrecy, as anybody could hear the discussions and know about the decisions taken. In order to overcome such difficulties in future, a proper City Control Room was opened on the First Floor of the SSPs office, where it functioned very well. Security personnel on duty were also looked after well because of its proximity with Police Lines. As Collectorate was nearby, the public found it very convenient to approach the authorities. Some problems of office space were experienced as a few rooms were got vacated for this Control

Room but that was worth it. After a few years, when I went to Meerut as Additional Director General of Police, Law and Order, U.P., in connection with the caste riots in this city, I also visited this Control Room. To my utter surprise I found that it was not functioning properly and had virtually gathered dust and some space was allotted back to original units.

Installation of Wireless-Based Public Address System

Difficulties were experienced in addressing the public centrally, particularly in communicating the information about curfew relaxation etc.. In Aligarh city loud speakers, having connection through wires, were installed at important places but the drawback was security, its maintenance and possibility of interruption due to wire cuts. Sri Roshan Lal D.I.G. and Director U.P. Police Telecommunication, devised a new wireless-based system which could be installed easily and its security and maintenance was also easier. After obtaining necessary sanction this system was installed which proved very effective and was later on also provided in other cities of U.P. On this system broadcast could be made to various parts of the city simultaneously or to selected areas only from the Control Room.

Long Term Planning

The U.P. Government wanted us to submit a scheme which could prove effective in checking the riots in future. All of us scratched our heads, conducted a survey of the city and identified the riot prone areas. We suggested police presence in sizable numbers on various outskirts. Main localities on various parts were Hapur Road, Garh Road, Delhi Road and Muzaffarnagar Road. The Meerut Cantonment area and Sixth Bn. P.A.C. on Muzaffarnagar Road were already there. For other areas, it was suggested to have one unit each of either P.A.C., Police Training Centre or C.R.P.F. on each road. Consequently 44th Bn. P.A.C. and a Police Training Centre were established on Hapur Road, which catered to Shastrinagar, Pilokhari, and Nauchandi areas. A few years later when a building collapsed under which several Muslim students got entrapped, recruits under training and P.A.C. jawans of the nearby 44th Bn immediately swung into action, rescued them and won the Muslim applause. One Bn. of C.R.P.F.(RAF) was located on Delhi bypass road. This bypass was under construction and was got opened for traffic during May riots as through traffic could not be allowed on Delhi-

Haridwar Road, passing through the curfew bound localities of the city. The Garh Road could not get any establishment as one Training Centre meant for it was diverted to *Kali Mitti* (Ugoo), the remote rural area in District Unnao on political considerations as it was the constituency of the Home Minister.

Happy Diwali-1987

Curfew was completely lifted in first week of September, 1987. Thereafter normalcy returned very fast and Diwali festival was celebrated on a grand scale. Traditionally markets used to be illuminated but this year it was done on a grand scale in which shopkeepers of all the communities contributed and the main markets on all sides of Beghum Bridge were well illuminated, which surpassed the record of previous years. Persons exchanged gifts and greetings forgetting the recent riots. On one fine morning I received an unknown visitor, who on entering the room immediately touched my feet and introduced himself as one whom I had taken to the hospital, while he was lying injured on road in June. He offered a packet of sweets, begging apology for doing so as he knew that I was one who did not accept gifts. I could not refuse it as he said that he had decided to see me on the occasion of Diwali to express his gratitude, even if I were in Madras, I was deeply moved by his gesture.

Thereafter, Meerut remained peaceful and people maintained very cordial relations. I was moved from Meerut to Police Head Quarters Allahabad on promotion as I.G.P. the in first week of August 1989. At Meerut City Railway station people from all walks of life were present to give me a grand send off. Even now Meerut people are maintaining contact with me and other officers, which is very satisfying. I wish all the best for Meerut *walas* and sincerely pray that Meerut should ever remain free from riots.

Grateful Acknowledgements of

1. Sri S.K. Mukerji, I.P.S. (Retired) Former D.G. Home Guards U.P.
2. Sri V.K.Gupta I.P.S.
3. Sri D.N. Samal I.P.S.
4. Sri Gyan Dixit , Photo Journalist, Meerut

6

Bhartiya Kisan Union Agitation 1988

25 DAY LONG SERIOUS AGITATION MANAGED WITHOUT CURFEW

I had read about farmers' agitation of Gujrat led by Sri Vallabhbhai Patel during India's freedom struggle in which he came to be known as *'Sardar'*. Some other *kisan* movements were also launched during British regime and after country's independence. I happened to be the D.I.G. of Police Meerut range, when Bhartiya Kisan Union (B.K.U.) led by Chaudhary Mahendra Singh Tikait launched an agitation of '*Gherao*' of the Divisional Commissioner Meerut, from January 27, 1988 which continued for 25 days. There were many situations demanding use of force and clamping of curfew at many places but things were managed with tact without curfew, 'wait and watch' policy and also as to who tires out whom first. This agitation was an unique experience not only for me alone but also for many others, who were concerned with the issue from any angle like social, political, moral, media reporting etc. Here we share some aspects.

About Bhartiya Kisan Union (B.K.U.)

The B.K.U. was formed in January, 1987 and it immediately started its activities. In its meeting held at Baraut (District Meerut) on February 26, 1987, it drafted a memorandum to be given to Central Government, exhorting farmers to launch a big agitation if the Govt. failed to respond, demanding justice for *Kisans* and the end of capitalism. It was also decided to hold a huge rally at Shamli (District Muzaffarnagar) on 1-4-1987 to unite the farmers and to agitate about irregular/non-supply of electricity in rural areas.

The B.K.U. also framed its constitution based on social and economic reforms for farmers. They also prescribed a Social Code of Conduct banning pomp and show in social functions particularly marriages, which were to be limited to certain guests and dowry/items of fixed amount only. Inter-caste marriages amongst Jats, Gujars, etc. (backward castes) were to be promoted. The B.K.U. decided to remain non-political and unite farmers from all over the country. Present constitutional system of elections in India was decried and it was demanded that 60% seats in Parliament and State Legislatures be reserved for farmers and this be based on the basis of percentage of each union of farmers, labour, advocates etc. Copies of the B.K.U. Constitution were circulated to various affiliating units in Districts. Chaudhary Mahendra Singh Tikait of village Sisauli, district Muzaffarnagar became the National President with Sisauli as head quarters. It also tried to form a common front of farmers' organisations of various States. The social reforms, based on prescribed code of conduct could not make a visible impact in the years to come but kisans agitated on several occasions at several places, particularly in western U.P. demanding fair price for sugar cane and regular supply of electricity and waiver of dues and loans. Out of their several demands, some were met by the U.P. Government from time to time.

I was posted as D.I.G. Administration at D.G.P. H.Qrs. Lucknow in 1987 when farmers of Muzaffarnagar district launched an agitation at 'Power Station Shamli' from 1-4-1987 against the irregular supply of electricity etc. Though, I was not dealing with this subject, all the officers then posted at D.G.P. Head Quarters used to remain fully updated about the developments. As a very large gathering of farmers was expected and serious law and order problems were apprehended, the programme was banned. Elaborate police and magisterial arrangements were made to see that the farmers coming to Shamli were stopped at various places but on the day of agitation they could not be stopped. At a Police and P.A.C. picket deployed at a culvert over a nullah the farmers ran their tractor trolleys over *jawans* in a bid to go ahead. The police used force which infuriated the *kisans* and they in turn killed 4 policemen, including an officer, Radhey Shyam Yadav ,of the rank of platoon commander of XV Bn P.A.C.. Agra, two P.A.C. Jawans, and one constable of District Police and injured several policemen. They held their demonstration at Shamli despite ban. This was the beginning of adamant and violent agitation by the B.K.U.

पी.सी. राधेश्याम यादव

Same year (1987) after this incident, several rounds of negotiations between the B.K.U. and ministers of U.P. Govt. (Congress Govt. led by Sri Vir Bahadur Singh) were held. Sri Gopi Nath Dikshit, Home Minister U.P., Sri Hukum Singh another Minister hailing from Muzaffarnagar and Chief Minister Sri Vir Bahadur Singh visited Sisauli on different dates, where farmers collected in huge numbers for meetings, but nothing tangible could emerge. Due courtesies were also not extended to these VIPs by Mahendra Singh Tikait and he tried to show to his followers that he did not care for the Govt. because the B.K.U. and its president Mahendra Singh Tikait had started growing larger than their size. The B.K.U. came in open conflict with the administration and launched several agitations for fulfilment of their demands, which included (1) removal of impediments in renewal of fire arms licenses, (2) implementation of the assurances given by the Chief Minister U.P. at meeting in Sisauli, where he had sought one month's time to do so and B.K.U. had asked him to take two months time which had since then elapsed, (3) all old bills of electricity and land revenue (*Lagaan*) be completely waived, (4) regular and uninterrupted power supply be ensured and new connections released immediately, (4) price of agricultural produce be fixed commensurate with the cost of inputs. There were several other demands too, and the charter kept on changing from time to time. Two days' (January 11 and 12, 1988) demonstration led by Tikait was held at Daurala Sugar Mills (Meerut) to demand increase in sugarcane prices.

The B.K.U. created problems in normal functioning of district administration at cutting edge levels. They refused to pay electricity and other revenue bills and accosted lower functionaries, whenever they visited their villages, compelling them to beat a hasty retreat. Hindrances were also created in police investigation and effecting of arrests etc. Govt. servants, belonging to Jat community were spared at times as they were considered their own brethren. Agitations at Tahsil and Power Sub Stations and road jams became order of the day. In most of the villages, dictates of local community panchayat prevailed, partly due to fear and partly due to B.K.U. influence.They developed the illusion that they could run a parallel administration. The Government's policy was to avoid confrontation as far as possible. On the whole the morale of B.K.U. went U.P., whereas, the district functionaries' morale at the cutting edge levels gradually started going down. The lower administrative functionaries could not dare to go to villages without adequate police protection. Policemen too, going in small numbers did not feel safe.

Call for Agitation and Gherao of Divisional Commissioner Meerut

The B.K.U. gave an ultimatum to start indefinite *'Dharna'* and *'Gherao'* of the Divisional Commissioner Meerut, wherever he was found, in office or residence, from 27-1-1988 by a large number of farmers, if their demands were not met by then. This was with a view to showing their might and compel the State Govt. to accept their demands. No written memorandum or charter of demands was given to authorities but the details could be known from the speeches made at rallies held at various places exhorting farmers to reach Meerut in huge numbers on the appointed day. They said that their agitation was bound to succeed as all the mutinies had started from Meerut only, provided they turned up in large numbers breaking all previous records including that of Shamli. Excerpts from religious scriptures like *Ramayan, Mahabharat* and *Quran Shareef* were extensively quoted to impress that 'good' always prevailed over 'evil'. They said that B.K.U. was fighting for the right cause and the Govt. which had refused to concede their demands represented the evil. As a ruse Govt. may relax the tariff rates and may ask them to start paying the bills, but farmers should not fall a prey to it. The farmers of western districts of U.P., mainly those having sizeable Jat population and other rich persons, irrespective of their caste or community, were asked to participate, threatening that those who failed would face social boycott. The farmers belonging to Brahmin, Kshatriya and Vaish communities, who neither possess big holdings, nor are numerically strong enough, were hardly approached. The landless labourers and small farmers, particularly belonging to lower classes, were neither mobilised nor they lent their support to this agitation.

Meetings were held weeks in advance to mobilise the *kisans*, particularly from districts Saharanpur, Muzaffarnagar, Meerut, Ghaziabad, Bulandshahar (Meerut Division), Aligarh, Mathura, Agra (Agra Division), Moradabad and Bijnor (Moradabad Division). In these meetings, farmers were exhorted to send at least one to two youths from each family including young girls and ladies. Each village was to contribute a minimum amount of Rupees two thousand but higher contributions were welcome. Fire arms were not to be brought but each member was to carry *danda* (cane) with *Jhanda* (B.K.U. flag–green and white colours) so that in case of *lathi* charge by the police, these *dandas* could easily be used against them. *Kisans* from nearby areas were to come on tractor trolleys and those coming from distant places were to travel on buses. As it was winter season, they were not to forget to bring sufficient winter clothing. Each family was asked to bring cooked food for one day and rations for five to six days along with cow dung fuel (*kandas)* as they might be required to cook their food at the site itself. *Ransinghas* (local bugles), *Hukkas* (tobacco smoking pipe) and material for preparing ropes etc. were also to be brought as it may be used during spare time. B.K.U. caps (Gandhi Caps in green and white colours) were to be worn.

Chaudhary Sukhbir Singh of Baraut, to whose son the daughter of B.K.U. supremo Tikait was married, belonged to different faction and he did not see eye to eye with Tikait, but Sukhbir Singh had hardly any following. A meeting of all chaudharies of various castes and *khaps* was called at Ramala (border of Baraut and Shamli) on 25-1-1988, two days before the agitation was to begin, to iron out differences. The strategy of this agitation was chalked out in this meeting but the internal differences could not be sorted out. It was decided that volunteers would come in large numbers, collect at appointed time and place on each approach road of Meerut city. From there they were to proceed in convoys to place of *dharna* with Union *jhandas* flying on *dandas*. Tikait was to join at Sakoti-Tanda (Meerut-Muzaffarnagar road) from where, he was to lead the convoy. B.K.U. Youth Brigade and volunteers were to control the traffic and maintain internal law and order at dharna site. The *kisans* were also told to turn up in large numbers so that Govt. did not dare to use force against them and be also forced to realise that they were really strong and could dictate terms. In case they were stopped on way, Shamli could be repeated and B.K.U. volunteers should give a tough fight and pose serious law and order problems. Unless the Govt. uses force against them, their demands will not be met, hence they should sit on indefinite *dharna*. The Govt. did not dare to recover the arrears amounting to several crores of rupees pending against industrialists , but was unnecessarily harassing the farmers and several *kisans*, against whom Govt. dues were pending, had been sent to jail in District Aligarh. A psychological appeal was also made that the policemen, who may be ordered to use force, were their own brethren.

Administrative Preparedness

After the Shamli incident, B.K.U. had been on top of the agenda of the Govt and of the local administration of districts and divisions concerned. U.P. Government and higher police authorities were kept fully informed about developments on this front from time to time. As soon as the call for *Dharna* and *Gherao* of the Divisional Commissioner was received, authorities concerned prepared their machinery to remain in top gear for meeting any eventuality. Sri M.A. Faruqui. A.D.M. (City) and his counterpart Sri V.K. Gupta, S.P. City Meerut kept a very close watch on the situation and also made preparations for meeting this challenge. District Magistrate Sri Vijay Sharma and

Senior Superintendent of Police Sri G.L. Sharma, also kept themselves fully abreast and made adequate preparations in Meerut District, both in rural and urban areas. As farmers from all the districts of Meerut Division were being mobilised and B.K.U. had strong following in all the districts namely, Shaharanpur, Muzaffarnagar, Meerut, Ghaziabad and Bulandshahar, I as Deputy Inspector General of Police (D.I.G.) of Meerut Range and my counterpart Sri V.K. Diwan, Divisional Commissioner, who was to be *gheraoed*, toured all the districts and took stock of the situation and gave necessary instructions. Sri Satish Kumar Mukerji, Zonal Inspector General of Police Meerut, whose jurisdiction extended over Meerut and Dehradun Divisions, was of great help to us in every respect. The Intelligence Machinery was galvanised and they kept us fully informed. We in turn took adequate measures to face the situation and also kept higher ups informed and used to seek their assistance and advice from time to time. I and Sri Diwan also used to brief Chief Minister Sri Vir Bahadur Singh, during his visits to Delhi as it was easier for us to go to Delhi being closer to Meerut, rather than Lucknow, which was about 500 KMs away. He told us to be firm and not to succumb to undue pressures of B.K.U.. Adequate resources like executive Magistrates, police and P.A.C. contingents, traffic police, Fire Brigade units etc., were mobilised from various districts of the State. Local municipal authorities were asked to galvanise their resources as huge congregation of people for several days was going to affect electricity, sanitation, water supply and other civil services. Local hospitals were also alerted to attend to the sick and wounded. All of us used to meet almost every day and some times more than once to take stock of the latest situation and prepare accordingly.

As Collectorate, Commissioner's office, Office and residence the of SSP were very close to apprehended site of *dharna*, we decided to have tactical H.Q. and operational Control Room in the office of Range D.I.G., which was neither far off from the office and residence of the Divisional Commissioner nor very close to the expected site. Police Lines was also close by, from where necessary force could immediately be mobilised.

Uncertainty

The B.K.U. kept their cards very close to their chest and did not disclose as to where they would accost the Divisional Commissioner and what was going to be the venue of *dharna*. In a few preparatory meetings it was said that *gherao* would take place, wherever the Commissioner was found, his office or residence. Apprehensions were also expressed that the Commissioner may not be in Meerut on 27-1-1988. There was no big ground of State Govt. near Collectorate/Commissioner's office, which could accommodate such a large gathering. As the venue was uncertain most of the civic amenities could not be arranged in advance. We did not think that they would occupy the Central Government ground, without prior permission of the competent authorities. Barricading of Commissioner's office and residence was got done and sufficient police force along with the Magistrates and senior police officers was deployed to meet any threat.

Actual Day

After the Republic Day functions on 26-1-1988 were over, we focused our attention on next day's threat. On 27-1-1988, messages started pouring in from various districts and places that *kisans* in thousands and in belligerent mood were on the move towards Meerut on tractor trolleys and buses. We kept a very close watch on the situation and kept on monitoring the happenings. Sri A.K. Mukerji, Zonal I.G., Sri V.K. Diwan, Divisional Commissioner and I, were sitting in my office Control Room from that early morning. Convoys started collecting on the outskirts of Meerut at appointed places on the roads coming from Hapur, Garhmukteshwar, Parikshitgarh, Mawana, Daurala, Sardhana, Binauli, Baghpat and Modinagar. Mahendra Singh Tikait led the convoy from Sakoti Tanda (on Delhi-Haridwar National Highway) in a bus. As decided, *kisans* were hoisting their union flags mounted on canes and shouted slogans while travelling on their tractor trolleys and buses and were also blowing *Ransinghas* to herald their march. They were surprised that their convoys were not stopped by the police any where, hence they could not get any chance for confrontation. We could guess about the venue when B.K.U. volunteers started arriving at C.D.A. (Controller of Defence Accounts) ground to make their own arrangements of traffic etc. This ground belonged to the Defence Department of Central Govt. and was very close to the residence of the S.S.P. and not far off from the Collectorate and the Divisional Commissioner's office. We did not anticipate that they would be naive enough to occupy Defence land without obtaining prior permission of the competent authorities. The proposed venue was kept a well-guarded secret by the B.K.U. and our intelligence machinery also could not let us know in advance. Around noon of 27-1-1988, *kisans* started arriving from all directions shouting provocative slogans. We were surprised when they did not try to reach the office or the residence of the Commissioner and collected at the C.D.A. ground only. Thousands of tractor trolleys and buses created traffic jams on highways and all roads which led to the C.D.A. ground, but it was gradually cleared when they moved towards the *dharna* site. Traffic, other police and Para-Military forces were kept a little away from the site to avoid confrontation either on roads or at the C.D.A. ground. This was our tactical move and not that the local administration had given it up. Soon the ground was full and the spill over could be seen on all adjacent places and roads. Roads in Cantonment area were used for parking and C.D.A. ground became the *dharna* site but no attempt was made to *gherao* the Divisional Commissioner at any place. The district authorities led by Mr. Vijay Sharma, D.M. and Sri G.L. Sharma S.S.P. remained very alert and were in full command of the situation. The Army and Defence Accounts authorities too did not react to this unauthorised occupation of the Defence Land.

The rumour spread that Sri Diwan, the Commissioner had fled from Meerut due to their fear. This was reported even in evening newspapers without verifying from any one of us. The fact was that we were all along present in the office of the Range D.I.G. and kept on monitoring the developments from there. Since things were highly uncertain on the first day, my wife had invited Mrs. Diwan to be with us at our residence, so that no harm was caused to her. Though, situation was still hot, after a few days of the agitation Dr. (Mrs.) Diwan started going boldly on duty to her hospital. The rumour of their having fled was deliberately spread to create panic in the administrative machinery and to boost up the morale of the B.K.U. crowd. We soon cleared the doubts and let it be known that Mr. Diwan along with his family was very much at Meerut and was performing his duties. While Zonal I.G.P. Sri Mukerji used to be present in the Range Control Room for monitoring and giving advice and orders, I, Commissioner Sri Diwan and other officers used to move about to take first hand stock of the situation.

At the C.D.A. ground, a makeshift rostrum was erected by putting tractor trolleys together and mounting loud speakers. Tikait and others started making speeches, exhorting the volunteers not to leave till their demands were met. B.K.U. had not given any memorandum of demands regarding this demonstration, hence we could not inform the State Government in advance for action at their level. On the evening of 27-1-1988, a feeler came that B.K.U. representatives wanted to meet the local authorities. Their representatives were asked to come that very evening to the office of the Divisional Commissioner for talks. The district authorities made elaborate security arrangements to ensure that nothing went wrong and no harm was caused to the authorities, particularly the Commissioner. Around 10 P.M. on 27-1-1988, about one dozen B.K.U. activists came in a delegation to attend the meeting but Tikait did not join. Several farmers were present on the adjacent roads of Commissioner's office and SSP's residence. All of us including Mr. Diwan and District authorities were present for talks. They insisted that their demands be met by the State Govt. When they were asked as to what their demands were, they said that demands had already been projected from time to time. When they were firmly told that no talks were possible in the absence of specific charter of demands, they came out with a haphazardly hand written and unsigned paper which indicated about 13 demands. On being asked as to whether this be treated as final list of demands, they said 'no', as their demands could further increase. The meeting ended around midnight without any result. The B.K.U. people were highly unpredictable and unreliable about their demands, which could not be met by the authorities and the Govt.

By the evening a large number of farmers started returning to their villages but quite a few thousand remained at the site. Tikait duly guarded by his volunteers, camped under the make-shift rostrum and that became his abode for the weeks to come. As Vallabhbhai Patel was given the title of '*Sardar*' during movement of *kisans* in Gujarat, Tikait was given the title of '***Mahatma***' by his followers. It being very cold in nights, *kisans* often slept on the open ground or took refuge under the tractor trolleys or went to the houses of their relatives at Meerut. Several of them used to go to family quarters in Police Lines Meerut and stayed with their relatives. Some of them stayed at night in the out houses of the residence of the Commissioner where his subordinate staff lived. It was like *Mahabharat*, where policemen were used to be on duty against them, but being relatives, gave them refuge in nights at their houses. No body ever left duties and no farmer ever put any hindrance in their official work.

Tikait on Dharna

Ransinghas were freely and occasionally blown at Meerut and many other places to warn and prepare the crowd. Many of them used to return to their villages in their trolleys every evening and be back next morning with sufficient cooked food packets. On one hand, no farmer at site ever remained hungry, beggars, rickshaw pullers and other poor persons had gay time, as they used to collect their food every morning and evening which was never denied to them.

Tikait Addressing the Farmers

Visits of Opposition Political and Kisan Leaders

After a few days, opposition leaders of political parties started making a bee line to Meerut to meet Tikait to express their sympathy and support to the B.K.U.. As per newspaper reports Chaudhary Devi Lal, the then Chief Minister of Haryana, also wanted to join them but could not do so as he was then heading the ministry in his State. Sri H.N. Bahuguna, former Chief Minister U.P. and former Union Minister, Sri Ajit Singh, Lok Dal(A) leader and son of former Prime Minister Chaudhary Charan Singh and a few others visited the site but none of them was allowed to share the plateform. Smt. Gayatri Devi, widow of Chaudhary Charan Singh and mother of Chaudhary Ajit Singh also visited. Tikait came down from the make-shift rostrum, touched her feet but politely refused to give her a chance to address the gathering as she was a political person and the B.K.U. was a non-political organisation. Maulana Bukhari, chief priest of Jama Masjid Delhi was allowed to address as he was a non- political person and he appealed to the farmers to rise above the religious barriers and fight their battle unitedly. Sri V.P. Singh former Chief Minister U.P. and former Union Minister, who later became the Prime Minister and film personality Raj Babbar also came to meet Tikait and express support. Swami Agnivesh, a social reformist, Sharad Joshi, *kisan* leader from Maharashtra also came to express their solidarity. Ruling Congress men were most unwelcome and whenever any body happened to come, he/she was manhandled. Local Youth Congress leader Om Prakash Sharma, who went there along with his police security guard, was manhandled and revolver of his shadow snatched after giving him thorough thrashing. Policemen were kept at a distance to avoid immediate confrontation but ever ready to move when ordered to do so. Officers used to keep a very close watch but avoided provocation and confrontation due to obvious reasons. The *Kisans* were repeatedly addressed by the B.K.U. leaders including women and girls appealing that they must remain firm and united as they were fighting for right cause and ultimately victory was bound to be their's.

Deaths

Several participants started dying because of severe cold and tractor accidents. First death was of the old man Bhagwan Singh, who died in night at C.D.A. ground. He was termed as martyr and his dead body, wrapped in B.K.U. flag, was kept there for a few days. They did not let anybody know as to what were they going to do of that dead body. Ultimately the cremation was performed on that ground itself. Later on several deaths occurred due to trolley accidents but bodies were not handed over to police for inquest and *post-mortem* .They were taken to C.D.A. ground and kept as martyrs wrapped in B.K.U. flags for a day or so and then cremated there only in every body's full view. Several leaders, whose names have been mentioned above used to come to express sympathy and pay homage with the intention of gaining political support of the *kisans*. Residents of Meerut city including ladies and children, visited the site out of curiosity to see the ongoing agitation and the crowd.

Brisk Business

This agitation proved a boon to local small vendors of edible items, who made bumper sales and also used to collect free food packets. It is noteworthy that nobody ever took items without proper payments, unlike other rallies where participants indulged in hooliganism and looting vendors. The local shop owners, particularly of handloom fabrics too made brisk business. Newspapers also reported that the flesh business flourished during those days as village youths frequently visited the red light area. Two local Hindi news papers, namely *'Dainik Jagran'* and *'Amar Ujala'*, which had started their publications from Meerut about a year back and also other small local news papers used to come out with special morning and evening editions extensively covering this agitation and having biased reporting favouring the B.K.U. As most of the farmers were illiterate and could not read, these papers used to publish several photographs of the rally on more than one page, so that the kisans could see them and feel happy about their so-called success. Nobody ever took any paper without payment. *'Dainik Jagran'* and *'Amar Ujala'*, the business rivals of each other, besides making huge business during agitation, were also successful in creating a sizeable market for future in rural areas of various districts. Other national newspapers, both Hindi and English, covered this agitation in their Delhi editions. But for state owned *Door Darshan*, there were no TV channels, hence *kisans* placed more reliance on newspapers, particularly of Meerut editions.

Civic Amenities but Stink All Around

Local administration made all efforts to provide civic amenities like water, sanitation etc., but this was not sufficient to meet the huge requirement of a big crowd of about one lac people who were there for 25 days. As villagers were not used to flush or temporary latrines, they eased out any where on the adjacent open grounds, roads and lanes, as they do in villages. This created very foul stink at and around the *dharna* site and also the close by SSP's residence and residential colonies of officers and public. Smoke of firewood, cow dung-cakes *(kandas)* used for cooking food and for keeping warm during chilly winter nights and pyres used for cremation, further added to the foul smell and unhygienic conditions. Though efforts were made but nothing much could be done to match the requirement.

Political Agitations in Support of B.K.U.

Hectic activities by the opposition political parties were started and Sri V.P. Singh appealed for opposition unity to support Tikait. Several people including public representatives sat on '*dharna*' etc. at various places to press the Govt. to accede to their demands. Opposition legislators, particularly of the Lok Dal, hailing from western U.P., sat on '*dharna*' at the Chief Minister's residence at Lucknow to express solidarity with farmers' cause and press the U.P. Govt. to accept the demands. They also threatened to disrupt the Budget Session of U.P. Assembly if demands were not met. Five Lok Dal legislators started relay hunger strike and about 10 of them threatened to resign. Few days later about 350 agitators including 14 legislators were arrested at Lucknow. Mr. Virendra Verma from Muzaffarnagar, former U.P. Home Minister, along with few hundred *kisans*, courted arrest urging the President of India to intervene in the matter.

Agitation Takes Violent Turn Outside Meerut

It was a battle of wits and patience between B.K.U. and local administration. The *kisans* adopted various tactics to tire out the administration and force the Govt. to accept their demands. They used to preach something from open platform but behaved differently at various places. A call for 'Meerut bandh' did not receive very favourable response. Few persons courted arrests at Delhi. Some of the agitators sat on hunger strike, some on fast unto death and others on relay basis, but it was also called of after a few days. The Chief Minister's *gherao* was also threatened. They threatened to offer bangles to the Divisional Commissioner and roamed around his office, giving the impression that they were carrying out the '*gherao*' there.

After three–four days of the start of this agitation the *kisans* sat on '*dharna*' on Panipat (Haryana)–Kairana (Muzaffarnagar-U.P.) road blocking the highway.

After about two weeks of the ongoing agitation, *kisans* started resorting to confrontation, rowdyism and violence at many places outside Meerut. *'Rail Roko'* agitation was launched in Meerut Division; several trains were forcibly stopped and attacked, forcing the authorities to cancel some trains. There was violence in Shamli, distirct Muzaffarnagar, during *'bandh'* there. In rural areas of district Meerut they clashed with police at several places. Near Chhota Mavana, they blocked the road, burnt roadways buses and when police intervened, they attacked them and also burnt two police jeeps. They also disrupted communication by cutting telephone lines and pulling down the poles. Confrontation also took place at Hapur (Ghaziabad) where two police jeeps were burnt while police was dealing with them. Violence was also reported from Bhopa, district Muzaffarnagar. Despite all this, administration maintained cool and did not clamp curfew any where, so that public was not put to inconvenience, police could be spared from the burden of enforcing it and adequate force could be conserved for deployment any where as per need. As a precautionary measure educational institutions of Meerut were closed till normalisation of the situation.

Incidents of Violence in Moradabad District

Several incidents of violence occurred in rural areas of district Moradabad as a result rail and road traffic between Delhi and Moradabad remained disrupted for several days. While writing this, I talked to Sri S.K. Chandra, the then Senior Superintendent of Police Moradabad and got the first hand briefing from him. He was the SSP and Sri R. Chandra was the District Magistrate and both of them made a nice team and were known as 'duo-Chandras' in the district. According to him the Moradabad B.K.U. activists participated in large numbers in Meerut agitation. the B.K.U. was a budding organization with a lot of following everywhere in western U.P. including Moradabad. From their behaviour, it appeared that they were under the misconception of being above the law.

While sporadic incidents of violence were taking place in Meerut division the B.K.U. supporters in district Moradabad, who were actively associated with the ongoing *'Dharna'* at Meerut from the very beginning and were contributing to it, both in men and material, quite, significantly indulged in large scale violence and vandalism on February 17 and 18, 1988 in an organised way. They blocked the Delhi-Lucknow Highway (NH 24) at a road crossing near Rajabpur in Joya-Gajraula section at 11A.M. on 17th February, 1988.

Kisans Brickbatting at Village Narangpur near Joya on NH 24

The Sub Divisional Magistrate (SDM) and the circle officer of the police (CO), who along with a posse of the district police and P.A.C. were deputed to clear the road, were subjected to heavy brickbatting. Several policemen were injured and the CO suffered serious hit on the nose and had to be shifted for medical aid. Meanwhile the SPRA (Sri Lalta Prasad Misra) reached the spot and the SSP also followed with reinforcements. The agitators, who came from the nearby villages, were in high spirits, shouted provocative slogans and appeared determined. Finding no other alternative the police used force and dislodged the mob from the road. But this proved to be only a tactical withdrawal by the agitators who reoccupied the road soon after the police had proceeded to remove other road blocks, which were put up by the B.K.U. at various places. At these places also the police had to face stiff resistance and fierce brickbatting from B.K,U. and although they succeeded in removing all the road blocks one by one, the B.K.U. put them back soon after the departure of the police from the particular spots. As a result, the traffic on this one of the busiest highways, came to a complete stop. A large number of policemen including the SSP himself sustained injuries and a constable fractured his nose. Some of the rowdies numbering about 30 had been captured by the police from various confrontation spots. The sun had already set and the darkness gradually started spreading. As running from one road block to the other had proved to be an exercise in futility, it was necessary to rethink about the strategy and to revise it suitably as also to commit more resources in the fray. So the operation was stopped to start the same next day. Accordingly the SSP left with his convoy for Moradabad.

The journey back to Moradabad was through numerous roadblocks, which had been put up again. At all these places the stone pelting B.K.U. men had to be first chased away before the convoy could pass safely. The B.K.U. had virtually taken control of the 24 Km stretch of the NH 24 between Joya and Gajraula.

Despite heavy odds the SSP and the SPRA went to PS Rajabpur, the centre of agitation in night of February 17/18 reaching there at 1 A.M. to try to find out a peaceful solution. As the main road to Rajabpur was blocked, they had to take circuitous route. Important local leaders of the agitation were invited and all out efforts were made to persuade them to call off the agitation. Their demand for the release of the arrested persons was accepted. The 3 hour long negotiations failed due to the B.K.U. leaders repeatedly bringing in fresh demands. At 4 A.M. the officers left for Moradabad after giving stern warning to the agitation leaders to clear the road by 10 A.M., failing which the police would proceed to clear it by force, which may include the use of fire-arms.

While these negotiations were going on at Rajabpur, the B.K.U. men were engaged in vandalism. They pulled down hundreds of road-side trees and telephone poles which were scattered on the road. Many culverts were broken or damaged. Sambhal-Hasanpur road was given similar treatment. Railway property was also ransacked. Railway track between Amroha and Gajraula was uprooted at a number of points. The communication system and some cabins were also damaged. As a result, the operation of trains on this section had to be completely stopped.

It was decided to first concentrate all energies on the clearing of the NH 24. The operation clearance started at 10 A.M. on

February 18 with full preparations. The agitators including women were also collected in strength at different places between Joya and Gajraula and some of them carried country made firearms. They were in high spirits and put up determined resistance but were finally overcome and made to flee. Pitched battles took place at several places. Firearms had to be used resulting in unfortunate death of 2 persons and injuries to several others. It took 3 hours to clear the road and the obstructions placed. By 1 P.M. on February 18, 1988 the movement of traffic was resumed on the highway. The SSP and the DM remained present at the spot throughout the operation and media along with their photographers were allowed to witness it. Thereafter attention was paid to the railway line. Heavy protective arrangements had to be put in at several places all along the track between Amroha and Gajraula. After the necessary repairs were completed by the railway authorities, the traffic on railway line was also resumed. The district had no respite, as the B.K.U. held its Mahapanchayat (8,000) at Rajabpur after a week and started *'jail bharo'* agitation. These programmes, however, were peaceful as the B.K.U. appeared visibly mellowed down after February 18 encounter. The *'jail bharo'* programme continued for 100 days and it was called off after a judicial enquiry was ordered. The judicial enquiry, however, gave a clean chit to the district administration.

"Full Marks" to B.K.U. for Discipline and Patience

Though, this agitation continued for 25 days, there was no act of indiscipline by any B.K.U. worker at Meerut. In order to keep the crowd occupied, farmers were asked to keep themselves busy in preparing ropes and other items of daily use of the raw material that they had brought. Besides speeches, folk songs, recital of poems, other items of entertainment of rural interest, etc. kept the crowd happy. Whenever any worker sat on the barricading or any other item of security put up by the administration, their volunteers intervened and nothing was disturbed. It is really amazing that despite violence at other places, no wrong was committed in Meerut, though repeated threats were given from the dais by different speakers. Ladies and girls did not lag behind and they too used to deliver fiery speeches and recite heroic poems, and in turn crowd addressed them as *'Jhansi Ki Rani'*. Other items of logistics were also managed very well.

Administrative and Govt. Efforts to Sort Out the Matter

From the very moment when a call for this agitation was given, the administrative efforts were made at the Divisional level to get the details of their demands and to ask them to come for talks. They did not listen as they were adamant for a show down. During agitation at Meerut, officers used to meet the B.K.U. representatives very often, but they deliberately did not give a written memoranda of demands at any stage, so that Govt. could be approached for decision. Chief Minister Sri Vir Bahadur Singh used to hold discussions with the senior leaders. Ministerial level talks held by Sri Saeed-ul-Hasan, (M.L.A. an d Minister from Bulandshahar) and Sri Hukum Singh (M.L.A. and Minister from Muzaffarnagar) yielded no results. Chief Minister also issued an appeal to say that since 99% farmers were against this agitation, those at Meerut should return back to their villages. He also said that Tikait may say any thing but Govt. will take right decision at the right time and their demands will not be met, for whatever period the *'dharna'* continued . Sri Kedar Nath Singh, Union State Minister, who was taking keen interest, also said that Tikait was responsible for the violent incidents. The Central Congress Govt. led by Prime Minister Rajiv Gandhi also advised the State Govt. to remain firm but avoid confrontation.

When the violent incidents, particularly of Moradabad, took place, we decided to apprise the Govt. again in writing, expressing our concern and to urge for early decision at the Govt. level. A joint letter under signatures of Sri Diwan and mine was addressed to various authorities at Lucknow with a copy to the Secretary to Chief Minister who was camping at Delhi. Our letter was delivered late in the evening at Delhi and the Chief Minister had read it immediately. A call came to us desiring that both of us should meet the C.M. early next morning at Okhla, Irrigation Guest House. We reached there next morning around sunrise and as soon as the C.M. was apprised about our arrival, he immediately called us in his bed room, where our letter was lying on his bed. It appeared that the C.M. got quite concerned on reading our letter. He had very detailed, free and fair discussions with us and also asked for our suggestions. We soon left for Meerut assuring him that we would continue to do our best to handle the situation and avoid use of force and confrontation at

Meerut. On return we confided with our officers and apprised them about CM's instructions and they in turn felt doubly assured.

Agitation Called off Unconditionally

Seeing the violence in district Moradabad and other places, with U.P. Govt. very firm in not succumbing to their demands, the agitation was called off unconditionally on 20-2-1988 (after 25 days). Most of the participants felt unhappy and returned cursing Tikait. We heaved a sigh of relief and profusely congratulated the D.M./ S.S.P. Meerut and other officials, who had worked day and night without losing nerves and not caring for their personal comforts. The Govt. also felt happy and relaxed and we received a pat on our backs. In lighter vein, we said that we came out successful as there were 3 '*Vijays*' namely Vijai Kumar Gupta, S.P. City, Vijai Sharma, D.M. and Vijai Kumar Diwan, Commissioner in our team. Sri Diwan said that two ' *Shashis*' namely Shashi Arun, my wife and Shashi Diwan, his wife, deserved mention for their role played from behind the scene. Without mentioning names of all the officers including their families, I would like to congratulate each one of them and all the security forces for their hard work and untiring efforts in meeting this challenge and morally forcing the B.K.U. to withdraw their agitation. How can we forget Sri S.K. Mukerji, our Zonal I.G.P., who acted as our friend, philosopher and guide.

After this the B.K.U. continued to adopt belligerent and non-cooperative attitude. Panchayats were held at various places to press for their demands. The Superintending Engineer of State Electricity Board at Meerut was *gheraoed* to demand immediate replacement of burnt and out of order transformers and also regular and uninterrupted power supply in villages. At several places they used to have confrontation with revenue authorities by not paying the bills.

The B.K.U. gave a notice of agitation at Delhi from 24-10-1998 at ground behind the Red Fort, wanting the Central Government to intervene in the matter. Meerut type of programme was chalked out and they were to reach there in thousands on tractor trolleys with other items of rural use. A co-ordination meeting was held at Delhi with Sri Vijay Karan, Police Commissioner and his officers. I gave an eye witness account of the Meerut agitation and warned them that the B.K.U. people were most unreliable, hence their assurances be taken with a pinch of salt. I told them that the B.K.U. were likely to create law and order problems by forcibly moving to other sites like India Gate or Boat Club and also other problems of sanitation etc. as they would ease themselves out on the roads. The Delhi Police took me lightly, being very confident that they would contain them at Red Fort only. Later on when the *Kisans* moved to Delhi in thousands on tractor trolleys, lot of traffic problems were created as they blocked the movement of fast moving traffic. They camped at Red Fort in evening but forcibly moved to India Gate to hold their *Panchayat* there. Delhi police could do very little to contain them at Red Fort and had to use force to disperse them from India Gate. A novel method was adopted for dispersal of the crowd by using police force under loud noise of disco music in night and *kisans* were driven out of Delhi. After this exercise was undertaken, police on our side was also warned to remain prepared to meet any eventuality as the dispersing crowd could have indulged in any kind of rowdyism.

The above narration has been given with a view to apprise the readers as to what kind of agitation it was and how was it handled by local administration and the Govt., particularly the Chief Minister. It may be of some use to all concerned. Tikait was never addressed as *'Mahatma'* thereafter.

With grateful acknowledgements of:

1. Sri S.K. Chandra, IPS (Retired)
2. Sri Raj Kumar Garg, Amar Ujala, Meerut
3. Sri Man Mohan Sharma, Photo Journalist, Lucknow
4. Commandant XV Bn. P.A.C. Agra, for providing photograph of Late PC Radhey Shyam Yadav.
5. Meerut District Authorities.

7

Muzaffarnagar Communal Riots – 1988

District Muzaffarnagar is situated on the western borders of Uttar Pradesh between rivers *Yamuna* in the west and *Ganga* in the east. It borders Haryana towards west and Uttaranchal towards north, which was part of U.P. till year 2001. It spreads about 50 kilometers from south to north and 90 kilometers from west to east. *Shukratal* a religious place where, Swami Kalyan Dev, famous spiritual leader and social reformist lived, is situated on the banks of *Ganga*, and its annual *Kartik Poornima Mela* attracts pilgrims in large numbers. Holy Jain pilgrim Centre 'Dholna' is also situated on the outskirts of this city on Meerut road. This District is famous for sugar cane cultivation, sugar mills and intensive farming. Muzaffarnagar *Gur* (jaggery) *Mandi* is said to be biggest in Asia. Delhi-Meerut – Ambala and Delhi-Saharanpur Railway Lines pass through this district. National highway from Delhi to Dehradun and Haridwar via Meerut passes through Muzaffarnagar city. Other important towns of the district are, Kairana, Shamli, Kandhla, Charthawal, Jansath, Khatauli, Shahpur, Purkaji and Meerapur.

According to 1991 census, the population of the district was about 28.5 lakhs of whom 70% were Hindus, predominantly Jats, 29% Muslims, 0.4% Sikhs and 1% others. The district, due to its prosperity, is notorious for crimes, particularly kidnappings for ransom and other heinous crimes committed by gangs armed with sophisticated weapons and operating on fast moving vehicles. People are God fearing but very conservative who believe in instant social justice delivered by the village *'caste panchayat'*. An incident of ordering immediate execution of two lovers, a boy of one caste and the girl of another caste of the village, who had eloped, is the worst example and it attracted the media headlines. Sisauli in this district, is village of Sri Mahendra Singh Tikait, influential farmer Jat leader and president of *Bhartiya Kisan Union*.

Communal atmosphere of the district gets vitiated every now and then on some pretext or the other. Major communal riots had occurred in Khatauli town and Muzaffarnagar city. In Muzaffarnagar *mohalla* Khalapar, predominantly inhabited by Muslims and Shiv Chowk on main highway in city surrounded by Hindu population have witnessed riots on several occasions. In October, 1976 serious riots broke out in *Mohalla* Khalapar of Muzaffarnagar city as Muslims had opposed the forced family planning during emergency rule. Curfew remained clamped for several days as incidents of attack on policemen including Sri A.P. Sharma, Superintendent of Police, rioting etc. took place. They were the worst anti-family planning riots of U.P., another being of district Sultanpur, where also police firing was resorted to on Muslim crowd.

The Ayodhya Movement for construction of a magnificent temple at disputed place, launched by Vishwa Hindu Parishad from 1986 onwards, led to serious communal incidents of breach of peace, necessitating clamping of curfew. These riots occurred in October, 1988, October, 1990 and December, 1992. I remained posted as Deputy Inspector General of Police, Meerut Range from June, 1987 to July, 1989 and Muzaffarnagar Communal riots of 1988 broke out during my tenure and I had occasion to supervise the handling of these riots. Meerut communal riots of 1987 led to tension all around, affecting Muzaffarnagar and its suburban town Khatauli. In July, 1987, Shiva devotees called *'kanvarias'* marched on foot in lakhs for about 10 days with holy 'Ganga Water' from Haridwar which they carried on shoulders in specially made hanging device called *'kanvar'*, to be offered in temples of their destination, particularly Pura Mahadev under police circle Binauli of Meerut district. Details have already been mentioned in Chapter on Meerut Riots. Ugly incidents of killings of Muslims by '*kanvarias*' in mango groves between Muzaffarnagar and Khatauli created lot of communal tension everywhere in the district. Katauli too experienced serious problems which were created by the marching crowd of '*kanvarias*'. Hindu activists created problems of law and order in Muzaffarnagar city at Shiva Chowk. I along with Sri V.K. Divan, Divisional Commissioner visited Khatauli and Muzaffarnagar for spot assessment of the situation and discussions with local D.M./S.P. Other details find mention in chapter on Meerut Riots of 1987. The entire area from Haridwar to Ghaziabad remained communally surcharged during 1987–88.

In October, 1988 state wide movement was launched by Vishwa Hindu Parishad/Bajrang Dal to mobilise Hindus for the cause of construction of temple at disputed site in Ayodhya. In Khatauli town early in the morning of 8-10-1988, a '*Prabhat Pheri*' was taken out by '*Ram Janam Bhoomi Mukti Sangharsh Samiti*', and the crowd damaged an egg shop of a Muslim. Little later this crowd went to various educational institutions, got them forcibly closed and the students also joined the crowd. In the meantime a motor cyclist went on spreading rumors causing serious adverse reaction in local Muslims and leading to incidents of stabbing and brickbatting at a few places leading to injuries to several persons including policemen, some of whom were shifted for treatment to Medical College Meerut and District Hospital Muzaffarnagar. Curfew was clamped around evening the same day and Additional District Magistrate and Additional Superintendent of Police Muzaffarnagar reached Khatuli with extra force for law and order duties and camped there for several days. After getting some respite from Muzaffarnagar city, D.M. Sri N. Ravi Shankar and S.P. Sri M.S. Bali also rushed to Khatauli the same night and held Peace Committee meeting of influential citizens. During curfew relaxation on morning of 11-10-1988 panic was caused following rumours of further outbreak of riots which led to a few stabbings and the curfew had to be clamped immediately, which continued the next day on Friday and *Namaz* was offered in local houses only. Curfew was relaxed during day time on 13-10-1988 and thereafter 'Peace Committee' meetings were held regularly during curfew relaxations. Initiative shown by Jain leaders in restoration of peace was commendable. Curfew was relaxed during daytime but night curfew continued. During these riots, two persons, one of each community, were killed, 13 injured and 34 persons (22 Hindus and 12 Muslims) were arrested.

The *'Babri Masjid Action Committee'* had given a call for *'Ayodhya March'* on 14-10-1988. On the occasion of U.P. *'Bandh'*, observed on 8-10-1988 the local Hindu activists took out procession and started forcing the shop-keepers to close their shops. On objection by Muslims they (Hindus) misbehaved with them and also beat a few following which police arrested some miscreants and took them to police station. Hindu local leaders, who had collected at the police station, demanded release of their men lodged there, who in the confusion mingled with the crowd and fled away. Rumour that Hindus were attacking Muslims, caused reaction in Muslims leading to incidents of brickbatting, arson, stabbings etc. Serious communal riots broke out in Muzaffarnagar city leading to imposition of curfew, which remained in force from 8-10-1988 to 5-11-1988 with periodical relaxations. 26 persons (12 Hindus and 14 Muslims) were killed and 77 (35 Hindus and 42 Muslims) were injured. Due to arson and thefts both the communities suffered huge losses of property.

On getting the information of these riots on the first day, I, Sri S.K. Mukerji, Zonal IGP and Sri V.K. Diwan, Divisional Commissioner sat together at Meerut, discussed strategy for controlling the riots and ordered mobilisation of extra police, Coys of P.A.C. and C.R.P.F.. Thereafter, we also rushed to Muzaffarnagar to supervise the arrangements. D.M. Sri N. Ravishankar and S.P. Sri M.S. Bali and their teams of Magistrates and police officers were already busy in controlling the riots. We took stock of the situation, went around the affected areas, visited hospital to enquire about treatment of the injured, with the local Chief Medical Officer and the Superintendent of the District Hospital. In the meantime Army Columns also reached from nearby station Roorkee. In the evening, when situation came under control, we sat in a meeting with the local officers, enquired about the extra help needed from outside District, gave them necessary instructions keeping in view the lessons learnt from Meerut riots. D.M./S.P. issued orders for the Magistrates and the police officers and allocated 12 hourly shift duties for them and the forces. After a little while we found some time for interaction and briefing. After the briefing Sri Mukerji left for Meerut so that he could attend to other areas from there.

On 9-10-1988 in a 'Peace Committee' meeting duly attended by influential and peace loving people, though, an appeal was made for keeping peace but for first few days sporadic incidents continued to occur. Outside curfew area on 10-10-1988 few 'Shiv Sena' workers tried to take out a procession in Nai Mandi area, shouting slogans against police and Mr. Saeed-U-Zaman, State Minister for Home, U.P., who resided in *Mohalla* Khalapar. On 11-10-1988 Hindu activists of various outfits again took out procession and tried to block the road making allegations against police and the Minister. When D.M./S.P. were holding talks in Kotwali, a few persons present outside Kotwali, came on Roorkee road and started damaging Muslim shops to which Muslims also reacted. Police immediately controlled the situation and curfew was clamped in other localities also. Stray incidents of stabbings were reported from some areas. Some Hindu women, who tried to come out in procession against arrests of Hindus, were sent back. A few stray incidents of arson, slogan shouting etc. took place in night of 12/13 -10-1988 and the situation remained tense for several days.

I and Sri Diwan camped there for several days. Briefing meetings were held in the 'Police Lines' every morning and evening before the change of shifts, where, after taking stock of the ongoing shift duties and the prevailing situation, suitable instructions were given for the next shift mounting on duty. In the beginning itself I told the police and P.A.C. officers that they should remain present with their *jawans*, lead and guide them properly so that high handedness is not committed. I also narrated experiences of Hashimpura and Maliana of Meerut and exhorted all concerned to wipe out the stigma of those riots. A separate meeting of P.A.C. officers was also held, where I also addressed them. All of them with one voice assured us that nothing irresponsible will happen; proper control will be kept on rank and file and force will be used on crowd only according to legal and procedural requirements.

A separate meeting was held of Magistrates, civic officials and senior police officers, wherein they were briefed about the experiences of Meerut riots. During relaxation of curfew, various groups and organisations used to distribute help in the form of food grains etc. in areas of their community, which was besides the help rendered by the local administration. It gave rise to suspicion in opposite groups that in the garb of help, arms and ammunition and other objectionable material was being passed on to respective communities for perpetuating violence. It was decided by the administration that nobody will be allowed to distribute any help directly in the *mohallas*. Instead all the relief material/assistance coming from various organisations etc. was collected at a given centre and pooled together and then distributed to the affected people and to those who could not come out due to curfew. This proved very useful and was free from the stigma of communal bias as it was difficult to distinguish as to which items came from which community and to which community they were distributed to. The local political leaders also tried to reach help directly in their respective communal constituencies but they were politely but firmly told to desist from doing so. Due publicity of this arrangement was got done through media and people were exhorted to extend helping hand to the district administration. This sent the right signals, which helped in winning over the confidence of the people. Due care was exercised by the sector officers in their respective areas to see that no help was distributed directly by anybody in any area but at the same time, the local administration ensured supplies to the needy persons in affected areas.

Not a single political person was allowed to visit affected areas for the first few days. The Congress was the ruling party in U.P. with Sri Saeed-ul- Zama, M.L.A. from Muzaffarnagar rural constituency, as State Minister for Home. We politely persuaded him not to move out of his locality in Khalapar. Ms. Charu Sheela, local Congress, M.L.A. was politely but firmly told to keep off the scene. She fully cooperated and helped the local administration in keeping peace. V.I.Ps from Delhi and other places were also not allowed to visit the city. This happened with persuasion only and restrictive orders under section 144 Cr.P.C. had to be issued sparingly. This arrangement was implemented without making any exceptions but after a few days, when the situation improved, this restriction was relaxed. Leaders of various outfits started coming in, but most of them were asked to come first to our Control Room in Police Lines, from where they were provided security and guides and were sent to places to be visited by them. Before they went to affected localities, they were briefed about the situation and their help was also solicited in restoring normalcy. Sri Syed Sahabuddin, activist for Muslim cause, also came to Police Lines, where I got an occasion to brief him. I told him to go around the areas, talk to the people on various matters including the role played by security forces in general and P.A.C. in particular. He also acceded to my request of coming back to Control Room for exchange of information and not to talk to the media, untill we had discussions. After round of the city, particularly Muslim localities, he dropped in the Control Room, to give us his feed back. I specifically asked him about the shortcomings of the P.A.C., to which he said, that this time P.A.C. has acted in fair manner and no complaints were reported to him by either community. While leaving, he thanked me, telling that though, he had not met me earlier, he had heard about me and therefore, I must continue to live up to the expectations of the people.

While I was camping there, I got a phone call from my wife on 16th evening that my mother had expired at Lucknow that day. I informed my IGP at Meerut, who permitted me to go to Lucknow and also said that in my absence he would be camping at Muzaffarnagar. Commissioner Sri Diwan expressed his condolences and asked me to leave immediately without worrying for this place. I also talked to Sri R.N. Gupta, D.G.P., U.P. and sought his permission. He immediately agreed to my request and permitted me to leave by road as no train was available then. He also told me not to worry for Lucknow as he would instruct the local officers to take care of the cremation etc. I left for Lucknow via Meerut from where I picked up my wife and reached Lucknow on 17th early morning after travelling the whole night. After cremation on 17th October, we left for Haridwar on 18th by road, where we reached the same evening and immersed the ashes in *Ganga*. Next day I reached Muzaffarnagar for duty. During my absence, I was always worried about this riot torn city.

The situation started improving and curfew was relaxed in phases. After about two weeks, when things became normal, curfew was lifted. Loss of lives, 26 deaths (12 Hindus and 14 Muslims) and 77 injured (35 Hindus and 42 Muslims) and destruction of property in arson etc. gave a huge blow to this city. 457 arrests (247 Hindus and 210 Muslims) were made. I

prayed that such things may not happen again, but the peace was disturbed in next two years during Kar Seva calls of 1990 and 1992. Who is to be blamed ? Let us again pray that Almighty God (Ram and Rahim) give humane feelings to those, who do not hesitate in unleashing violence including killings and believe that it is the best service that they are rendering to their community.

8

Kanpur Riots

During my childhood in villages (my village being 80 Kms west of Kanpur now in District Kannauj, earlier in District Farrukhabad), elders used to talk a lot about the importance of this city and the popular song about Kanpur was:–

कानपुर कनकइया,
जहां पर चले रेल का पहिया।
नीचे बहतीं गंगा मइया,
ऊपर घाट बना सरसइया।।

Meaning thereby that Kanpur is city of kites, where rail wheels ply and underneath flows mother Ganga and above it is Sarsaiya Ghat (bank).

Kanpur, one of the oldest cities of Uttar Pradesh, is situated on the right banks of holy river Ganga (Ganges). On the left side of this river is district Unnao and jurisdiction of Kanpur City does not extend beyond the mid stream on that side. Capital City Lucknow is about 80 Kilometers away from here. Kanpur has been the main industrial city of central India, having several industries like tanneries, cotton textile mills, ordnance factories etc. It was known as Manchester of India as major textile mills (now all sick and closed) were located here. Kanpur has been the main trading centre particularly for textiles, leather goods, mainly *chappals* and *saddlery*. It has several educational institutions of repute like IIT, Agriculture University, Technological Institute and Kanpur University. It is well connected by rail and road from all sides as Delhi–Kolkata main railway line and Grand Trunk Road (National Highway No. 2) also pass through this city.

Population and Areas

Kanpur is metropolitan city having about 35 lakh (3.5 million) population of whom about 7 lakh (20%) are Muslims, 4 lakhs (9%) Sikhs and eleven thousand Christians. Hindus are in sizable majority. In old city Muslim (Sunnis) population is predominantly in Nai Sadak, Moolganj, Bekanganj, Chamanganj, Colonelganj and Gwaltoli, where Shias are in majority. Majority of the Hindu population is in Pheelkhana, Collectorganj, Chowk, Badshahi Naka, Meston Road, Juhi etc. Anwarganj, Bajaria, Latouche Road, Rail Bazar, Jajmau and Raipurwa are the main mixed localities, which besides having Muslim population also have sizeable Hindu population of Scheduled Castes consisting of *Chamars* (engaged in leather work), *Khatiks* (engaged in vegetable selling and piggery) and *Koris* (weavers community). People of both the communities living in these areas, being very poor and illiterate, are used as pawns by their fanatic co-religionists during communal riots and these poor people also become the worst victims. The post-partition Sikh migrants from Pakistan are settled in Govindpuri, Najirabad and Harjinder Nagar. New colonies, which have come up recently, have people from all communities but Hindus are in majority.

Festivals and Fairs

Popular festivals of various communities are celebrated with devotion and enthusiasm. Main Hindu festivals are *Diwali* and *Holi* and during Holi colours are played for about a week till the Holi Milan Mela at Sarsaiya Ghat is over. Hindu devotees come for holy dip in Ganga at various ghats, particularly at Sarsaiya Ghat on Magh Poornima, Jeth Dashera and Kartik Poornima days. A grand procession is taken out by followers of Guru Ravidas (Chamars) on Magh Poornima, his birth day. Sikhs take out processions on birth days of their Gurus and also congregate in large numbers at Gurudwaras. Muslims celebrate traditional festivals of *Id-ul-Fitr* (Id), *Id-ul-Azha* (Bakrid) and *Id-ul- Milad-ul-Nabi* (Barawafat) with great enthusiasm. Grand processions are also taken out during Barawafat and Moharrum. On the following days of *Id* and *Bakrid* fairs of *'Arr'*, *'Tarr'* and *'Parr'* are held where Muslims, particularly boys and girls, collect in large numbers. Incidents of eve teasing cause tension. During *'Tarr Mela'* in 1988, incident of eve teasing at Latouche Road near Gurudwara took a serious communal turn. Local civil and police administration have to be very watchful during all these festivals, particularly in the mixed localities from where the processions pass.

Riots

Before India's independence, Kanpur witnessed worst communal riots in 1931. Ganesh Shankar Vidyarthi, a great patriot and son of Kanpur, devoted to maintain communal harmony, was killed on 25-3-1931during riots. Thereafter the peace prevailed. Even during post-partition days, the country witnessed worst communal riots but Kanpur remained free from communal frenzy. From 1975 onwards this city had several sectarian and communal riots as is evident from the following table 8.1:

MY EXPERIENCES OF KANPUR RIOTS

I was student of DAV College Kanpur, then affiliated to Agra University, from 1957 to 1963 and lived in its hostel from where I did my B.A., M.A. and L.L.B. During the winter of 1959, there was a serious riot (*Satia Kand*) in old Kanpur City allegedly over detention and rape of a woman namely Satia by the policemen, of Chauki Badshahinaka, under police station Collectorganj. Public violently protested against this incident and there were serious anti-police riots, following which curfew remained in force for several days. Civil Lines side, where our hostel was located, remained unaffected. One evening some of us were going on stroll towards Company Bagh in Phulbagh area, when an elderly gentle man stopped us and advised not to go towards Phulbagh side as the adjoining areas were under curfew and we were likely to be arrested. We understood the gravity and immediately returned to our hostel and thereafter did not go out till the city was normal. I left Kanpur in August, 1963 to join the I.P.S. and foundational training at National Academy of Administration Mussooorie.

TABLE 8.1

S. No.	Year	Nature and Cause of Riot	Other facts
1.	January, 1975	Communal (Hindu-Muslim) Clashes over Moharrum procession near BSSD College.	One person of each community killed, remained confined to Nawabganj and Bekanganj.
2.	September, 1977	Sectarian (Shia-Sunni) Due to fall out of Lucknow Shia-Sunni riots.	Several persons of both the communities were killed and injured. Justice C.D. Parekh retired Judge High Court Allahabad conducted Judicial Enquiry of Lucknow and Kanpur riots.
3.	September, 1978	Sectarian (Akali-Nirankari) It was fall out of attack on Nirankaris in Delhi.	Several Sikhs including ladies attacked Nirankaris in Nirankari Bhawan Kanpur on 29-9-1978 where Baba Gurbachan Singh was preaching.5 Nirankari, men and women killed and about 300 injured. Of Sikhs, 7 men and 1 woman killed and 14 injured.
4.	February,1979	Communal (Hindu-Muslim).	On 28-2-1979 two communities (Muslims and Khatiks) clashed in Latouche Road-Anwarganj area over petty matter which turned into a riot.

Contd....

S. No.	*Year*	*Nature and Cause of Riot*	*Other facts*
5.	November, 1980	Communal (Hindu-Muslim).	On 15-11-1980 a Muslim was murdered by *Khatik* Hindus in Coolie Bazar area. Stones were pelted on *Tazia* procession, which turned into communal riot and curfew had to be imposed.
6.	November, 1984	Anti-Sikh Riots.	Following assassination of Prime Minister Indira Gandhi on 31-10-1984, anti Sikh riots broke out at Delhi and several other places. From 1-11-1984 onwards Kanpur witnessed worst riots where mobs indulged in killings, arson and looting of houses and shops etc. of Sikhs and curfew had to be imposed. Entire city was affected. About 225 Sikhs were killed and 750 incidents of arson and looting were reported. These were the worst riots in history of Kanpur.
7.	April, 1990	Communal (Hindu-Muslim).	Two motor cyclists of rival communities collided in Sisamau-Bajria area, following which crowds collected and rioting took place. Muslim youths hurled bombs on a passing P.A.C. truck. Arson and looting was also reported. 5 Muslims were killed.

Contd....

S. No.	Year	Nature and Cause of Riot	Other facts
8.	November-December, 1990	Rioting due to Kar Sewa at Ayodhya	Several persons including 20 Muslims, 5 Hindus and one police constable were killed. About 1000 persons were arrested.
9.	May, 1991	Elections Related Communal Riots	During electioneering for Lok Sabha and U.P. Vidhan Sabha, a B.J.P. procession passing through Muslim locality near *Yatim Khana* (orphnage) was accosted when provocative slogans were raised by the processionists. This turned into serious communal riots and curfew was clamped. About 18 persons including 11 Hindus and 7 Muslims were killed. About 1200 Hindus and 250 Muslims were arrested
10.	December, 1992	Communal Riots following demolition of disputed structure at Ayodhya by *Kar Sewaks*	Disputed structure of Babri Masjid-Ram Janam Bhoomi was demolished by *Kar sewaks* on 6-12-1992. Local Muslims felt hurt and took to streets. They attacked police and security forces alleging that when they could not do any thing to protect their mosque at Ayodhya, what were they doing in their localities in Kanpur. Serious riots broke out

Contd....

S. No.	Year	Nature and Cause of Riot	Other facts
			and curfew was imposed. While stray Hindus were killed in Muslim localities, stray Muslims were killed in new colonies having predominantly Hindu population. Rioting claimed more than 60 lives (17 Hindus-45 Muslims and one police constable and a few more whose bodies were disposed of by relatives without reporting to police,
11.	November, 1993	Political clashes during electioneering	On 14-11-1993, an election procession of SP-BSP, combined candidate for U.P. Assembly election was accosted by B.J.P. supporters at Sisamau crossing under PS Bajria. Following provocative slogans from both sides situation took ugly turn resulting in serious violence. 2 Hindus and 1 Muslim were killed, while 13 Hindus and 16 Muslims were injured. One SP, one Magistrate, one Dy. SP several police personnel were also injured. 31 Hindus and 6 Muslims were arrested and sent to jail.
12.	February, 1994	Communal (Hindu-Muslim)	One Munna Sonkar *alias* Kala Bachcha, B.J.P. corporator and known criminal was murdered by hurling bombs on 9-2-1994 in Babupurwa area. Persons of *Khatik* community reacted violently indulging in arson

Contd....

S. No.	*Year*	*Nature and Cause of Riot*	*Other facts*
			and attack on Muslim community. Curfew was imposed to control the situation. 4 persons were killed and 6 injured.
13.	December, 1994	Communal (Hindu-Muslim)	During friendly cricket match in Khalasi Line, played between two teams of two *mohallas*, each having players of Hindu-Muslim communities, clashed over the result. This took serious communal turn. Two persons were killed and several injured.
14.	August, 1997	Communal (Hindu-Muslim)	On 31-8-1997 boys of a community wanted glasses for drinking wine from cold drinks shop at Parade Chauraha, which was refused. Boys beat the shopkeeper, damaged shop and smashed the cold drinks' bottles. The rival communities brickbatted and also threw bottles on each other. Police intervened and brought the situation under control. Cases were registered against 400 rioters.
15.	October, 1997	Communal (Hindu-Muslim)	Over old rivalry two sides clashed in Parampurwa (Juhi) in which a Muslim was found missing whose dead body was found later. This took ugly communal turn but police intervention brought the situation under control. 28 Hindus and 11 Muslims were arrested.

Contd....

S. No.	*Year*	*Nature and Cause of Riot*	*Other facts*
16.	January, 1998	Communal (Hindu-Muslim)	On 9-1-1998 morning, a *Pesh Imam* of a mosque at Laxmipurwa under PS Chamanganj was slapped by a Hindu boy, which was resented to. During the same evening Muslims collected at Deputy Ka Padao to protest against electricity failure and also demanded immediate arrest of accused of earlier incident. When police intervened, crowd pelted stones, hurled crude bombs and also fired at them. One policeman on security duty of S.P. City was killed. About 75 rioters were arrested and illicit fire arms recovered
17.	March, 1998	Communal (Hindu-Muslim)	At Latouche Road (PS Anwarganj) on the last day of Holi festival on 29-3-1998, revellers threw colour on the passing car of a Muslim which was objected to. This took serious communal turn, resulting into rioting, arson and stone pelting. Authorities immediately reacted and controlled the situation. Several persons of the two communities were arrested.
18.	March, 2001	SIMI (Student Islamic Movement of India) Movement	CD Pathak, ADM killed.

I was Inspector General of Police Kanpur Zone in 1990-91. Vishwa Hindu Parishad duly supported by Bharatiya Janta Party (B.J.P.) gave a call for *Kar Sewa* in Ayodhya from end of October,1990 and started preparations for mobilisation of volunteers in large numbers, not only from U.P. but from all over India. Routes, both rail and road, for Ayodhya from Haryana, Rajasthan and Madhya Pradesh were through my Zone right from Aligarh, Mathura, Agra, Etah, Mainpuri, Kannauj, Etawah and Kanpur. The U.P. Government, with Sri Mulayam Singh Yadav as Chief Minister decided not to allow the movement of *Kar Sevaks* with a view to keep Ayodhya free from huge crowd so that no harm was caused to the disputed structure of Babri Masjid/Ram Janam Bhoomi there. I visited every district of my jurisdiction and discussed details with local authorities. All over U.P., elaborate advance arrangements were planned to stop the inflow of *Kar Sewaks*. As large Hindu crowds were expected, open air temporary jails were created at various places in buildings and campuses of educational institutions, mandi parishads etc. so that *Kar Sevaks* moving towards Ayodhya are intercepted and detained there with a view to stopping their onward movement. *Kar sevaks* were kept in these temporary jails. Hindu activists from Kanpur used to take thousands of food packets every morning and evening for those detained at Fatehgarh. These detenues used to move locally, particularly for bathing in holy *Ganga* as authorities could not be very strict due to obvious reasons.

The communal frenzy of the highest order was created all over paving fertile ground for riots any time and at any place. In Kanpur Hindus took to streets by singing devotional songs and ringing of *ghantas* and *ghadials* on the day of *Kar seva* at Ayodhya. In October 1990, I had to camp at Aligarh, where serious riots had broken out in city which was put under curfew. One afternoon, I received instructions from D.G.P., HQrs. that I should immediately rush to Kanpur, where serious breach of peace was apprehended. Sri B.S. Bedi, I.G., P.A.C. and my predecessor as I.G.P., Kanpur Zone, was asked to reach Aligarh at the earliest for supervising arrangements there. I immediately left Aligarh and reached Kanpur the same night. Sri Bedi met me at Kanpur, on his way to Aligarh, where I briefed him about the prevailing situation there. As Sri Bedi had remained posted as S.S.P. Aligarh, he took no time to grasp the details.

Next morning serious riots broke out in Kanpur, curfew was clamped and conditions remained disturbed for several days. Innocent Hindus passing through Muslim dominated areas in Chamanganj were suddenly attacked, killed and their bodies dumped in gutters, from where they could not be recovered easily. Muslims too were targeted in Hindu localities. Employees engaged in essential services like electricity and water supply and belonging to either community fled for their lives deserting their duty. This led to utter confusion and untold miseries to people as most of the areas had to be without water for several days as there were neither pump attendants nor electricity supply workers. While I was on round in curfew areas, I found anti-police, P.A.C. and anti-administration slogans written on walls in Muslim localities and reverse was the situation in Hindu localities, where anti-Central Para Military Forces slogans were written. In Muslim localities Central Forces were welcome but local Forces and administration were most hated and unwelcome. Firearm shots aimed towards police, P.A.C. and Magistrates were also heard. At Roopam Talkies Magistrates and police officers used to remain on duty in shifts. On my enquiry about their welfare, I was told that they did not receive any help from the local Muslims. As the cinema hall, where they were camping was closed, and shows could be run because of curfew, no eatables or tea could be available. Its toilets, which were used by these officers, started stinking for want of water supply and cleaning. Contrary to this Hindus not only provided shelter but also tea, snacks and food to some of the officers and State Forces, but most of the personnel on duty did not accept it. Muslims felt too happy to entertain the Central Para Military Forces, though they too did not accept their hospitality. The communal divide was loud and clear; rumours added fuel to the fire and nobody was willing to listen to reason. Smt. Subhashini Ali, local M.P. used to say that Bhanmati park in Bajria area, on either side of which the two communities lived was very badly affected and if Bhanmati had been alive, Subhashini would have asked her as to why were people hungry of each others' blood in that area.

One evening we were having a joint meeting of the officers in Kotwali Kanpur where Army, C.P.M.F., police, civic officers and Magistrates were present. Around 10 P.M. loud noises of rioting with religious slogans from either community and firearm shots started coming from nearby curfew bound areas. We immediately called off the meeting and officers rushed to the locality, where they found that things were normal and people, instead of being on the roads were indoors. Police parties on duty also did not report of any such incident. This was handiwork of mischief-mongers who wanted to create panic by loudly playing the pre-recorded tapes but security forces could not immediately make any recoveries. People of the area were taken into confidence and there was no untoward reaction.

In October/November, 1990, Kanpur, like any other city became very tense. The day *Kar Seva* was to be done in Ayodhya, Hindu devotees, singing *Bhajans* on devotional music, came out in large numbers in every locality, where security forces found it very difficult to keep the people indoors in curfew bound areas. Things were controlled tactfully and major incidents avoided but the frenzy was unimaginable as seeing was believing. On that fateful day I remained present in my office, continuously monitoring the situation in districts of my Zone and in contact with Lucknow to get the feed back of happenings elsewhere, particularly at Ayodhya so that I could advise the districts for appropriate measures. Sri Narendra Mohan, editor *'Dainik Jagran'* and my good friend came to my office in Motijheel and said that he had definite information (from local army authorities) that *Kar Seva* had begun at Ayodhya and the disputed structure was being pulled down. I said that I had no such information, but that did not satisfy him. To be doubly sure I rang up D.G.P., HQs, from where a very high ranking officer told me that though a few persons had climbed the domes of the disputed structure, there was no damage to the edifice and *Kar Sevaks* were well under control. Sri Narendra Mohan insisted that he would publish a special evening edition. I tried to dissuade him but he did not agree. He did his job and the local administration performed their duty by not allowing the paper to reach the public. This never came in our way of smooth relations and we remained good friends till his death after several years.

Kanpur suffered huge losses of life and property and the victims took several years to recover from the shock. Shops of rival communities in various markets were marked by displaying some signs, which were known in advance to very few planners, which facilitated the loot and arson by the anti-social elements and this strategy did not come to the notice of the district authorities, as a result the remedial measures could not be taken.

In February, 1994 I was Additional Director General of Police, Law and Order, U.P. and was camping at Varanasi as serious incidents of atrocities including murders of Scheduled Castes and others had taken places in some villages of Chandauli area. This led to serious repercussions in Varanasi city and certain localities had to be put under curfew following the attack on Scheduled Caste students of a local reputed college. Around 9 P.M. Sri V.P. Kapur, D.G.P. U.P. rang me from Lucknow saying that following the murder of Kala Bachcha, a local criminal and B.J.P. worker, Kanpur was put under curfew and therefore, I should rush to Kanpur and reach before dawn of the following morning. I told him that my presence was needed at Varanasi also, but he ordered me to leave immediately as Chief Minister Sri Mulayam Singh Yadav wanted my presence at Kanpur. I rang up my wife at Lucknow to prepare set of fresh uniform, so that I could collect it for use at Kanpur. I travelled the whole night, reached Lucknow around 3 A.M., collected things and was at City Control Room Kanpur by 5 A.M.

In Kanpur after getting briefing from the local officers, I visited the affected areas in Babu Purwa locality, where Kala Bachcha resided and was fatally attacked in broad day light the previous day. In retaliation *Khatiks* (Scheduled Caste), who have sizeable population there, attacked Muslims which resulted in arson, killings, damage to houses and other property. As a reaction and retaliation trouble spread in other localities, particularly in old Kanpur, where too curfew was clamped. During a round of the affected areas in Babu Purwa, I found that Muslims had fled as they were attacked and their houses gutted. I saw a young Muslim lady with children sitting in her hut which was next to that of a *Khatik* neighbour. I asked her as to why did she not leave her house when others had fled. The *Khatik* lady of the adjoining house told that husband of this Muslim lady, who was a vegetable vendor had not returned since *Kar Seva* days of 1992 and was presumably killed by the rioters. Since then security of this widow and her children was being taken care of by the Hindu neighbours and this time also they took care of her and no damage was done. We were really moved by this humane gesture.

While taking round of curfew bound areas in old city we were approached by the affected people, who said that patients were not getting emergency medicines. Owners of medical stores, who resided in the same premises, were asked to open them under adequate police protection and this effort earned public applause for the police pickets. Same day around noon I saw an old Muslim couple standing outside a nursing home waiting for a lift to their nearby residence and because of curfew, nobody was willing to come out in their help. I stopped there and got them sent in my car. Happiness was evident on their faces and they thanked me profusely for this little but timely help.

The police men on duty said that they were not able to get hot tea, though, it was being served from Police Lines in big containers on the orders of Sri D.N. Samal, S.S.P. In the evening briefing meeting we discussed these problems and took remedial measures. Tea stalls in the neighbourhood of police stations, outposts and strategic points, where security pickets were deployed, were got opened. Security personnel on payment started getting hot tea and biscuits whenever they needed and the shopkeepers too had a good business. The proper care was also taken to cater for the milk, tea, sugar and biscuits etc. as they had to be arranged from outside the curfew areas. Local supply department did commendable job in this respect.

The central public address system, based on wireless network was earlier installed at every police station and outpost so that officers could centrally address the people and the security staff from the City Control Room. This system was lying unused since its installation, a few years ago and the test broadcasts did not work., therefore, the police wireless staff was ordered to set the things right without loss of time. From next morning, officers started addressing the public. They would prepare a draft of their brief address which included information about curfew in various areas, the likely time of its relaxation, urging people not to believe various rumours which were afloat. Officers, particularly, D.M., S.S.P., Range D.I.G. and Divisional Commissioner used to disclose their names and rank before addressing, which went a long way in restoring peace. Local newspapers on the first day of broadcast came out with a joking caption "*Bhonpu Bola*". After things calmed down, I returned to Lucknow.

Sri D.N. Samal, the then SSP made commendable personal efforts to mobilise public opinion for communal harmony and peace. He held several seminars in which people from all sections of society including politicians and religious leaders participated. Children and students of various localities and institutions took out marches appealing for peace. All these peace time efforts did not last long because in subsequent years, several serious incidents occurred, which besides other losses included attack on security personnel, killings of a few constables, and one ADM. It is difficult to say that Kanpur will remain quiet in future.

9

Ganjdundwara (Etah) Riots – 1990

Ganjdundwara town of district Etah in Agra division, which is located about 40 kilometres towards north east from district headquarters, is connected by metre gauge railway line on Kanpur-Kasganj section of North Eastern Railway. River Ganga flows towards north of this town. It has population of about 25,000 with 40%Hindus and 60% Muslims and neighbouring villages too have more or less the same ratio. The chairman of this municipality had been generally a Muslim and one Munawwar Hussain happened to be the Chairman in 1990, who was removed from office same year after a no-confidence vote, in which Hindu members played a prominent role. Thus Munawwar Hussain bore a grudge against his opponents, particularly the Hindu members of the municipality.

In October/November, 1990 *Kar Sewa*, several Hindu activists including those who had played a key role in the removal of Munawwar Hussain, had gone to Ayodhya, who on return were felicitated at several places. Babri Masjid Action Committee Ganjdundwara was also active in mobilising Muslims against Hindu *Kar Sewa* at Ayodhya. This generated communal tension in this area as was witnessed elsewhere in U.P. and the country. The anti-social elements also often exploded crackers adding to tension in the town. Ms Uma Bharti, firebrand B.J.P. M.P., was to address meetings at Aliganj, Kasganj and Jalesar towns of this district on 4-12-1990 to mobilise Hindus in favour of Hindu cause for construction of Ram temple at Ayodhya. Last minute changes were made in her programme and she was asked to address meetings at some other places also including Ganjdundwara. At all the places slogan shouting staunch Hindu youths sporting saffron scarves and riding on two wheelers used to pilot their leaders in cities and towns. She delivered very provocative speech at Patiyali town before leaving for Ganjdundwara. On December 4, 1990 morning, when Ms. Uma Bharti was approaching Ganjdundwara town, several such youths who were piloting her, raised provocative slogans but Muslims were also prepared to meet the challenge. Munawwar Hussain too had mobilised his supporters including anti-social elements and as soon as Uma Bharti's convoy entered the town, one scooter collided with somebody which led to altercation and heavy brickbatting by Muslims from the nearby mosque. Hindus had to run for their lives and police tackled the situation. Violence spread in the town which was tackled by a few police men present tnere. Police managed to take Ms Bharti to Panchayatibagh, where she addressed the gathering inside the closed campus and after giving fiery speech left the town.

One Hindu goldsmith, who was coming to town with his bag of ornaments from outside was attacked and stabbed. Somehow he could save his bag and managed to reach Panchayatibagh, where Hindus were still present. After seeing the injured and hearing him, these Hindus got infuriated and started damaging the shops etc. of Muslim community. Rumours spread fast and the entire town was gripped by riots by 1 P.M. Incidents of arson, loot and attacks on rival communities took place all over and police, because of insufficient numbers, could not effectively control the situation. Around 4 P.M. some reinforcements arrived but they too could not help in bringing the situation under immediate control. Persons, who had gone outside the town for work in morning, started returning around sunset and one Gajendra Singh, a pressman from other town who was coming from outside, was stabbed and killed near house of Munawwar Hussain. This led to still worse rioting and both the communities indulged in attacking, injuring and killing each other, particularly those who were either leaving the town after day's work or were returning from outside. Some vehicles along with their drivers and staff were burnt. Riots also spread to neighbouring villages following the tales carried by the persons returning from Ganjdundwara town. Curfew was clamped around midnight and additional reinforcements of police, P.A.C. and Fire brigade were rushed which helped in controlling the situation. During next few days the town remained under curfew and at the same time neighbouring towns and villages like Sikanderpur Vaisya, Sidhpura, Kasganj, Sahawar, Patiyali, Marhara etc.were also affected.

In these communal riots police had to fire several rounds to disperse the crowds. In all 14 persons (7 Muslims and 7 Hindus) were killed and 9 (5 Muslims and 4 Hindus) were injured. In arson and loot etc.of shops and houses of 70 Muslims and 50 Hindus, loss worth about Rs. 32 lacs was estimated. Misbehaviour with ladies and children was also reported and police recovered 9 missing persons. 30 cases under various laws were registered and investigated of which 12 were later on transferred to Crime branch of U.P. C.I.D. House searches for recovery of looted property, preventive arrests and monetary help given to victims, helped in early normalisation of the situation.

I was Inspector General of Police of Kanpur Zone in 1990-91 and District Etah was in my jurisdiction. Sri M.S. Bali was Senior Superintendent of Police Etah, whereas Sri Suresh Pal Singh was the Range D.I.G. Sri Bali along with his District Magistrate had rushed to Ganjdundwara with whatever force they had. Sri Singh sent additional reinforcements and I too had rushed forces from other areas. I kept on monitoring the situation from Kanpur. Next day I reached Ganjdundwara *via* Farrukhabad and by that time the Divisional Commissioner and the Range D.I.G. had also arrived. The situation was really bad and it was shocking to see the burnt shops, houses and talking to the victims particularly the ladies, children and the innocent old people. The usual drill of riot control was followed and the normalcy was restored in next few days.

Looking from the hindsight now it could be debated as to where did administration lack in timely prevention of these riots. The communal atmosphere was tense and fragile not only here but all over due to the ongoing agitation on Ayodhya issue. The police and P.A.C. were heavily committed and over deployed due to communal riots at many places. In these circumstances they could not have been deployed in sufficient numbers at all those places where not only Ms Uma Bharti but others too were visiting almost simultaneously to mobilise Hindus for Ayodhya cause. Last minute inclusion of programme of Ganjdundwara and a few other places resulted in further depletion in deployment of police and P.A.C. in this District. Slogan shouting Hindu youths riding two wheelers did not listen to advice for maintaining peace and the communal frenzy was at its peak. Due to programmes and counter programmes of Vishwa Hindu Parishad and Babri Masjid Action Committee the entire atmosphere was surcharged and the tolerance was at its lowest ebb as nobody was prepared to listen to the saner advice of maintaining peace and communal amity. In such circumstances it will be unfair to raise any accusing fingers towards officers. Nevertheless sincere efforts by both the communities duly supported by the local authorities could have helped in avoiding these riots. The post riot efforts in restoring peace with the active cooperation of the local people of both the communities wore fruits and thereafter peace prevailed.

10

Ayodhya Rocks the Nation

Introductory

Ayodhya agitation came on the forefront during last two decades of 20th century which caused serious law and order problems from time to time and led to imposition of curfew at various places in the country. In 1990 and 1992 a number of cities and towns of India, simultaneously remaining under curfew, was unprecedented and perhaps a record. Repercussions were also felt outside India, particularly in some of the Islamic countries. It will be worthwhile to know about Ayodhya tangle, as it may be of help in planning the security and law and order arrangements for such situations by the future generations of the administrators, particularly the executive Magistrates, police officers and political leadership.

Location of Ayodhya

Uttar Pradesh has several places of pilgrimage for various religions, particularly for Hindus. Three most important Hindu seats namely Ayodhya, the birth place of Lord Rama, Mathura, the birth place of Lord Krishna and Varanasi (Kashi) the place of Lord Shiva are located in this State. Ayodhya is located on the right bank of holy river *Saryu*, also known as *Ghaghra*. On the left side of this river are the rural areas of districts Gonda and Basti. This holy city falls under Faizabad district and its divisional headquarter is also Faizabad. The twin cities of Faizabad and Ayodhya are about eight kilometres away from each other but now it is difficult to find as to where one city ends and where the other starts as they have rapidly grown towards each other. Faizabad is 127 kilometres away from State capital Lucknow while Ayodhya is 135 kilometres. In 1991 population of Ayodhya was around 50,000, of whom about 46,000 (92%) were Hindus and 4,000 (8%) Muslims. Faizabad city has population of about 1,25,000, of whom about 85,000 (68%) are Hindus and 40,000 (32%) are Muslims.

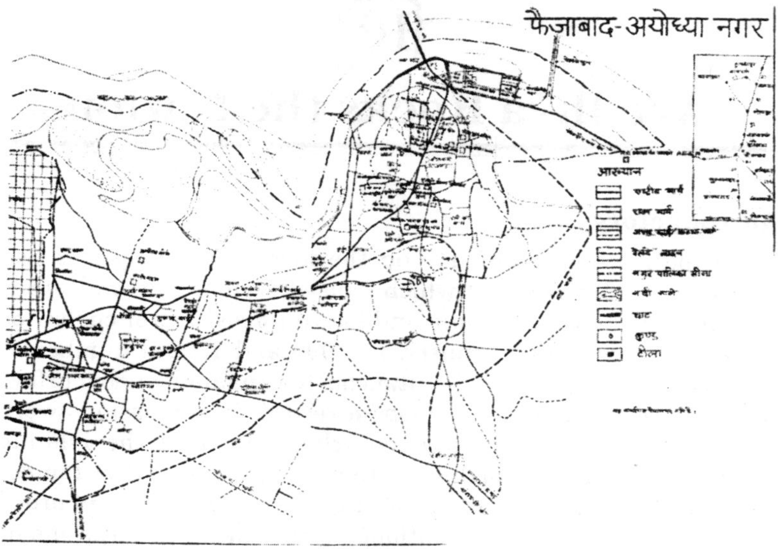

Map of the Twin-Cities, Faizabad and Ayodhya.

Importance

Ayodhya, besides being a holy place, has historical importance to Hindus, Muslims, Jains, Sikhs and Buddhists. According to Hindu legend it was established by Manu and developed by his son Ikshvaku and in the sixty fourth generation of this Suryavanshi clan, God Ram Chandra was born as son of Dashrath, the King of Ayodhya and queen Kaushalya. Hindus consider Him as an incarnation of Lord Vishnu.

Muslims consider that the burial place of one Sheesh Ali, a saint, is located at Mani Parvat in Ayodhya and Hazrat Nooh (Noah), who on his ship saved the various species of life on earth, is buried at a place at the rear of Ayodhya Police Station (presently known as Ayodhya Kotwali). Ayodhya is considered as Mecca Khurd (mini Mecca) by several Muslim saints.

Jains believe that the first Teerathankar, Sri Rishbhdev was born at this holy place and He established the Jain religion. It is said that four other Teerathankars were also born in Ayodhya and therefore, it is a place of pilgrimage for Jains.

Ayodhya was also visited by Sri Guru Nanak Dev, the first guru, to meditate and Guru Gobind Singh, the last Guru to organise Hindus and seek their assistance against Aurangzeb. A very old Gurudwara still stands loftly which attracts many Sikh pilgrims.

The Buddhists believe that Lord Buddha stayed there for twelve months. It is also believed that the Chinese pilgrim Fahian visited this place called Saket (Sachi) in 400–410 A.D. and Huen-Tshiang visited Vaiskaka (Ayodhya) in 692 A.D.

Important Temples, Fairs and Festivals

The important Hindu temples in Ayodhya are, (1) Hanuman Garhi, (2) Kanak Bhawan, (3) Sita Rasoi, (4) Manas Bhawan, (5) Vishwamitra Mandir (6) Mani Parvat Temples and several others. Disputed place of Ram Janam Bhoomi and Babri Masjid has its own importance. Though pilgrims from all over India keep on coming to this holy city round the year, most important fairs and festivals are (1) Ram Naumi Mela, date of birth of Lord Rama, falling in March or April, when large number of devotees collect to have holy bath in river *Saryu* before visiting temples, (2) Savan Jhoola Mela held at Mani Parvat during month of *Shravan*, (July-August), (3) *Panch kosi* (16 kilometers) and *Chaudah kosi* (42 kilometers) Parikrmas, when pilgrims walk on foot to cover the route and visit temples, (4) *Kartik Poornima Snan*, falling in November, when lakhs of devotees take holy dip in river *Saryu* and (5) Hanuman Garhi Mela held during summers, when large number of devotees throng at Hanuman Garhi Temple for having '*Darshan*' of almighty Lord Hanuman, devotee of Lord Rama.

HISTORY OF UNRESOLVED AYODHYA DISPUTE

I am neither a historian nor any authority on this subject, yet I venture to put a few details here which I could gather from various sources, the authenticity of which cannot be guaranteed. Still these details may help the readers in knowing about and appreciating the vexed Ayodhya tangle which has been rocking our society off and on and the amicable solution does not appear to be in sight.

According to popular Hindu belief three Hindu shrines of Ayodhya, (1) *'Janam-sthan-temple'* where Lord Rama is believed to have been born, (2) *'Treta-ka-Thakur'*, where Rama performed *'Maha Yagna'* installing images of Sita and His own and (3) *'Swarg Dwar'*, gate through which Lord Rama passed to paradise, were destroyed by Mughal emperors. It is claimed by a section of Hindus that a temple was built at the site of birthplace of God Rama in eleventh century. In 1528 during the reign of Mughal emperor Babar, Mir Baqi Tashqandi, Shia Muslim, commander of Babar and Governor of Avadh is said to have built a mosque after destroying Ram Janam Sthan temple, giving rise to the tussle between Hindus and Muslims which still continues. Subsequently a *Ram Chabutra* (plateform named after Lord Rama) is said to have been built within the same precincts. During the reign of Aurangzeb, a small temple is said to have been destroyed and thereafter, attacks and counter attacks continued. This tussle also continued during the rule of Nawabs of Avadh.

In 1853 there were riots between Hindus and Muslims in Ayodhya in which 75 persons lost their lives. Avadh was annexed by the British in 1856. It is said that in 1857, a Hindu *pujari* (worshipper) arranged worship by occupying a portion of the mosque. The first war of independence was fought jointly by both the communities in 1857. Freedom fighters, both Hindus and Muslims, were hanged on a tree near *Kuber Tila*, adjacent to that disputed *shrine.* In 1858 the rule of East India Company ended, giving place to sovereignty of British Crown. In 1859 the British Government got a wall erected in the mosque precincts, segregating the areas of worship for the two communities. In 1860 the settlement operations were conducted by the British Government.

There was a minor battle in this part of Ayodhya (Kot Ram Chandra). In 1885 in which a large number of casualties had taken place. The Mahant of Ram Chabutra filed a suit, which was dismissed with the finding that the Hindus had a right to worship there. Ayodhya witnessed communal riots in 1912, following which the cow slaughter was banned. In 1934 dispute between Hindus and Muslims over the structure led to communal riots in which the structure suffered some damage which was later repaired. The Muslim Waqf's Act was enforced in 1936.

In the night of 22/23 -12 -1949, idols of Ram Lala (*Virajman with jhoola*) were transferred from the chabutra to the inside central dome of the structure, called by the British as' '*Masjid Janamsthan*'. First information report (F.I.R.) of this incident was lodged *suo-moto* by the local police saying that thousands of Hindus collected at Sri Ram Janam Bhumi to have '*Darshan*' of Bhagwan Sri Ram Lala who were chanting "*Bhaye Prakat Kripala, Deen Dayala, Kaushalya Hitkari*". The report was sent to higher authorities mentioning that nothing untoward happened due to good arrangements. This incident led to attachment proceedings under section 145 Cr.P.C. and appointment of a receiver. Since then to commemorate this occasion, a small section of local Hindus have been taking out annual procession called '*Prakatoshav*'.

Prolonged Litigation

Several civil suits were instituted during last half of the twentieth century. Following four civil suits were originally filed.

1. Civil suit No. 2/1950, Gopal Singh Visharad *Vs*. Zahur Ahmad and others.
2. Civil suit No. 25/1950, Mahant Ramchandra Paramhans Vs. Zahur Ahmad and others.
3. Civil suit No.26/1959, Nirmohi Akhada *Vs*. Priya Dutt Ram and others.
4. Civil suit No.12/1961 Central Sunni Waqf Board *Vs*. Gopal Singh Visharad and others.

These suits have not yet been finally decided and are now being heard on priority by the 3 Judge bench of Lucknow Bench of Allahabad High Court. There does not appear any need to go into details of these cases but people say that though, half a century has passed, the judiciary has not been able to give its verdict.

'B.J.P.'s White Paper on Ayodhya & The Ram Lala Temple Movement (April 1993)' mentions that "the first legal case for repossession of Ramjanambhoomi was filed by Mahant Raghubardas in 1885 and the judgement of the Faizabad District

Court was delivered in March, 1886. An English Judge Col. F.E.A. Chamier acknowledged as :

> " It is most unfortunate that a Masjid should have been built on land specially held sacred by the Hindus, but, as that event occurred 356 years ago, it is too late now to remedy the grievance. All that can be done is to maintain the party in *status quo*. In such a case as the present one any innovation may cause more harm than derangement of order than any benefit."

Thus the Hindus won the case but could not get the *Janamsthan*. Purely in legal terms, this judgement was correct.

The role of law and the judiciary in the Ayodhya case clearly confirm the confession of the judiciary that some aspects of the Ayodhya case are incapable of judicial determination. It also brings out the fact that the judiciary had condemned itself as far back as 1955, that 38 years before, for keeping the Ayodhya case pending; it is ironical that it should be pending even today. The effect, regardless of the intent, of the interim judicial orders in the Ayodhya case was to prevent the construction, while the delay, unprecendented in legal history, indefinitely prolonged the suit. It is evident that the English system of jurisprudence which is intended to settle bipartite property disputes cannot adjudicate on an explosive issue like Ayodhya.

Period of Peace 1950 to 1983

From 1950 to 1983, about thirty three years, were the years of peace when no major incident involving law and order took place, though the civil litigation continued between Hindus and Muslims. During these years no entry, either of Hindus or of Muslims, was allowed into the disputed structure. Hindus could have '*Darshan*' from outside the iron gate and put offerings in the '*Daanpatra*' hung outside. *Bhajan* and *Kirtan* continued without break on the *chabutra* (platform). In the name of security one armed police guard consisting of one head constable and four constables used to be present and that too did not call for much vigilance. I was Superintendent of Police Gonda in 1968 and my jurisdiction extended right up to the other side of river Saryu on which Ayodhya is situated. I got the opportunity of visiting the place then but did not notice any thing special which could be of importance to me from security or law order angle in bordering areas of district Gonda.

May, 1983

Sri Dau Dayal Khanna of Congress, who had been a minister in U.P. Government, wrote to Prime Minister Indira Gandhi demanding restoration of Vishwanath Temple Kashi, Bhagwan Krishna's temple at Mathura and Sri Ram Janam Bhumi Temple at Ayodhya to Hindus saying that they had been forcibly destroyed by the Mughals.

VISHWA HINDU PARISHAD AGITATION FROM 1984 ONWARDS

April, 1984

First *Dharam Sansad* (Religious Parliament) sponsored by *Vishwa Hindu Parishad*, hereafter referred as V.H.P., was held at Delhi on April 7 and 8, 1984, where they demanded restoration of three religious places/temples of Varanasi, Mathura and Ayodhya to Hindus. Liberation of *Ram Janam Bhumi* was to be taken up first and *'Ram Janam Bhumi Yajna Samiti'* was formed to launch the agitation.

September–October, 1984

To mobilise Hindu public opinion *'Rathyatra'* was taken out from Sitamarhi (Bihar) (started on September 25, 1984) to Ayodhya. A Hindu sammelan (*Sankalp Diwas*) was held at Ayodhya on 7-10-1984 where vow was taken at the banks of river Saryu to liberate Ram Janam Bhumi (R.J.B.) by peaceful means. Similar vows were also taken at 'Sangam Allahabad'. Second 'Rathyatra' was taken out from October 8 to 14, 1984 from Ayodhya to Lucknow. A public meeting was held at Lucknow and a memorandum was handed over to the Chief Minister U.P. demanding restoration of the three shrines. These Rathyatras continued via Naimisharanya (District Sitapur) and Chitrakoot (then district Banda) but were voluntarily called off soon after assassination of Prime Minister Indira Gandhi on 31-10-1984.

1985

***Rathyatras* recommenced – riots broke out at several places**

In October, 1985 seven *'Rathyatras'*, six in U.P. and one in Bihar started on 23-10-1985, which toured various places. I was posted as D.I.G. (Communal Intelligence) U.P. those days and had to monitor the day to day happenings. Communal tension started mounting and where-ever these '*Yatras*' reached they used to be piloted by hundreds of zealous Hindu youths riding two wheelers sporting *Ramnami Gamchhas* (scarfs) and chanting slogans "*Garv se kaho hum Hindu hain*" (say with pride that we are Hindus), "*Jai Sri Ram*" and several other provocative slogans. Muslims at a few places took exception to such acts which resulted in breach of peace including riots and clamping of curfew particularly at Musafirkhana town of district Sultanpur. Police personnel, deployed to escort the '*Yatras*', were taken care of by the organisers in respect of food and daily needs. Some volunteers applied *tilaks* on the foreheads of policemen and also gave them '*Ramnami*' scarfs, which some of them carried on shoulders while in uniform. Lower police functionaries without realising the implications of their secular credentials of functioning, did not object to such things and the senior officers also did not realise their implications. This gave the impression to a section of the Muslim population that police were getting partisan and may not be committed to protecting them.

Dharam Sansad at Udipi (Karnataka)

The second *Dharam Sansad* held on October 31 and November 1, 1985 at Udipi reiterated the call for liberation of *Ram Janam Bhoomi* and handing over of its management to Jagadguru Ramanandacharya Swami Shivaramacharya of Kashi and threatened that if the same was not done by 8-3-1986 (Shiva Ratri) country wide Satyagraha would be launched for the same. On December 18, 1985, Ram Janam Bhoomi Nyas (trust) was formed. Mahant Ram Chandra Paramhans Das threatened to commit self-immolation on forthcoming Ram Naumi Day (1986) if R.J.B. was not restored to the *Nyas* by then. A delegation of V.H.P., which met the Chief Minister U.P. on 19-12-1985 demanded unlocking of the R.J.B.

1986–Year of Confrontation and Muslim Reaction

In a public meeting held by V.H.P. at Lucknow on 19-1-1986, call was given for county wide Satyagrah from 8-3-1986 (Shiva Ratri). On February 1, 1986, the District Judge Faizabad ordered the unlocking of the disputed complex. B.J.P.'s White Paper mentions that "the case was decided with lightning speed as an unknown advocate (Umesh Chandra Pandey) filed an application on 21st January, 1986, within two days after the sant's ultimatum in the Munsif Court at Faizabad; on 28th January, 1986 the Munsif refused to pass any order; an appeal was filed forthwith, in the Court of District Judge Faizabad; on 1st February, 1986, i.e. within three day's of the Munsif Court order, the District Court passed an order directing the Government of Uttar Pradesh to unlock the gate, and further directed that they shall not impose any restriction or hurdle in the *darshan* or *pooja* by the Hindu community; within hours of passing of the above order, the temple was unlocked and even the Doordarshan cameramen were present to cover the occasion which was widely telecast all over India." This was rejoiced by the Hindus and bemoaned by the Muslims, adding to the already mounting communal tensions. Muslims filed a writ petition in Lucknow bench of High Court Allahabad, against the judgment of the District Judge Faizabad.

Soon after the orders of the unlocking, *Babri Masjid Action Committee* (B.M.A.C.) under the presidentship of Maulana Muzaffar Hussain Kichochhavi was formed to take care of the Muslim interests. BMAC launched several programmes to mobilise Muslims and most of these programmes were kept on Fridays when Muslims turned up in larger numbers for Juma Namaz. On 14-2-1986 *'Yom-e-Shyah'* (black day) was observed all over U.P. and *'Bandh'* was observed on 21-2-1986.

In April, 1986 Muslims courted arrests on Fridays at various places. On 13-4-1986 while courting arrests, crowd got unruly at Barabanki and 16 persons were killed in police firing. This added fuel to the already prevailing tension and administration in the State had a very tough time in handling the situations. On 19-4-1986 Muslim youths courted arrests defying prohibitory orders. *'Youm-e-Dua'* (prayers' day) was observed on Friday, May 9, 1986. On June 6, 1986, *'Shahid Diwas'* was observed to mourn Barabanki deaths. Muslim leaders courted arrests at Delhi near Jama Masjid on August 7, 1986 to highlight their cause in Ayodhya dispute. 'All India Babri Masjid Conference' held in Delhi on December 21 and 22, 1986 resolved to (1) boycott the forthcoming Republic Day on 26-1-1987, (2) socially boycott the Muslim Members of Parliament and State Legislatures, who do not toe their line, (3) organize a *'bandh'* on February 1, the anniversary of the orders passed for unlocking of the gates, (4) hold a rally at Boat Club Delhi on 1-2-1987, (5) march to

Ayodhya on a future date to offer Friday *Namaz* at the disputed place and (6) to form a 'Babri Masjid Co-ordination Committee ' with Syed Shahabuddin as convenor.

1987 (Year of Intense Activities)

Muslims remained busy in mobilising their community in the months of February and March. A nation wide protest '*bandh*' with phenomenal success was observed on 1-2-1987, which was the first anniversary of the unlocking of the gates of the disputed structure. Maulana Abdullah Bukhari, Shahi Imam of Jama Masjid Delhi, organized a meeting on 29-3-1987 at Jama Masjid Delhi, where he denounced the Hindu approach and mentioned it as '*mazloomistan*' (land of atrocities on *akliat*-(minorities). On the following day on 30-3-1987 Muslims marched from Jama Masjid to Boat Club and organized a big rally there, where one of the speakers allegedly said that *Bharat Mata* (mother India) was '*Dayan*' (witch).

An attempt was made to bring both the warring communities together for talks. Prince Anjum Qadar, President *'All India Shia Conference'*, brought Hindu and Muslim leaders to a round table conference on March 3, 1987, but the talks failed.

The V.H.P. remained busy from April to December, 1987 in mobilising their community for the cause. On April 4, a *'Virat Hindu Sammelan'* was organized at Ayodhya to demand restoration of R.J.B. to facilitate construction of a magnificent temple at the disputed site. Meanwhile several *'Rathyatras'* were taken out by the V.H.P. resulting into breach of peace and harmony as communal violence broke out at several places. Following these disturbances the *Rathyatras* were banned and the *Raths* were detained at police stations/outposts of the places, where-ever they happened to be at that point of time. V.H.P. threatened further agitation and '*bandhs'* against indefinite ban on their *Rathyatras*. The detained *Raths* were moved from police stations/outposts to the nearest V.H.P. places. Since the communal atmosphere got highly surcharged everywhere, serious communal riots broke out in Meerut city in April/May 1987, detailed mention of which has been made in chapter dealing with ' Meerut Communal Riots'.

The U.P. Government moved Allahabad High Court in December, 1987 to transfer all cases from District Court to High Court Lucknow Bench.

The V.H.P. held a *'Hindu Sammelan'* at Ayodhya on 29-12-1987, where it was demanded that R.J.B. be transferred to them on forthcoming *'Ram Naumi'* (26-3-1988) (birth day of Lord Rama), failing which further agitation would be launched.

The divisional level *'Babri Masjid Action Committee'* in a meeting held at Faizabad on April 30, 1987, endorsed the call for a *'Muslim March'* to Ayodhya and demanded restoration of pre-independence status to all the disputed places of worship. It also urged that all the pending civil cases in the dispute be transferred to a tribunal in south India without any Hindu/Muslim judge on it.

1988 (Turning Point)

The Babri Masjid Conference held at Faizabad on 22-5-1988 was another turning point in the struggle for restoration of Babri Masjid to Muslims. The conference attended by many Muslims including Syed Shahabuddin, M.P., gave a call for a Muslim 'Mini March' to offer prayers at Babri Masjid Ayodhya on 12-8-1988 and also a 'Long March' on 14-10-1988 for similar purpose. The 'Mini-March' was called off due to differences of Muslim leaders and issuance of *Fatwa* by Muslim *Ulemas* of Deoband (very important Muslim theology seat).

Earlier in May the V.H.P. had demanded enactment of law by the Central Government for handing over of sites to Hindus of three temples at Kashi, Mathura and Ayodhya. In September the Union Home Minister made unsuccesful attempts to find out amicable settlement.

To pre-empt the Muslim march 'Bajrang Dal', a hawk wing of the V.H.P., organised a local *'bandh'* on 8-10-1988 to consolidate Hindu opposition to 'Muslim Ayodhya March'. *'Ram Maha Yagna'* was also organised at Ayodhya from October 10 to 15, 1988, and Bajrang Dal volunteers were posted *en route* from Fizabad to Ayodhya to prevent the Muslim march. At this *'yagna' Ram shilas* (plain bricks) were sanctified and preserved for the foundation laying ceremony of the proposed temple. Sporadic communal violence was witnessed in some parts of U.P. following which the 'Long March' was called off in the last minute. A bomb explosion took place on October 12, 1988 at Tatshah Masjid Faizabad and a few days later the communal violence broke out in Faizabad city on 21/22-10-1988, when a *'Ram Barat'* procession crossed the path of *'Muslim Jalsa'* near a mosque in a predominantly Muslim locality.

1989 (Foundation laying and after)

The year 1989 remained the period of intense activities for both the communities , as they remained busy in mobilising their respective people for their cause and the Union Government too was busy in finding a solution to this vexed issue.

The Ardh Kumbh Mela Allahabad was held in first quarter of 1989, where third *'Dharam Sansad'* was held by the V.H.P.. Here it was resolved that if the Government failed to hand over the R.J.B. land to *'Ram Janam Bhoomi Mukti Yagna Samiti* (RJBMYS), then the foundation of the proposed temple would be laid on November 9, 1989. The V.H.P. in its meeting held at Haridwar in May, 1989 said that the foundation laying could be pre-poned if the Government decided to pre-pone the forthcoming general elections. In this meeting it was also decided to organise a *'Diksha Samaroh'* (valediction function) on July 13 and 14, 1989 at Ayodhya, where *Sants* (saints) were to bless the young cadres of 'Bajrang Dal' who were being prepared to facilitate the task of the temple construction. The *'Sant Sammelan'* organized at Ayodhya on April 13,1989, gave a call for *'Ram Shila Poojan'* commencing from September 30, 1989. Prior to this *'Ram Yagnas'* were to be organized at Block/District levels all over India, prior to the foundation laying on November 9,1989. The *Sammelan* had also decided to organize *'Indraprastha Dharma Yatra'* from September 17 to 21 and a "*Vishal Hindu Sammelan'* at Boat Club Delhi on September 22, 1989.

On July 10, 1989, High Court (Lucknow Bench) transferred all civil suits for hearing by a three judge bench. As per programme chalked out earlier a *'Sant Sammelan'* was held at Ayodhya on July 13 and 14, 1989, where saints blessed the Bajrang Dal cadres. On September 19, 1989, the V.H.P. decided to go ahead with *'Shila Poojan'* programme without waiting for the High Court verdict. *'Ram Shila Poojan'* programme was launched from September 30, all over the country, which generated communal tensions resulting into riots at several places. The administrative and police machinery remained very busy in maintaining law and order as the sanctified bricks were taken around to various places/villages. After great persuasion the *'Shilanyas'* was performed outside the disputed area at Ayodhya on 9-11-1989 but further programme of doing construction from November 10 and 11, 1989, was not allowed by the administration.

'Sunni Waqf Board' filed a writ petition in Supreme Court of India on the question of law, which was heard on 24-10-89, 5-12-89 and 12-1-1990.

1990, Year of *Kar Seva*, Bitterness and Unprecedented Riots

'Kendriya Marg Darshak Mandal' of V.H.P. met at Allahabad from January 26 to 28, 1990 and decided to start temple construction from February 14, 1990, which was postponed on 9-2-1990 on Prime Minister's appeal. The V.H.P. in their meeting on February 13 and 14, 1990 chalked out programme of *'Jan Jagran'* (public awakening) to be carried out during next four months. *'Chetna Diwas'* was observed in March and April by beating of gongs (30 times in March and 60 times in April) simultaneously at appointed time in evenings at all the places in the country. These programmes created lot of communal tensions particularly in towns and cities having sizable Muslim population as evening *namaz* timings clashed with the timings of the beating of gongs. Police had very difficult and tough times in maintaining peace.

A *'Dharma Sabha'* (Religious Congregation) was held in Ayodhya on April 17, 1990. Another *'Dharama Sabha'*, of people coming from various places, was held at Mathura on 21-4-1990. A bus from Aligarh, carrying slogan shouting Hindu participants, instead of going straight to the site of *Dharam Sabha*, went towards 'Shahi Masjid' side, predominantly Muslim locality, which resulted in communal clashes in which 12 persons (7 Muslims and 5 Hindus) lost their lives. In the meantime Swami Swaroopanand of *'Dwarka Peeth'*, who was not in V.H.P. camp, declared to perform fresh *'Shilanyas'* at Ayodhya on 7-5-1990. *'Kendriya Marg Darshak Mandal'* of V.H.P. met at Haridwar on June 23 and 24, 1990 and decided to start temple construction at Ayodhya from 30-10-1990 and prior to that hectic preparations were to be made. On September 1, 1990, *'Arini Manthan'* (igniting the fire) was performed at Ayodhya and *'Sri Ram Jyotis'* were lighted and sent to various parts of India for worship by

Hindus. The V.H.P. took out victory processions on 29-9-1990, causing road jams and demonstrations.

The month of October 1990 was of serious troubles not only for U.P. but for the entire country. The V.H.P. started preparations for the *'Kar Seva'* and mobilised volunteers from all over giving slogans "*Garv se Kaho hum Hindu Hain*" (say with pride that we are Hindus), "*Jai Sri Ram*" and "*kasam Ram ki khate hain-Mandir vahin banayen ge*" (we swear by God Rama that construction of temple will be done there only). It was announced by the V.H.P. that the *Kar Seva* for the construction of temple will start, come what may and volunteers from all over the country were asked to reach Ayodhya in large numbers to participate in *Kar Seva*. Several meetings were held and programmes organized at various places to mobilise Hindus. Muslims too started preparing to meet the challenge. Hectic meetings etc. of both the communities vitiated the communal atmosphere and gave way to polarisation, causing serious damage to hitherto prevailing social amity and tolerance. Sri Mulayam Singh Yadav, Chief Minister addressed *'Ekta'* (unity) rallies all over U.P., particularly in areas having sizable Muslim population and Hindu activists started calling him 'Maulana Mulayam'. Riots broke out at several places. Sri Lal Krishna Advani (B.J.P. President) undertook a 'Rathyatra' from Dwarka (Gujarat) to various parts of the country which was to terminate at Ayodhya on the occasion of the commencement of *'Kar Seva'*. Sri Advani was arrested at Samastipur (Bihar) on the orders of Chief Minister Sri Laloo Prasad Yadav, following which bitter communal frenzy was generated every where. The V.H.P. and their supporters justified their cause, whereas other parties tried to justify the cause for secularism, though they were termed as pseudo-secularists by pro-Hindu people. As danger was apprehended from the crowd to the disputed shrine, administrative preparations were also ordered by the U.P. Government.

There were B.J.P. governments in Rajasthan and Madhya Pradesh, which were favouring mobilisation of *Kar Sevaks* from their areas. U.P. and Bihar were against this mobilisation as danger was apprehended from the highly emotive issue and committed crowd collecting in Ayodhya. A ban was imposed on movement of *Kar Sevaks* towards Ayodhya from any side of U.P.. Rajasthan and M.P. did not impose such ban and supported the

Hindu cause. A call was also given for Hindus to collect in large numbers at Chitrakoot side of M.P. of Satna district and then march towards abjoning Chitrakoot area of district Banda in U.P.. To stop the movement of kar sevaks by rail, train services for Ayodhya and the neighbouring areas were cancelled. Road blocks were erected and trenches dug on roads so that vehicles could not pass. Bus services for Ayodhya and Faizabad were also stopped. The V.H.P. accepting this challenge of U.P. Government, threatened to reach Ayodhya in very large numbers to perform *Kar Seva*, starting on 30-10-1990. As Hindus (V.H.P.) were preparing to court arrests everywhere in large numbers, special arrangements were ordered for keeping them in temporary jails. Schools, colleges and other official premises like *Kisan Mandi Samitis* etc. were converted into temporary jails. At that point of time I was posted as Inspector General of Police Kanpur Zone having jurisdiction over 10 communally sensitive districts of Kanpur and Agra Ranges which had highly trouble prone cities like Aligarh, Mathura, Agra, Firozabad and Kanpur. Etawah, home district of Chief Minister Sri Mulayam Singh Yadav and Aligarh, the home district of Sri Kalyan Singh, a powerful B.J.P. leader and pro-V.H.P., who subsequently became the Chief Minister, U.P., also fell in my zone. It had borders with Rajasthan and Madhya Pradesh from where *Kar Sevaks* were to come in large numbers. Chief Minister Sri Mulayam Singh Yadav addressed several *'Ekta'* (Unity) rallies all over U.P. including my jurisdiction and we had very tough time in ensuring law and order and security arrangements. I distinctly remember that in early October, 1990, when Sri Yadav visited Aligarh Muslim University (A.M.U.), he was given rousing reception and all the buildings including Students' Union office were beautifully illuminated, which was indicative of his popularity in Muslim community. Subsequently in November, after the incidents of Ayodhya *Kar Seva*, when Aligarh city was under curfew, he visited the curfew bound areas and I was accompanying him; noticeable Hindu hatred was found for him in certain parts of the city. While the V.I.P. convoy of vehicles was passing through a narrow road to burnt houses of Muslims, Hindus drove pigs from one lane to the other and shouted derogatory slogans for Sri Yadav from housetops.

In middle of October, 1990, preparations were on to meet any likely law and order situation. A team of senior officers from Lucknow namely Sri V.K. Jain, Special D.G.P., U.P., Sri Ram Asray

Additional D.G.P. Intelligence, U.P. and Sri A.K. Rastogi Home Secretary visited several places of the State to take stock of the situation and planned arrangements. I had to accompany them, in helicopter from Lucknow. They first went to Allahabad, Chitrakoot and Jhansi of Allahabad Zone and then to Agra, Mathura and bordering areas of Rajasthan and M.P. of my Zone, Kanpur. It was practically a war like situation, the battle lines clearly drawn between the U.P. Government on one hand and the V.H.P. on the other, who were also being supported by the B.J.P. Governments of the bordering states of M.P. and Rajasthan, as the latter had thrown the challenge of reaching Ayodhya in large numbers at any cost and administration's job on U.P. side was to prevent them from reaching Ayodhya.

The "D" Day–October 30, 1990

A few days before October 30, *Kar Sevaks* started secretly trickling towards Ayodhya and many reached the villages on the other side of river Saryu in Districts Gonda and Basti. At Chitrakoot, Sadhvi Uma Bharti (who became Union Minister subsequently) appeared with thousands of supporters and the crowd caused serious law and order problems on U.P. side. Sri Ashok Singhal then Vice President of V.H.P. and Sri S.C.Dikshit, former Director General of Police U.P. and V.H.P. activist, managed to dodge the security forces and suddenly appeared at Ayodhya to lead the *Kar Sevaks* on October, 30.

However bitter communal feelings were generated leading to frenzy all over. About two lakh *Kar Sevaks* and Hindu volunteers were arrested in U.P. at various places and lodged in temporary jails. The Police and Magistrates had very tough times in managing these camps as educational institutions, mostly schools and colleges and other premises like *Mandi Parishad* sheds were converted into temporary jails and it became uphill task to manage these fanatic Hindu volunteers there. As sufficient police forces could not be deployed because of the non-availability due to very heavy commitment all over the State, they used to loiter about and many of them went out for bath in holy rivers including Ganga at Fatehgarh. Sufficient packets of cooked food were regularly sent from Kanpur to Fatehgarh every morning and evening by RSS and V.H.P. workers, from where it was about four hours road journey. I had never seen earlier that kind of commitment for Hindu cause. The administration and security forces remained at tenter hooks for several days in handling protests, road *jams* and *dharnas*, organized at several places. Muslims kept close watch but did not react as they had a feeling that Mulayam Singh Yadav's Government was fighting for their cause.

On 30-10-1990, canopy of *'Shilanyas Sthal'* was removed by the State machinery which was resented to by the V.H.P.. That very morning, despite ban, thousands of *'Kar Sevaks'*, many of whom had come from the other side of the river, suddenly appeared on Saryu bridge and started marching towards Ayodhya with a view to reaching the disputed shrine for *Kar Seva*. Police tried to stop them but they kept on marching and were ultimately dispersed after police firing.

A few *Kar Sevaks* from other areas could manage to reach the disputed place, climbed the domes and unfurled the saffron flags on their tops. Police had to fire on crowds at places in which six *Kar Sevaks* were killed and 84 injured. Fiftyfour police personnel also received injuries.

On this fateful occasion, I had to sit in my office at Kanpur for the whole day and night to monitor the situation and help districts of my Zone in maintaining law and order. In the

Scene at Saryu Bridge After Dispersal of the Crowd
Kar Seva 1990

Scene at Sary, Bridge after Dispersal of the Crowd Kar Seva 1990

afternoon of 30-10-1990, Sri Narendra Mohan, a prominent journalist, owner and editor of *'Dainik Jagran'* having wide circulation all over and my personal friend, came to my office and said that he had authentic information that *Kar Seva* had begun in Ayodhya and, therefore, he was bringing a special issue that evening. I said that according to my information *Kar Seva* had not started. For his satisfaction I contacted DGP's Control Room at Lucknow from where I was informed that though, *Kar Sevaks* could manage to climb the domes, they were brought down and no *Kar Seva* had started. Despite my persuasion of not bringing out a special issue, that Newspaper and one more local Hindi Daily brought out evening editions mentioning that *Kar Seva* had started, which was factually incorrect. Sensing that these editions will add fuel to the fire in already volatile communal situation in Kanpur, we had no option but to prevent their circulation.

In Ayodhya on 2-11-1990, thousands of *Kar Sevaks* marched towards disputed structure and tried to enter the shrine. Police had to fire in which 10 Kar Sevaks were killed and 93 injured. 46 police personnel were also injured. At some spots senior officers had to open fire. These incidents caused serious reactions and riots broke out at several places in the country. Wives of officers residing in officers' colony Faizabad got so much emotional due to action on *Kar Sevaks* that they went in a procession to the nearby residence of the Divisional Commissioner and offered bangles to him (Sri Madhukar Gupta). It is noteworthy that husbands of many of them were deployed on law and order duty in Ayodhya/Faizabad. Sri Subhash Joshi, Senior Superintendent of Police Faizabad, and Sri G.L. Sharma, Range D.I.G. of Police, were also treated uncharitably, because of their tough handling of the situation and firing at *Kar Sevaks* to prevent them reaching the disputed site.

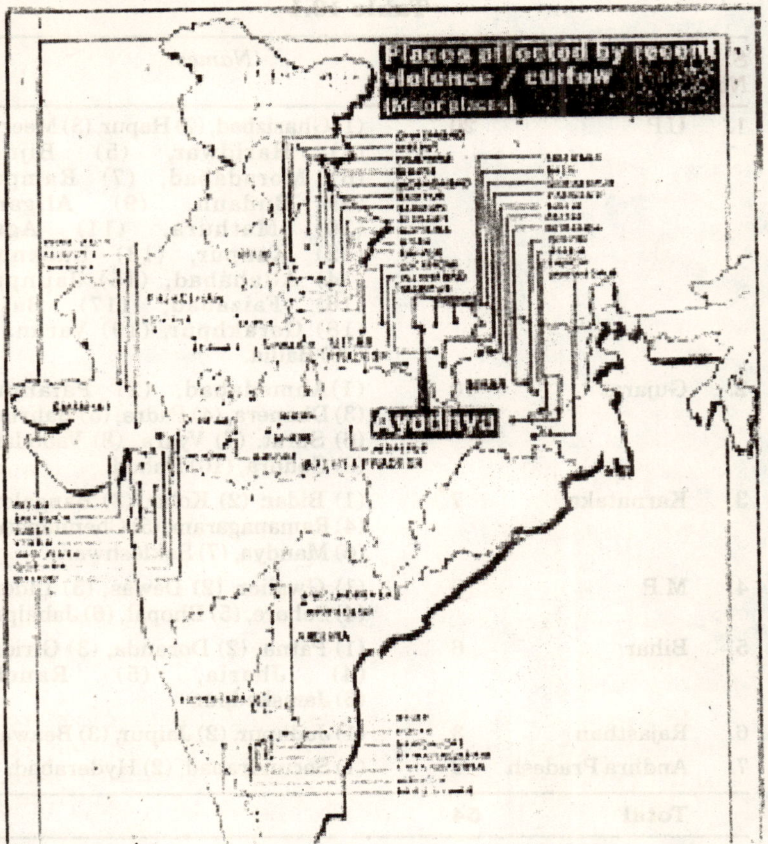

Courtesy Times of India, New Delhi Dated 7-11-1990

The ashes of the killed *Kar Sevaks* were put in 22 urns in Ayodhya on November 7 and 8, 1990 and sent to various parts of India. Wherever they reached serious law and order problems were created resulting in communal riots.

The map shows the cities and towns of the country which were under curfew in October and November, 1990 due to Ayodhya tangle.

An analysis shows that following 7 States were badly affected. The number of places which remained under curfew are mentioned below in the descending order of the numbers of each state in table 10.1:

Table 10.1

S. No.	*State*	*No.places Under Curfew*	*Names*
1.	U.P.	20	(1) Ghazizbad, (2) Hapur, (3) Meerut, (4) Haridwar, (5) Bijnor, (6) Moradabad, (7) Rampur, (8) Budaun, (9) Aligarh, (10) Mathura, (11) Agra, (12) Kanpur, (13) Lucknow, (14) Allahabad, (15) Jaunpur, (16) Faizabad, (17) Basti, (18) Gorakhpur, (19) Varanasi, (20) Ballia.
2.	Gujarat	10	(1)Ahmedabad, (2) Palanpur, (3) Dhanera, (4) Padra, (5) Bahruch, (6) Surat, (7) Vyara, (8) Vadodara, (9) Godhra, (10) Dahod.
3.	Karnataka	7	(1) Bidar, (2) Kolar, (3) Bangalore, (4) Ramanagaram, (5) Chennapatna, (6) Mandya, (7) Sakleshwar.
4.	M.P.	6	(1) Gwalior, (2) Dewas, (3) Indore, (4) Sehore, (5) Bhopal, (6) Jabalpur,
5.	Bihar	6	(1) Patna, (2) Doranda, (3) Giridih, (4) Jharia, (5) Ranchi, (6) Jamshedpur.
6.	Rajasthan	3	(1) Jodhpur, (2) Jaipur, (3) Beawar.
7.	Andhra Pradesh	2	(1) Secundrabad, (2) Hyderabad.
	Total	**54**	

The following places of Uttar Pradesh went under curfew from 29th October to 15th December 1990, and their names are mentioned in chronological order in table 10.2 :

Table 10.2

S. No.	Place	curfew clamped on	S.No	Place	curfew clamped on
1.	Rampur City	28-10-1990	19.	Basti City	31-10-1990
2.	Lucknow City	29-10-1990	20.	Barabanki	31-10-1990
3.	Varanasi City	29-10-1990	21.	Faizabad	31-10-1990
4.	Muzaffarnagar City	29-10-1990	22.	Hardoi City	31-10-1990
5.	Shamli Town (Muzaffarnagar)	30-10-1990	23.	Hapur City (Ghaziabad)	1-11-1990
6.	Aligarh City	30-10-1990	24.	Dibai Town (Bulandshahar)	1-11-1990
7.	Bijnor City	30-10-1990	25.	Muradnagar Town (Ghaziabad)	1-11-1990
8.	Budaun City	30-10-1990	26.	Saraimir Town(Azamgarh)	1-11-1990
9.	Kanpur City	30-10-1990	27.	Moradabad City	1-11-1990
10.	Gorakhpur City	30-10-1990	28.	Meerut City	2-11-1990
11.	Allahabad City	30-10-1990	29.	Bulandshahar City	2-11-1990
12 .	Jaunpur City	30-10-1990	30.	Ganjdundwara (Etah)	4-12-1990
13.	Atrauli Town (Aligarh)	31-10-1990	31.	Aligarh City	7-12-1990
14.	Modinagar Town (Ghaziabad)	31-10-1990	32.	Kanpur City	10-12-1990
15.	Firozabad City	31-10-1990	33.	Meerut City	10-12-1990
16.	Agra City	31-10-1990	34.	Jahangirpur Town(Bulandshahar)	13-12-1990
17.	Mathura City	31-10-1990	35.	Agra City	14-12-1990
18.	Jhansi City	31-10-1990	36.	Khurja Town (Bulandshahar)	15-12-1990

Table 10.3

S.N.	**Meerut Zone**	*Date when curfew clamped*
1.	Meerut City (First Time)	2-11-1990
	Meerut City (Second Time)	10-12-1990
2.	Muzaffar nagar City	29-10-1990
3.	Shamli Town (Muzaffarnagar)	30-10-1990
4.	Modinagar Town (Ghaziabad)	31-10-1990
5.	Hapur City (Ghaziabad)	1-11-1990
6.	Muradnagar Town(Ghaziabad)	1-11-1990
7.	Dibai Town (Bulandshahar)	1-11-1990
8.	Bulandshahar City	2-11-1990
9.	Jahangirpur Town (Bulandshahar)	13-12-1990
10.	Khurja Town (Bulandshahar)	15-12-1990
	Allahabad Zone	
1.	Allahabad City	30-10-1990
2.	Jhansi City	31-10-1990
	Lucknow Zone	
1.	Lucknow City	29-10-1990
2.	Hardoi City	31-10-1990
3.	Barabanki	31-10-1990
4.	Faizabad	31-10-1990
	Bareilly Zone	
1.	Bijnor City	30-10-1990
2.	Moradabad City	1-11-1990
3.	Rampur City	28-10-1990
4.	Budaun City	30-10-1990

S.N.	**Kanpur Zone**	*Date when curfew clamped*
1.	**Aligarh City (First Time)**	**7-12-1990**
	Aligarh City (Second Time)	**7-12-1990**
2.	**Atrauli Town (Aligarh)**	**31-10-1990**
3.	**Mathura City**	**31-10-1990**
4.	**Agra City (First Time)**	**31-10-1990**
	Agra City (Second Time)	**14-12-1990**
5.	**Firozabad City**	**31-10-1990**
6.	**Ganjdundwara (Etah)**	**4-12-1990**
7.	**Kanpur City (First Time)**	**30-10-1990**
	Kanpur City (Second Time)	**10-12-1990**
	Gorakhpur Zone	
1.	**Gorakhpur City**	**30-10-1990**
2.	**Basti City**	**31-10-1990**
	Varanasi Zone	
1.	**Varanasi City**	**29-10-1990**
2.	**Jaunpur City**	**30-10-1990**
3.	**Saraimir Town (Azamgarh)**	**1-11-1990**

Table 10.3 shows places of U.P. where curfew was clamped during one –and- half month from 29-10-1990 t0 15-12-1990 and in certain cities (1-Meerut, 2-Aligarh, 3-Agra,4- Kanpur) curfew had to be clamped more than once. Places in west U.P. were worst affected as they have sizable Muslim population and have history of repeated communal riots.

Rumours/Panic

Various kinds of rumours, which were floated, played an important role in fanning the riots everywhere. It may be of

interest to know about some such glaring cases. On the evening of October 30, 1990, we heard in Kanpur that because of the rumour of Sri Lal Krishna Advani, National President, B.J.P. having been shot at, (false) curfew had to be clamped in Hazratganj area of Lucknow (posh market and seat of power as Raj Bhawan and Vidhan Sabha are hardly a few metres away). This rumour created panic resulting in serious tension everywhere. One evening around 10 P.M., when Kanpur City was under curfew, a joint briefing meeting of all the officers including Magistrates, Police and Army officers was going on in City Police Control Room at Kotwali, loud noises were heard from Badshahi Naka (Hindu locality)/Nai Sadak (Muslim dominated places) areas. It was "*Allah-o-Akbar*", "*maro-kato*" and "*Jai Sri Ram*", "*Bachao Bachao*" etc. which gave a feeling that people of both the communities were fighting a pitched battle in that area. The meeting was immediately called off and senior officers rushed to that area. I continued to sit there to monitor the developments. The phone calls from panic-stricken citizens started pouring in asking for reinforcement of security forces. After some time officers returned to the Control Room and told that nobody was found in streets and situation was perfectly under control. We increased our night vigil. Similar noises were heard the next evening in curfew bound areas of Agra City. I asked the officers of Agra to be alert telling them that similar sounds were heard earlier in Kanpur city. A day later, Agra police traced a loud speaker fitted jeep on the outskirts of the city, which was having tape recorded versions of the noises that were being played here and there to create panic. Similar sounds were noticed at several places in U.P. This showed that this was being planned and circulated from somewhere else and think tank of trouble shooters was doing it deliberately to misguide the local administration and create panic and sense of insecurity in the minds of the general public of the two communities and also with a view to polarising the communities.

1991

The *'Kar Sewa Satyagrah'* was performed in Ayodhya from December 6, 1990 to January 14, 1991(Day of *Makar Sankranti* Festival when devotees turn up in huge numbers for holy bath in river Saryu). About 1.5 lakh Hindus courted arrests in U.P.

The General Elections for Lok Sabha and U.P. Assembly were held in May and June, 1991 and former Prime Minister Rajiv Gandhi was assassinated in Tamilnadu during electioneering. Ayodhya remained the main plank for electioneering in U.P.. Whereas Congress Party with Sri P.V. Narasimharao as Prime Minister came to power at the Centre, B.J.P. won in U.P. with thumping majority and formed the Government under the leadership of Sri Kalyan Singh. Samajwadi Party of Sri Mulayam Singh Yadav lost in noticeable Hindutva wave.

Hectic activities started towards the aim of construction of temple at 'Sri Ram Janam Sthan' in Ayodhya. The canopy of *'Shilanyas Sthal'* removed earlier, was re-installed on July 2/3, 1991 and U.P. Government also helped in removing the obstructions coming in the way of construction of Sri Ram Temple. On August 26 and 27, 1991, the V.H.P. obtained some shops, houses and temples etc. which was a step forward towards removal of obstructions for construction of Sri Ram Temple.

'Kendriya Marg Darshak Mandal' in its meeting held at Shimla from September 7 to 9, 1991 decided to perform 40 days' *'Bajrang Rudra Maha Yagya'* at Ayodhya in forthcoming October. This programme was endorsed in another meeting held at Rishikesh from September 27 to 29, 1991.

In early October, 1991, U.P. Government (led by Sri Kalyan Singh–B.J.P.) acquired 2.77 acres of land to facilitate the construction of the temple by the V.H.P.. Central Government (led by Sri P.V. Narasimharao–Congress) brought *'Dharm Sthal Vidheyak'* which was opposed by the V.H.P. and its copies were burnt at District Head Quarters from October 7 to November 3, 1991. Meanwhile suits were filed in High Court against acquisition of land and the High Court in its interim order banned permanent construction on the acquired land. At the same time levelling of the acquired land started which was widely reported by media causing panic in various groups.

The V.H.P. performed ' *Bajrang Rudra Maha Yagya'* at *Kar Sevak Puram* Ayodhya from October 18 to 26, 1991. On October 30, 1991 *Shaurya Samaroh*' (Bravery Function) was organized at Ayodhya to mark the first anniversary of Ayodhya *Kar Seva* incidents. On 31-10-1991, a few *Kar Sevaks* could manage to climb the 3 domes of the disputed structure and damaged their certain parts. Immediately after this a fact finding committee headed by Sri M.J. Akbar visited Ayodhya, which was protested by the *Kar Sevaks*. All these activities continued to build the communal atmosphere.

1992

Leaders of both the communities, Hindus led by the V.H.P. (Vishva Hindu Parishad) and Muslims led the B.M.A.C. (Babri Masjid Action Committee) remained busy in arranging various agitational programmes and counter programmes during 1992, ultimately resulting in the demolition of the disputed structure on December 6, 1992.

Levelling of acquired land was done from February to July, 1992. 'National Integration Council' and ' Joint Parliamentary Committee' visited the site at Ayodhya on 7-4-1992. On 9-4-1992 'B.J.P. Parliamentary Group,' led by its Vice President Sri Sikandar Bakht also visited the site and addressed press conference. The Chief Ministers of B.J.P. Governments of Madhya Pradesh, Rajasthan, Himachal Pradesh and Uttar Pradesh went to Ayodhya on 26-4-1992 and also visited the disputed shrine. The High Court held hearings on May 12, 14, 20 and 21, 1992 against unlocking of the disputed shrine and Sri R.K. Srivastava, retired District Judge was appointed receiver of the disputed structure on 22-5-1992. A delegation of the Muslims from Ayodhya led by Sri Vinay Katiyar (President Bajrang Dal) met Sri Kalyan Singh, C.M. U.P. and pleaded for the removal of the Babri Masjid to another place and facilitate the construction of the temple at Ram Janam Bhumi. On June 10, 1992 a few metres away from the disputed structure, but outside the disputed area, *'Bhumi Poojan'* of *'Sheshavatar'* temple was performed and a large number of Hindus participated in this programme. Apprehending danger the BMAC met the Prime Minister on 27-6-1992 and demanded protection of the Babri Masjid.

In July V.H.P. remained very active in Ayodhya. Kendriya Marg Darshak Mandal/Sant Sammelan was held at Ayodhya on July 8, where 'Temple Renovation Committee' was set up and role of Central Government was condemned for creating hinderance in the temple construction. Sri Ashok Singhal also announced the resolution of starting construction of the temple from 8-7-1992 and Rupees 75 lakhs were sanctioned for performance of '*Sarv Dev Anushthan*'. 200 truck load of stones, 60 trucks of cement and sand was unloaded at the site for temple construction and '*Sarv Dev Anushthan*' of different sects of Hindus including Sikhs, Buddhists and Jains started a few metres away from the disputed structure. A huge *Pandal* was set up having 'Havan Kund' for each sect and to accommodate the devotees, who were to remain present in large numbers. As announced earlier 3,000 *Kar Sevaks* started '*Kar Seva*' on 8-7-1992 from 3 P.M. They were asked to bring one *lota* (mug) of sand from river Saryu and drop it in a pit at '*Shilanyas*' site. This programme led to communal tension all over, creating serious law and order problems at several places in the country. On 13-7-1992 the Supreme Court ordered stoppage of work and maintenance of status-quo. On 20-7-1992, V.H.P. and other Hindu organisations protested against the Supreme Court's order. On stoppage of *Kar Seva* of Sri Ram Temple, *Kar Seva* of *Sheshavatar* temple started on 26-7-1992 which continued to generate communal divide and Prime Minister Sri Narasimha Rao held talks with Hindu Saints for defusing the situation. Ultimately ' *Kar Seva*' was postponed for three months on 26-7-1992 and in the meanwhile the Prime Minister was to find out some amicable solution

The Muslim organisations particularly the BMAC carried out several programmes from May to August, 1992. The Aligarh Muslim University Students Union in meetings held from May 6 to 9, resolved to " *Do or Die*" in case Babri Masjid was demolished. A Muslim *Karvan* (caravan) was taken out from July 5 to 10 by B.M.A.C. protesting against the commencement of *Kar Seva*. During this period Muslims also observed '*Bunds*' by closing their shops, hoisted black flags, wore black armbands and also courted arrests at Moradabad, Kanpur and Unnao. The B.M.A.C. leaders also toured various Districts of U.P. to mobilise Muslims on this issue. These activities of the leaders of both the communities created lot of tension and panic everywhere, particularly in urban areas

Next three months i.e. September, October and November, 1992 saw hectic activities from both sides which kept on adding to the tensions to already prevailing communal frenzy in the country as the *Kar Seva* was to begin from 6-12-1992. There was clash between Sadhus and C.R.P.F. *jawans* at Ayodhya on 11-9-

1992. On September 27 and 28, 1992 *'Charan Padukas'* (11,800 in numbers) were worshipped, consecrated and dispatched to various parts of the country for *pooja*. During October 'Charan Paduka Poojan' was performed; lakhs of Kar Sevaks were enlisted and their signatures obtained on oath papers; funds collected and Block and District level meetings were also held in November.

D.G.P., U.P. Replaced

Sri Prakash Singh was replaced by Sri S.V.M. Tripathi as D.G.P., U.P. on 30-9-1992.

' Nyay Yatra'

The B.M.A.C. took out *'Nyay Yatra'* in September and October demanding removal of idols from the Babri Masjid. 'Muslim Majlis' in a rally organized on 26-11-1992 exhorted Muslims to protect the Babri Masjid at any cost and remain prepared for any sacrifice. They were also asked to observe *Roza*, offer *Namaz* and to proceed to Ayodhya in case the Central Government failed to stop *'Kar Seva'* from 6-12-1992.

Hectic Week from November 29 to December 5, 1992

The V.H.P. had already made elaborate preparations for mobilisation of *Kar Sevaks* in large numbers from all over the country. *'Lalkar Saptah'* (challenge week) was observed all over the country from 9-11-1992 to December 5, 1992. *Kar Sevaks* from various parts of the country, numbering over two lakhs, were collected at Ayodhya, who were there for several days and were being indoctrinated about their goal of *Kar Seva*. Unlike 1992, no restrictions were imposed on collection of the *Kar Sevaks* there. It is noteworthy that total population of Ayodhya town was about 50,000 and another over two lakh committed persons were added which increased Ayodhya's population by five times. These *Kar Sevaks* were kept busy in religious activities, listening to devotional songs of saints and lectures of important leaders, at *'Ram Katha Mandap'* situated very close to the disputed area and also doing earth work at nearby *Kuber Teela*. There were no restrictions imposed by the local administration. *Kar Sevaks* were made to camp on open land on all sides of the disputed structure, except the 2.77 acres of the acquired land and this made the protected area highly vulnerable to crowd attack.

Additional police and P.A.C. Coys were mobilised by State authorities. The Central Government of its own mobilised 195 Coys of C.P.M.F. (Central Para Military Forces). According to the Government of India's White Paper on Ayodhya "the Chief Minister reacted very strongly to the stationing of Central forces near Ayodhya. The State Government was informed of the stationing of these forces on 24th November. The very next day the Chief Minister wrote to the Home Minister protesting against this precautionary move of the Central Government. At no stage, did the Government of U.P. indicate that it would not use force for the protection of the structure." As the B.J.P. Government of U.P., led by Sri Kalyan Singh, did not ask for the C.P.M.F. Coys, these forces were not provided accommodation and other facilities by the local administration. Therefore, they were made to camp at Central Government's premises in (Dogra Regiment Centre Faizabad) and around Ayodhya extending upto a distance of about 50 K.Ms. Officers of C.P.M.F., many of whom were deputationists from U.P. Cadre, could not have desired liasion with the local authorities. There was not only communication gap but also element of secrecy and distrust between the Central and the State authorities as the U.P. and the Central Governments were not having smooth relations. Whereas, the State B.J.P. Govt. was supporting the *Kar Seva*, the Central Congress Govt. was opposed to it. The Congress Party took out a 'Peace March' on 4-12-1992 from Lucknow to Ayodhya but their leaders were arrested before they could reach Ayodhya. On 5-12-1992, nine political parties led by former Prime Minister Sri V.P. Singh, started on 'Peace March' from Lucknow to Ayodhya but they too were arrested at Kalyani river bridge at Ram Sanehi Ghat (District Barabanki). This is the strategic place as no vehicle could pass without crossing this bridge and persons arrested particularly the V.I.P.'s could easily be lodged in the adjacent P.W.D. Inspection House.

The Supreme Court ordered stoppage of the construction activity over 2.77 acres of the acquired land. Prime Minister. Narasimharao called a meeting of the National Integration Council where Chief Ministers of various states were present. Where C.M. U.P. Sri Kalyan Singh gave an assurance for protecting the disputed structure.

A leaflet (photo copy given on next pages), which was found in circulation, was brought out by *'Akhil Bhartiya Vidhyarthi*

Parishad, Uttar Pradesh', exhorting Hindus to reach Ayodhya on December six. Certain questions were also addressed to the Supreme Court of India.

The *Dharam Sansad* decided to have symbolic *Kar Seva* from 6-12-1992. Sri L.K. Advani, the prominent B.J.P. leader went out on *Rath Yatra* from Varanasi to various parts of eastern U.P., whereas Sri Murli Manohar Joshi B.J.P. President, took out Rath Yatra from Mathura to central and western parts of U.P.. A B.J.P. public meeting, held at Lucknow on 5-12-1992 for *Kar Seva* at Ayodhya, was addressed by Sri L.K. Advani and Sri Atal Bihari Vajpayee. By 5-12-1992, the entire country was anxious about the likely events on 6-12-1992 as the V.H.P. had prepared their

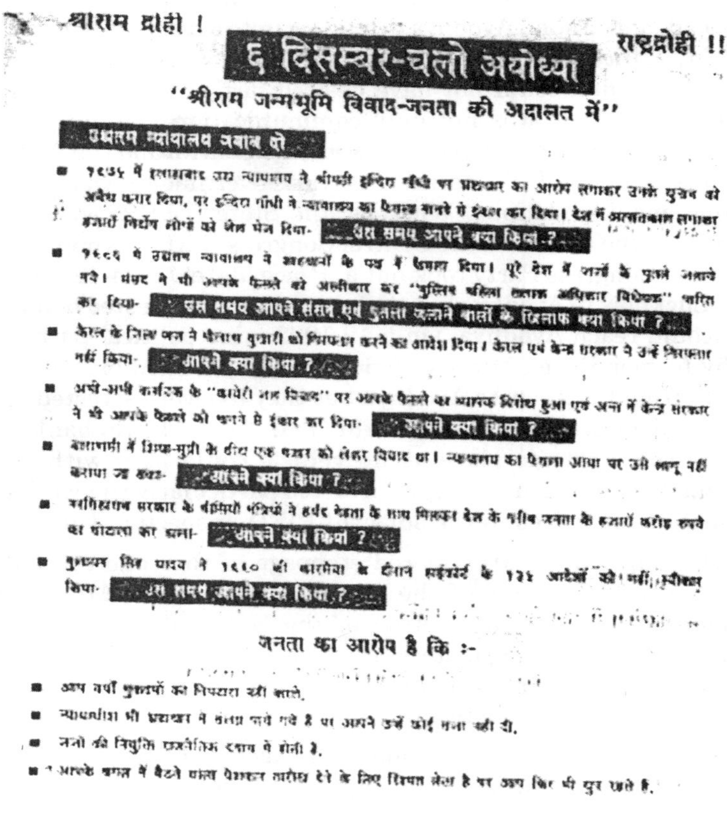

फिर-

- आप तो मात्र गवाहों के बयानं एवं दस्तावेजों के आधार पर ही फैसला देते हैं .

कौन गवाह है-

- कि भगवान राम का जन्म अयोध्या में हुआ था या नहीं दावे के साथ कह सके।
- दस्तावेज लाकर साबित कर सके कि जन्म भूमि वही है या नहीं।

सवाल गवाह या दस्तावेज का नहीं आस्था का है आप अपने को इससे अलग रक्खें

श्रीराम जन्मभूमि पर मंदिर निर्माण का संघर्ष है;

- उन ताकतों के खिलाफ जो विदेशी आक्रमणकारी बाबर की तुलना श्रीराम से करना चाहते हैं,
- बाबर के पुत्र हुमायूं के खिलाफ संघर्ष करने वाले एवं हुमायूं को पराजित करने वाले राष्ट्रवादी मुसलमान शेरशाह को भुलाकर एक विदेशी आक्रमणकारी बाबर के साथ भारत के मुसलमानों को जोड़ना चाहते हैं,
- भारतीय क्रिकेट खिलाड़ी अजहर के छक्के पर मातम मनाते हैं पर पाकिस्तानी खिलाड़ी इमरान खान एवं मियांदाद के छक्के पर पटाखे दागते हैं,
- पाकिस्तान के खिलाफ संघर्ष में शहीद हुए भारतीय अब्दुल हमीद को भूलकर पाकिस्तान के मुर्दों के शहादत पर शोक मनाते हैं,
- जिन्हें राष्ट्रगान "वन्दे मातरम्" को संसद में गाये जाने पर आपत्ति है,

भारत का नौजवान-देश का अपमान नहीं सहेगा,

आइये !

- कारसेवा में भाग लेकर राष्ट्रीय स्वाभिमान के संघर्ष को यशस्वी बनायें।

निवेदक :- अखिल भारतीय वियार्थी परिषद, उत्तर प्रदेश

अखिल भारतीय विद्यार्थी परिषद, 5, नवीन मार्केट, कैसर बाग, लखनऊ द्वारा प्रकाशित एवम् वैष्णो कलर प्रेस, 96/2, कर्नलगंज, कानपुर द्वारा मुद्रित

ground for the *Kar Seva* and the BMAC had also asked Muslims to remain prepared for facing any eventuality. Flags, saffron of Hindus and green or black for Muslims had already been hoisted on houses / establishments of the staunch supporters of the respective communities. That kind of frenzy was never witnessed earlier, as some people said that it did not happen even at the time of the partition of the country in 1947/ 1948 when mass exodus of the population took place.

KAR SEVA ON DECEMBER 6, 1992

The ultimate day, December 6, arrived. The top B.J.P. and V.H.P. leaders were present at Ayodhya, some to supervise the *Kar Seva* at *Shilanyas* site and others at *Katha Kunj* to address the crowd gathered there to wait for their turn of *Kar Seva*. Media persons particularly those with T.V. Cameras had found suitable sites for themselves; while many were on the roof top of the Manas Bhavan from where both the sides of disputed area and the *Katha Kunj*

DEMOLITION ON 6-12-1992

Top VHP Leaders with Media on 5-12-1992

(Left to Right) Sarva-Sri (1)SC Dikshit,(2) Ashok Singhal, (3) Mahant Ram Chandra Param Hans Das,(4) Mahant Avaidhya Nath.

Distribution of Food

Listening to 'Pravachan' & Speeches at Ram Katha Kunj

Kar Sevaks Listening to Speeches and 'Pravachan' at Ram Katha Kunj

Kar Sevaks all round–Frontal view of the Structure

Rear View of the Structure–Kar Sevaks Busy in Demolition

View of Two damaged Domes–One Demolished

Make–Shift Temple

Faizabad City Under Curfew

could be easily covered; others remained mobile to cover spot situations. Senior police officers, Magistrates and other officers including the receiver appointed by the court, were present on the top of *Sita Rasoi*, from where the Security Control Room had been functioning and from this place the disputed structure was clearly visible. Besides one Coy. of C.R.P.F., deployed from before for inner cordon security duty, police, P.A.C. and other security personnel were also present. RSS volunteers were also present on the wall and the security barricades of the disputed structure. The Symbolic *Kar Seva* started amidst the chanting of slogans, particularly "*Jai Sri Ram*". Sri Ashok Singhal, who was present at the site, was controlling the situation as was shown in the video tapes, but the *Kar Sevaks* rushed towards the disputed structure pushing aside security forces and caring little for the instructions that were to follow from the organisors. Sri D.B. Rai Senior Superintendent of Police and Sri R.N. Srivastava, D.M. Faizabad went to the security zone to manage the situation, which had suddenly gone out of control. Ultimately nothing could be done and the security personnel left their duties leaving the site and the disputed structure to the mercy of the *Kar Sevaks*, who not only climbed the domes but also started demolishing them. The media persons, particularly the cameramen, many of whom were covering from Manas Bhavan roof top, were targeted, cameras smashed, reels/tapes exposed, writing pads snatched and torn and some of them were also given thorough thrashing. The speeches from Katha Kunj continued and it is alleged that slogans like "*Ek Dhakka aur do-Babri Masjid tod d*o." (give one more push and break the Babri Masjid) were also raised. The whole nation/world watched the happenings on television sets. Central Para Military Forces stationed at places, could do nothing as they were not mobilised. Chief Minister Sri Kalyan Singh owned the responsibility for not ordering the police firing on *Kar Sevaks*. He was subsequently sentenced to one day's imprisonment by the Hon'ble Supreme Court. By the evening of sixth December, the three domes had been razed to ground and the symbolic construction activity of the Temple started. Several persons who were on the domes are said to have fallen with the debris and got buried under it. A poet said that this structure was demolished neither by *Rama nor Rahim* (Allah), but by the human beings who are supposed to live in peace.

The 'White Paper' of the Government of India mentioned that "Initial reports from Ayodhya on 6th December indicated an air of normalcy. About 70,000 persons had assembled in the Ram Katha Kunj for a public meeting with some 500 *Sadhus* and sants gathered on the foundation terrace for performing *pooja*. Everything seemed to be going according to the plan announced by the organisers for doing a symbolic *Kar Seva* and observing other formalaties of *Kar Seva* not involving violation of court orders. As the crowd was being addressed by leaders of B.J.P., V.H.P. etc. roughly 150 persons in a sudden move broke through the cordon on the terrace, regrouped and started pelting stones at the police personnel. All this happened a few minutes before noon and within a very little time, around a thousand persons broke into the R.J.B./BM structure. Around 12.20 Hrs. about 80 persons had managed to climb the R.J.B./B.M. structure and started damaging the domes. At this time the crowd inside the complex was around 25,000 with larger numbers milling around outside. By 14.40 Hrs crowd had increased to about 75,000." (Para 1.18)

"While this criminal activity was going on, the local authorities and the police appeared to be standing as mute spectators, ostensibly under the instructions of the Chief Minister of Uttar Pradesh. This dismal picture of inaction and the State Government's derelection of duty was because of orders of the Chief Minister of U.P. not to use force. Even the small contingent of Central Reserve Police was rendered inactive and powerless by express directions given to them by the local Magistrate and higher State Government authorities. A worse example of irresponsibility and abdication of power by those who had taken oath to defend the Constitution and uphold the rule of law cannot be imagined." (Para 1.19)

In the evening of 6-12-1992, Kalyan Singh Government was dismissed, President's rule imposed and the deployment of C.P.M.F. was ordered. They could not reach the site promptly as all approach roads had been blocked by putting logs, telephone poles and felling trees at several places and *Kar Sevaks* in large numbers remained present at those places for confrontation. It took very long, say several hours, to clear the roads and reach the places of deployment. The Government of India's White Paper reads "In view of the situation in R.J.B.-BM complex and the presence of over 200,000 Kar Sevaks in aggressive and militant mood, the decision about the timing of entry of the Central forces was left to themselves. Action was also initiated for evacuation of Kar Sevaks from Ayodhya. As a result, by the evening of the 7th December nearly 70,000 persons had left Ayodhya. The officers commanding the security forces decided to move the force in the night of 7th and 8th December so as to use minimum force. Action was taken accordingly and the R.J.B.-BM area was quickly secured. This was managed without having to resort to firing." (Para 1.21)

The B.J.P.'s 'White Paper' says "From the evening of Sunday the 6th December, 1992 to the morning of 8th December, 1992 it was under Sri Narasimha Rao's rule that the Kar Seva for temple construction took place. It was not under the rule of Shri Kalyan Singh. The 135 companies of Central Forces were the guardians for the Kar Seva. The White Paper of the Government lists phone calls after phone calls from the Home Ministry and the Home Minister to every official of the Uttar Pradesh Government, from the Chief Minister to the ADM of Faizabad, asking, pleading and directing them to use the Central Forces. This was from 12.00 a.m. to 5 p.m. on December 6, 1992. But after Shri Kalyan Singh resigned and Shri Narasimha Rao's Government ruled Uttar Pradesh through the Governor Shri Satyanarayan Reddy, the Central Government did not use these Central Forces! In fact, the Kar Seva started when Ayodhya was under President's Rule which means, the Prime Minister's rule." (Para2-5) " Considering the fact that for 36 hours the Central Forces did not think it proper to act, would the same judgement not have held good for Shri Kalyan Singh also? How could Shri Kalyan Singh be faulted if he had decided not to fire upon the unarmed Kar Sevaks?. . . . the decision of Shri Kalyan Singh not to intervene during the six hours on the afternoon of December 6, 1992 was also perfectly in order." (Para 2.6)

Serious Riots in the Country

Following the demolition of the structure the communal situation in several parts of the country, deterioted sharply.

Serious riots broke out in various parts of India from evening of 6-12-92 onwards necessitating deployment of Army and other Para Military Forces for very long periods. The security forces had to face the Muslim ire for alleged failure to protect their Babri Masjid. As a protest several temples were destroyed in Bangladesh, Pakistan, Dubai and U.K. Indian diplomats were also attacked in Dacca (Bangladesh) and Islamabad (Pakistan). In Bombay serious riots broke out in January, 1993 and explosions took place on 6-3-1993 resulting in demolition of important buildings and very heavy loss of life and property.

'Bharat Bund' was observed on 8-12-92 on the call of non-B.J.P. parties including Congress against demolition of the disputed structure. Prime Minister Narasimharao also announced that 'mosque' will be reconstructed there. In the meantime several top B.J.P. leaders including Sri L.K. Advani and Sadhvi Uma Bharti had been arrested and kept at Mata Teela Dam Inspection House in Lalitpur district of U.P., which was converted into a temporary jail. *'Bharat Bund'* was observed on 9-12-92 by the B.J.P. in protest of these arrests and the announcement of the Central Govt. to reconstruct mosque at the disputed site. Sri Atal Bihari Vajpayee expressed shock over the demolition and termed it as unfortunate. Other B.J.P. leaders also said that the demolition was never intended.

The Lucknow Bench Of Allahabad High Court in its judgment on 11-12-1992, set aside acquisition of 2.77 acres of land by the U.P. (B.J.P.) Govt. On 15-12-1992 B.J.P. Governments of Rajasthan, Madhya Pradesh and Himachal Pradesh were dismissed and President's rule imposed. This led to serious objections by the B.J.P..

The B.J.P.'s White Paper said, "During the period from December 7 to December 14 there were riots in different parts of the country. In India, Pakistan and Banladesh many temples were destroyed and Hindus attacked. Not a word against the desecration came from any political party in India other than the B.J.P. Worst among the riot-affected states were Maharashtra, Gujarat, Karnataka, Assam and Andhra Pradesh. The casualties in Congress or Centre ruled states were 907 and in the B.J.P. ruled states 154. The riots that followed were not Hindu-Muslim riots, but clashes mostly between the rioters and the police. . . . Ayodhya provided the context, it was not the cause." (Para 2.10)

The following map published in 'Sunday Magazine' of (20-26 December,1992) captioned "BLOOD SPOTS, Scenes of Violence after the 6-December demolition" is being reproduced (with their grateful acknowledgements) which clearly indicates the cities and towns of India which were under curfew at that point of time. This was perhaps, a record of the places simultaneously being under curfew in India:

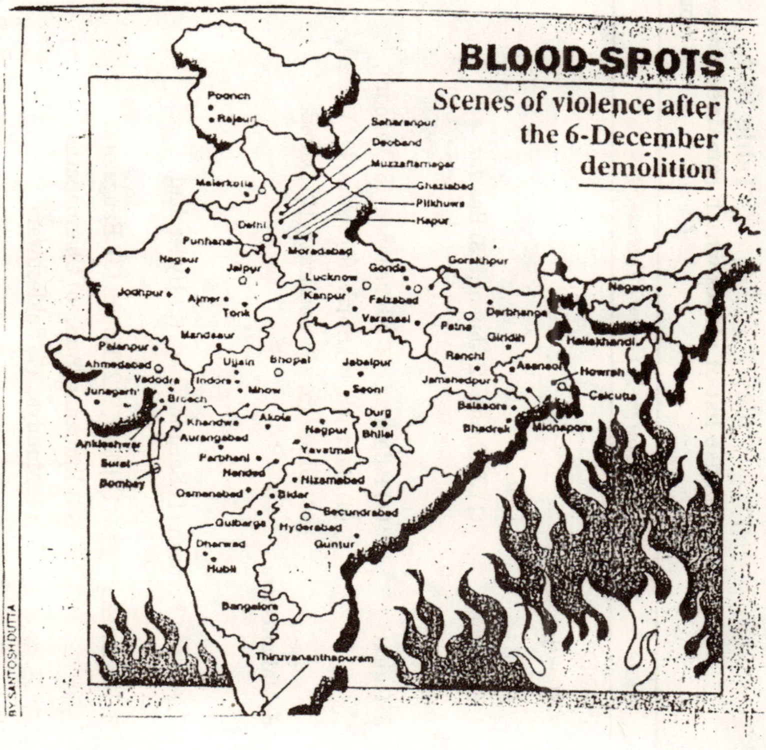

Table 10.4

State wise list of places which remained under Curfew in 1990 and 1992

(Source – two maps displayed on pages 185 & 213)

State	*1990 States–7, Cities / Towns–54*	*1992 States–15, Cities/Towns–69*
1. J&K	—	(1) Poonch, (2)Rajauri.
2. Haryana	—	(1) Malsekotia.
3. Delhi	Delhi	Delhi
4. Rajasthan	(1) Jodhpur, (2) Jaipur, (3) Beawar.	(1) Punhana, (2) Nagaur, (3) Jaipur, (4) Jodhpur, (5) Ajmer, (6) Tonk, (7) Mandsaur.
5. Gujrat	(1) Palanpur, (2) Ahmedabad, (3) Vadodra, (4) Bahruch, (5) Surat, (6) Padra, (7) Vyara, (8) Dhanera, (9) Godhra, (10) Dahod.	(1) Palanpur, (2) Ahmedabad, (3) Vadodra, (4) Bahruch, (5) Surat, (6) Junagarh, (7) Ankleshwar.
6. Maharashtra	——	(1) Akola, (2) Nagpur, (3) Yavatmal, (4) Aurangabad, (5) Parbhani, (6) Nanded, (7) Bombay, (8) Osmanabad,
7. Andhra Pradesh	(1) Secundrabad, (2) Hyderabad,	(1) Nizamabad, (2) Secundrabad, (3) Hyderabad, (4) Guntur,
8. Karnataka	(1) Bidar, (2) Kolar, (3) Bangalore, (4) Ramanagaram, (5) Chennapatna, (6) Mandya, (7) Sakleshwar.	(1) Bidar, (2) Bangalore, (3) Gulbarga, (4) Dharwad, (5) Hubli.
9. Kerala	——	(1) Thiruvanantpuram.

State	1990 States- 7, Cities / Towns- 54	1992 States- 15, Cities / Towns- 69
10. M.P.	(1) Gwalior, (2) Dewas, (3) Indore, (4) Sehore, (5) Bhopal, (6) Jabalpur.	(1)Ujjain, (2) Indore, (3) Mhow, (4) Bhopal, (5) Jabalpur, (6) Seoni, (7) Durg, (8) Bhilai.
11. U.P.	(1) Ghazizbad, (2) Hapur, (3) Meerut, (4) Haridwar, (5) Bijnor, (6) Moradabad, (7) Rampur, (8) Budaun, (9) Aligarh, (10) Mathura, (11) Agra, (12) Kanpur, (13) Lucknow, (14) Allahabad, (15) Jaunpur, (16) Faizabad, (17) Basti, (18) Gorakhpur, (19) Varanasi, (20) Ballia.	(1) Shaharanpur, (2) Deoband, (3) Muzaffarnagar, (4) Ghaziabad, (5) Pilkhuwa, (6) Hapur, (7) Moradabad, (8) Lucknow, (9) Kanpur, (10) Gonda, (11) Faizabad, (12), Gorakhpur (13) Varanasi.
12. Bihar	(1) Patna, (2) Doranda, (3) Giridih, (4) Jharia, (5) Ranchi, (6) Jamshedpur.	(1) Patna, (2) Darbhanga, (3) Giridih, (4) Ranchi, (5) Jamshedpur.
13.West Bengal	——	(1) Asansol, (2) Midnapore, (3) Howrah, (4) Calcutta, (5) Hallakhandi.
14. Orissa		(1) Balasore, (2) Bhadrak.
15. Assam	——	(1) Naugaon.

Officers Transferred

After the demolition of the disputed structure and the imposition of President's rule on 6-12-92, the shifting of officers started. Sri Arvind Verma IAS (1963), who happened to be my batch mate, was posted as Divisional Commissioner Faizabad in the late hours of 6-12-92 and was asked to rush from Allahabad to Faizabad to take over the same night from the outgoing Commissioner Sri S.P. Gaur. Sri Vijai Shankar Pandey replaced Sri R.N. Srivastava as District Magistrate Faizabad, who was placed under suspension. Sri P.P.S. Sidhu, who on return from central deputation, was awaiting posting orders at Lucknow, as there was some hitch in the issuance of his promotion as DIG due to litigation about seniority between promotees and direct recruits, was suddenly asked to proceed to Faizabad to take over as range DIG, where he took over around midnight of 6/7-12-1992 replacing Sri Uma Shankar Bajpai. Sri D.B. Rai was suspended and replaced by Sri Har Bhajan Singh, who had earlier been SSP Faizabad. I was then posted as Inspector General of Police, Economic Offences Wing, C.I.D. at Lucknow and was keeping track of the events as I had to go to S.V.P. N.P.A. Hyderabad for a lecture to the IPS officers on management of communal riots. On the evening of December 10, I happened to be at Intelligence Head Quarters Lucknow. Sri P.S.V. Prasad, D.I.G. Intelligence who had gone to U.P. secretariat, soon on entering his room congratulated me informing that I was being posted as I.G.P. Lucknow Zone. I told him that it was hardly a matter for congratulation. It is noteworthy that Faizabad District is under the jurisdiction of Lucknow Zone. After talking to him I went to D.G.P. H.Qrs., where I met Sri S.V.M. Tripathi, D.G.P., who said that my orders are coming. I requested him to permit me to join the next day when my predecessor Sri A.K. Sharan would be returning to Lucknow from Ayodhya, where he had been camping and Sri Tripathi agreed to my request. I returned to my residence, where I gave this news to my wife. That evening around 10.30 P.M. Sri Radhey Shyam, I.G.P., Karmik who was in his office, told me on phone that I must take over in the night itself. I told him that as the E.O.W. office was closed, it would not be possible for me to hand over charge in the night. He said that I need not worry as he was getting the papers prepared in his office for handing over and taking over. I got in touch with the

D.G.P. again telling him that it would not be in the fitness of things for me to take over, as Sri Sharan was out to Faizabad. Sri Tripathi told me that as desired by the Government, I should take over in the night itself and Sri Sharan had already been sounded to return, who was on his way to Lucknow. I went to D.G.P. Office and signed the papers. A few days later, (on 23-12-1992) Sri S.V.M. Tripathi was replaced by Sri Prakash Singh as D.G.P., from whom Sri Tripathi had taken over on 30-9-1992. Home Secretary U.P. Sri Prabhat Kumar was also replaced. Sri T.S.R. Subramanian took over as Chief Secretary, U.P., from Sri VK Saxena following the imposition of President's rule.

Certain Obsevations

After taking over charge, I went to Faizabad, where I had to camp for several days. But for Lucknow, I could not visit the other curfew bound areas of my Zone, as my continuous presence was needed at Ayodhya/Faizabad. I saw certain things in and around Ayodhya, which were undisturbed till then, and I feel that a mention of some of them may be of interest:-

1. The arrangements made by the V.H.P. for *Kar Sevaks* in respect of stay, essential requirements, briefing, liasion etc were exhaustive and some thing to learn about. Left behind camping material and several tents were still lying which were later removed by the contractors.
2. Media management was excellent. I fail to appreciate as to how and why did they fail in controlling the *Kar Sevaks*, who attacked and manhandled the media persons, particularly at Manas Bhawan on 6-12-1992.
3. Loud speakers were provided all over Ayodhya city so that people could listen the announcements and speeches made centrally. But for wireless sets and loud speakers fitted in official vehicles, administration did not have the matching arrangements, hence they were not in a position to communicate centrally to the people for maintaining law and order.
4. Muslim houses, shops and other establishments were marked in advance by a special sign written in red (by *geru*), which helped the outsider *Kar Sevaks* in identifying and destroying them. Practically all visible houses, shops, graves, mosques etc. were burnt or destroyed.

5. As Muslims had already fled to safer places, apprehending danger, very few were killed/injured.
6. Highly provocative slogans were written and signs painted on walls of the acquired land and adjacent buildings and they could easily be seen by all those who happened to be there.
7. *Kar Sevaks*, men and women of different age groups, were highly motivated people, who had come prepared to do and die. The three domes of the structure in normal situation could not have been razed to ground without bull-dozers, but *Kar Sevaks* pulled them down within hours and dumped the debris including huge domes in the adjacent low lying land. These boulders could be seen even now.
8. The security barricades erected to regulate the crowd and infiltration could not withstand the crowd pressure and the Kar Sevaks climbed over them like monkeys; later they removed them and used for demolition and other purposes.
9. The work on make–shift temple was done with record speed. After the fall of the structure, there were no security personnel and *Kar Sevaks* had no fear of the law. As is already known, the security forces could take control of the place on the early hours of 8th December. Some of the implements and construction material including cement, sand etc. were still lying there. It is apparent that blue print of the make shift temple had either been prepared in advance or the architects were there who did it then and there. Some of the material like logs used for supporting the canopy might have been brought subsequently but without loss of time. Boundary walls on all 4 sides were erected and climbing steps were also prepared. "*Vijai Diwas* 6-12-1992" was inscribed in cement on the first step, so that anybody stepping towards make shift temple could easily notice it.
10. The carved pillars, stones, statues etc. claimed to have been recovered from the debris, were taken to *Katha Mandap* and stored in a room, which was subsequently got sealed by the administration. These are now being

examined by archeological experts in order to help the court in deciding the case.

11. Some of the security personnel, who were first to arrive at the make–shift temple, worshipped, did *parikrama* and offered money. For next few days there were no visitors except Magistrates, police officers, security personnel on duty and the Mahant of the deity. Visitors started coming when High Court ordered that *Pooja* could be performed there.

12. It took about 3 days to clear the *Kar Sevaks* from Ayodhya, though special trains and buses had started running from the evening of 6th December. It was Herculean task to remove them from there. On way they created problems between Faizabad and Lucknow. At Rudauli Railway Station, Hindus were bringing food for the *Kar Sevaks*, where local Muslims were also seen, who were asked to chant "Jai Sri Ram". They fled towards the town for safety but many of them were chased and attacked. Later several Muslim houses and shops were burnt. Governor Sri B. Satya Narayan Reddy visited the affected town after about 10 days of the incident and I had accompanied him, where the destruction was still visible. *Kar Sevaks* travelling by another train chased the Muslims from over-bridge of the Barabanki Railway Station to nearby Muslim Mohalla, Rassi Batan and killed some of them. It was also said that while travelling by passenger trains they manhandled the Muslim passengers by pulling beards of men and burquas of women and forced them to chant "Jai Sri Ram". This kind of behaviour is said to have been repeated in many trains and at most of the places.

13. While checking night duties in curfew bound Faizabad city, I found police men bearing berret caps. As P.A.C. *jawans* had been putting on such caps, I asked some of them as to which Battalion they belonged to, but they told me that they were from the District Police. Then I realised that Sri Prakash Singh, D.G.P., had introduced these caps replacing traditional forage caps. Subsequently the traditional forage caps were restored as police personnel and the public had been used to them.

14. After Ayodhya had been cleared of *Kar Sewaks*, it remained under curfew for several days but the locals did not feel the pinch of it as they did nothing wrong and co-operated with the administration, hence curfew was not enforced very strictly.

Afterwards certain actions were taken and a mention of some of them may be of interest:

1. Security scheme was prepared immediatly for the area. Besides others, we the three batch mates, Sri Hari Das Rao, A.D.G., Law and Order U.P., Sri C.K. Mallick, I.G.P. Security U.P. and I, as I.G.P. Lucknow Zone, were mainly involved in this exercise.
2. Government of India in consultation with the U.P. Government ordered the investigations of the demolition cases etc. by the C.B.I.
3. The investigation of cases about attack on media persons was handed over to a special team of investigators of U.P. Police which was to be headed by me. Most of the media persons co-operated with us but they said that since they would be required to cover such situations in future also, they would not like to depose against any body. We talked to foreign media persons also at Delhi but they,too, did not depose against any body. Before we could finalise these cases they were handed over to C.B.I.
4. The anniversary of '*Prakatosav*' fell on 23/24-12-1992 and the persons, who had been traditionally taking out procession, insisted on taking it out again this time. Since the town had hardly come out of the tensions of *Kar Seva*, the district administration initially did not allow them but a few days later they were permitted and the processon was taken out peacefully. Those were the days of tension for all of us.
5. The Government of India by an Act of Parliament acquired 70 acres of land and buildings in and around the disputed place. We prepared its security plan and got it implemented. Divisional Commissioner Faizabad was appointed the receiver of the land and also the make-shift temple.
6. The High Court Allahabad, Lucknow Bench, ordered that *status quo* be maintained at the make-shift temple, *Pooja*

be carried on and Darshan of *'Ram Lala Virajman'* be allowed to public. We had to ensure *Darshan* in an orderly manner and without causing security risk, hence arrangements were made accordingly, initially by putting wooden ballies and planks and subsequently by erecting structure of steel rods and plateform without disturbing the *status-quo* .

7. Few days after the lifting of curfew in Faizabad city, *SAHMAT* (Safdar Hashmi Memorial Trust), an organisation with leftist leanings organized a photo exhibition in Town Hall Fiazabad, where an objectionable painting of F.M. Husain about Sita was exhibited, which was resented to by the Hindus as according to them it hurt their feelings. The administration had tough time in keeping things under control.

8. Several dignitaries of the Government of India used to visit Ayodhya, for official purposes and they were keen to visit the site and make-shift temple, the security and law and order arrangements were ensured by the local administration. On several occasions I had to accompany some of them and my experiences of their visits are still fresh in my mind. Whereas H.E. the Governor Sri B. Satya Narayan Reddy and Sri Madhav Godbole, the Union Home Secretary inspected the entire area but did not enter the make-shift temple as till then *Darshan* had not been allowed, Sri Rajesh Pilot, Union Minister of State for Internal Security who came with Sri Salman Khurshid another Union Minister of State, went inside and also asked Sri Khursid to come in as he had been standing outside in the courtyard. Sri Khursid could not say 'no' to Sri Pilot.

9. Sri Chandraswamy, who was very close to ceratin powers at the Centre, wanted to have *'SomYagya'* on a ground near Hanuman Garhi. Local Administration was not in favour of it as law and order could be disturbed, but since he had support of the top leadership of the ruling party at the Centre, he was allowed to have his function for a few days, but that could neither attract public attention nor could yield any political mileage to the ruling Congress Party.

10. After the demolition of the structure on 6-12-1992 the first traditional major festival of *'Ram Naumi'* fell on 1-4-1993. Heavy police and security arrangements were planned and executed as large number of devotees were expected and the security structure erected was to be tested for the first time. On this day devotees, most of them hailing from neighbouring rural areas of the adjoining districts, turned up for holy dip in river *Saryu* and then for *Darshan* in various temples including Hanumangarhi and the make-shift temple. There was lot of curiosity in people to see the place for the first time after demolition. Till about 1P.M. the crowd was contained in barricades and those in line had 'Darshan' smoothly. Around 1 P.M. huge crowd turned up therefore, we had to put them in zigzag barricades especially provided for such eventualities. This proved very useful and we had to continue with it for about 3 hours. Some of our officers said that around 2 lakh devotees had turned up there for '*Darshan*'. I said that it was not feasible as minimum one second was required for each person to pass in front of the deity and that too from the distance of about 4 metres. This being so, only 60 persons could have '*Darshan*' every minute and 3,600 persons every hour. '*Darshan*' was allowed for about 22 hours and in the remaining two hours the temple was temporarily closed for '*Bhog*' and rest of the 'deity'. So in about 22 hours at the rate of 3,600 persons per hour, not more than 80,000 persons could pass from there. I told my officers that unrealistic assessment and exaggeration of figures is never in the interest of planning arrangements for future. Thereafter, zigzag barricades were never used in the years to come. We had briefed our Force that nobody will leave the place of duty or will go for *'Darshan'* till the duty was over. I had been monitoring the situation from the Control Room at Manas Bhavan as every thing was visible on three sides from there. Lunch packets were distributed to security personnel on duty after 2 P.M. I saw some of the *Jawans* without uniform standing in queue of the normal devotees. On being asked, they said that as per normal Hindu practice of the area they were supposed to have food only after *'Darshan'*, hence after their shift duty was over at 2 P.M. they were waiting for their turn for '*Darshan*'. I felt happy to know that duty came first

for them and also that they chose to stand in queue rather than jump it and have *'Darshan'* out of turn. The festival passed of peacefully and we heaved a sigh of relief. Though, it was the first of April, the 'All Fool's Day', God helped us in managing the things smoothly. Of course God helps those who help themselves.

SCENES OF RAM NAUMI 1993

Ram Ki Pairi – Saryu Ayodhya

Pilgrims for Holy Dip in River Saryu

Devotees in Ayodhya City

Devotees having 'Darshan' at 'Make–Shift Temple'

LIBERHAN COMMISSION

A few days after the demolition of the structure, the Government of India, on 16-12-1992, appointed a one man Commission of Enquiry headed by Mr. Justice Manmohan Singh Liberhan, Hon'ble Judge of the Punjab and Haryana High Court. The terms of reference of this Commission were:–

(a) The sequence of events leading to, and all the facts and circumstances relating to, the occurrences in the Ram Janma Bhoomi-Babri Masjid complex at Ayodhya on the 6th December 1992,

(b) The role played by the Chief Minister, Members of the Council of Ministers, officers of the Govt. of Uttar Pradesh and by the individuals, concerned organisations and agencies in or in connection with, the destruction of the Ram Janma Bhoomi-Babri Masjid structure.

(c) The deficiencies in the security measures and other arrangements as prescribed or operated in practice by the Government of Uttar Pradesh which might have contributed to the events that took place in the Ram Janma Bhoomi-Babri Masjid complex, Ayodhya town and Faizabad on 6th december, 1992.

(d) The sequence of events leading to and all the facts and circumstances relating to the assault on media persons at Ayodhya on 6th December, 1992, and

(e) Any other matter relating to the subject of inquiry.

Twelve years have passed but the Commission's enquiry report is still awaited. In this light it would not be in the fitness of things for me to say any thing about the matters which are within the terms of reference of the Commission.

GUJARAT TORCHED BY AYODHYA FLAMES IN 2002

For about a decade after the demolition of the disputed structure in December, 1992, no major programme of mass mobilisation of Hindu volunteers for Ayodhya was undertaken. The country did not have any major communal riot arising out of the Ayodhya tangle from 1993 to 2001.On October 24,1994 the Supreme Court rejected the single-point presidential reference on whether or not a temple existed before the mosque and also upheld the acquisition of land of 1993.

In February, 2001, the V.H.P. in Kumbh Mela Allahabad, decided to start the construction of the temple from March, 2002. The carved pillars kept somewhere in Ayodhya, were to be moved to the disputed/acquired site for the erection of gateway and the construction was to start from March 12, 2002. In February, 2002, the V.H.P. mobilised volunteers called, *'Ram Sevaks'* for a programme of *"Aahuti"* of *Yagna* to be performed at *Kar Sevak Puram* Ayodhya on different dates by different groups of volunteers coming from various States. As their programmes were chalked out in advance, train reservations in groups for inward and return journeys were also got done. They used to come to Ayodhya, perform the programme and then returned back. They reportedly travelled in groups, in trains chanted religious slogans and at times forced the fellow Muslim passengers to chant *"Jai Sri Ram"*. On 26-2-2002, a group of *'Ram Sevaks'* on way to Ayodhya by Sabarmati Express train, forced local Muslims at Rudauli (between Barabanki and Faizabad) to chant *"Jai Sri Ram"* and on their refusing to do so, they were attacked, resulting in serious injuries to them and the communal tension in Rudauli town, which was the trouble spot in 1992 also.

Train Burnt at Godhra

As per media reports, Sabarmati Express daily and direct train from Faizabad/Ayodhya to Ahmedabad, covering distance of about 1400 Km.s, was running late by about 4 hours before reaching Godhra (District Head quarters of Panchmahal District of Gujarat) on 27-2-2002. Several *'Ram Sevaks'*, men, women and children, travelling in second class reserved coaches, particularly, S-6, S-7 and S-8, had allegedly been teasing fellow Muslim passengers and somebody might have conveyed about it to Muslims at Godhra. It is also said that in the early morning of 27-2-2002, when the train was at the Godhra platform, some *Kar Sevaks* had altercation with the vendors, majority of whom were local Muslims. When the train left the station, the alarm chain was pulled as a result the train stopped within the Godhra railway yard. Unruly crowd, which had collected there, by then, attacked the train upon which the passengers closed the shutters and locked the gates from inside. The coaches caught fire and the hapless passengers, mainly 'Ram Sevaks', particularly of coach number S-6, could do nothing and 57 of them including 25 women and 14 children were burnt alive. Who did it and how it happened is the subject matter of 'Judicial Enquiry Commission'. What a ghastly, gruesome and inhuman act it was?

Reaction in Gujarat and Elsewhere

'Gujarat Bundh' was observed on 28-2-2002 by the V.H.P. which was also supported by the ruling B.J.P. Government. The news of Godhra tragedy spread like a wild fire in Gujarat and the revenge attacks led to serious communal riots, the worst affected places being Ahmedabad, city and rural, Vadodara, Sabarkhantha, on that day.

VHP's call of 'Bharat Bundh' on 1-3-2002, supported by B.J.P. resulted in violence including imposition of curfew at several places (25 cities) of Gujarat. Religious places were also attacked in Punjab, Haryana (Kaithal), U.P. (Aligarh) etc. Unprecedented violence and inhuman acts of barbarism. were reported from all

Gujarat Violence 2002

CENOCIDE

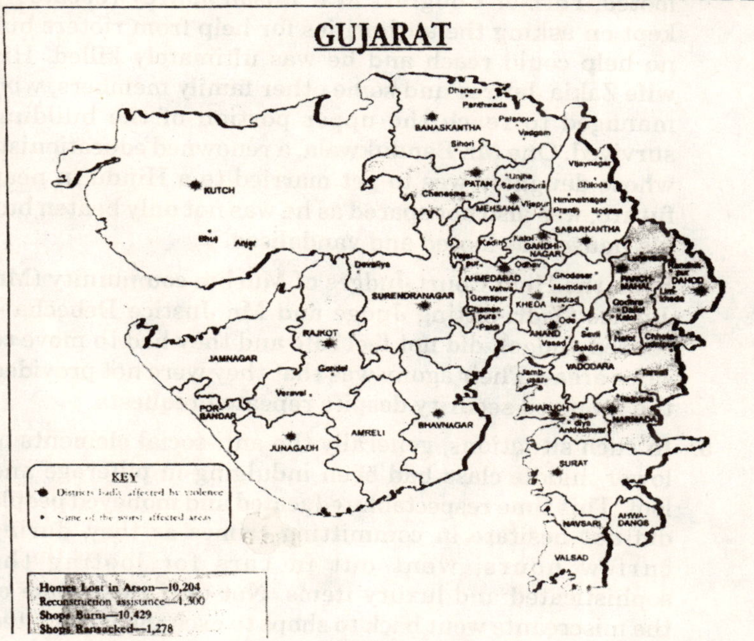

Source : **Communnalism Combat, March-April 2002.**

over Gujarat, particularly Ahmedabad, Junagarh, Banaskantha, Vadodara, Rajkot, Anand and other places. Army was called but its arrival was delayed as troops, deployed in forward areas on Indo-Pak borders, had to be moved from distant places. Police fired at several places in which rioters were killed but the situation remained grim and out of control as rioters indulged in crimes without any fear of law. Matter came up for discussion in Parliament which was in session and serious concern was expressed over the brutalities committed in Gujarat and elsewhere.

Serious riots continued in Gujarat till 6-3-2002 and some notable features of these incidents, as reported in media, are:

1. Arson and killings continued unabated for several days.
2. Muslims were the target of attack everywhere.
3. Even influential and open-minded Muslims, living in Hindu localities were not spared as they were attacked, killed and injured, their houses ransacked and property looted. Former Congress M.P. Ehsan Jaffrey repeatedly kept on asking the authorities for help from rioters but no help could reach and he was ultimately killed. His wife Zakia Jaffrey and some other family members, who managed to reach the upper portion of the building survived. One Mr. Bandukwala, a renowned educationist, whose daughter was to get married to a Hindu in near future, was also not spared as he was not only beaten but his house was looted and vandalised.
4. Even the High Court Judges of Muslim community (Mr. Justice Qadri-sitting Judge and Mr. Justice Debecha – retired Judge), did not feel safe and they had to move to safer areas. Their agony was that they were not provided the required security despite repeated requests.
5. In such situations, generally the anti-social elements of lower middle class had been indulging in pilferage and loot. This time respectable, educated and moneyed people did not hesitate in committing crimes as they, during curfew hours, went out in cars for looting the sophisticated and luxury items. Not only this, some of the miscreants went back to shops to exchange the looted items, particularly shoes, so that they could fit them.

6. In rural areas the weaker sections, majority of whom were scheduled tribes, who hitherto had been very simple and law abiding and friendly with Muslims, were kept on the forefront in committing atrocities and were allowed to take away the looted material also.
7. Girls and women were raped and killed in full view of every body including their relatives.
8. Factories and commercial places, majority of which belonged to Vohra community were also not spared. They were not only looted but were also torched rendering them unfit for future production.
9. Muslim religious places including mosques, *Dargahas* and *mazars*, were specially targeted, razed to ground and destroyed.
10. The convoy of Defence Minister Mr. George Fernandes was also attacked in Ahmedabad on 1-3-2002, which showed the fearlessness of the rioters.
11. There was no fear of law, the authorities, the police and the security forces for several days. It is said that the shops and a *Dargah*, located in main market and right at the boundary wall of the Police Commissioner's office in Ahmedabad, were looted and gutted by using gas cylinders etc. in the broad day light.
12. The role of executive Magistrates, particularly the District Magistrates, was not significantly reported. It appears that some of them did not perform the desired role as required by law, particularly the Criminal Procedure Code.
13. The refugee camps, which had thousands of Muslim victims, had their own problems as accusing fingers were raised at the authorities, who allegedly failed to provide timely relief, food, water, shelter etc. On return to their native places they had to face not only the problems of rehabilitation but also of social and economic boycott of fellow Hindus, with whom they hitherto had been living amicably.
14. Problems were also faced in providing treatment in hospitals because hospitals were not equipped to treat

the larger number of patients, particularly the victims of serious burn and bullet injuries, requiring urgent and specialised treatment.

Certain other Developments of Gujarat and Elsewhere, Requiring Attention are :–

1. While Gujarat riots were continuing, pamphlets were circulated on 6-3-2002 in Ahmedabad telling people not to purchase goods and eat in hotels etc. of a particular community (Muslims).
2. Around 6-3-2002, bookies were arrested in Jaipur (Rajasthan) for betting on the point that whether Rajasthan in general and Jaipur in particular will witness riots, the rates being 1: 6 and 1: 4 . People were asked to make telephone calls to others to spread rumours in order to keep the situation hot. On this very day curfew was relaxed in Kishangarh, Bhilwara and Udaipur cities of Rajasthan.
3. On the persuasion of Prime Minister Sri Atal Bihari Vajpayee, and the initiative of Swami Jayendra Saraswati Shankaracharya of the Kanchi Kamakoti Peetham, talks were held at Delhi from 4-3-2002 to resolve the Ayodhya issue by religious leaders of the two faiths. The representatives of the V.H.P., All India Muslim Personal Law Board, the All India Imams Organisation and other religious groups, though met to resolve this vexed problem the solution remained a distant dream. Shankaracharya said "The time has come for all religions to unite. Let religion become more important than politics. Only then will politicians see the light."
4. Visits of various political figures on different dates were of no help in restoration of peace. Accusations and counter accusations of not condemning Godhra episode and subsequent violence elsewhere in Gujarat did not help in restoration of peace. Political parties did not come out with any joint appeal for restoration of peace.
5. Heated discussions made in Parliament also failed to pacify the rioters and the communal frenzy continued unabated.

6. President Mr. K.R. Narayanan remained highly concerned about the sad events and also the activities of certain outfits/organisations but his concern also went in vain in restoration of very early peace in Gujarat.

CONCERN OF NATIONAL HUMAN RIGHTS COMMISSION

A team of National Human Rights Commission (N.H.R.C.) comprising Justice J.S. Verma, Chairman, Justice Sujata V. Manohar and Sri Virendra Dayal both members, visited Gujarat from March 19 to 22, 2002. The excerpts of their report, given below, should be of concern to those, responsible for such situations and the authorities concerned, who could not protect the innocent citizens of the inhuman acts of violence and failed to maintain the law and order.

1. The Commission would like to observe at this stage that it is the primary and inescapable responsibility of the State to protect the right to life, liberty, equality and dignity of all those who constitute it. It is also the responsibility of the State to ensure that such rights are not violated either through overt acts, or through abetment or negligence. It is a clear and emerging principle of human rights jurisprudence that the State is responsible not only for the acts of its own agents, but also for the acts of non-State players acting within its jurisdiction. The State is, in addition, responsible for any inaction that may cause or facilitate the violation of human rights.
2. The first question that arises, therefore, is whether the State has discharged its responsibilities appropriately in accordance with the above. It has been stated in the report of the state government that the attack on *Kar Sevaks* in Godhra occurred in the absence of "specific information about the return of *Kar Sevaks* from Ayodhya. It is also asserted that while there were intelligence inputs pertaining to the movements of *Kar Sevaks* to Ayodhya between 10-15 March; 2002, there were no such inputs concerning their return either from the state intelligence branch or the central intelligence agencies; and that the "only message" about the return of *kar sevaks*, provided

by the Uttar Pradesh police, was received in Gujarat on 28 February, i.e., after the tragic incident of 27 February and even that did not relate a possible attack on the Sabarmati Express.

3. The Commission is deeply concerned to be informed of this. It would appear to constitute an extraordinary lack of appreciation of the potential dangers of the situation, both by the central and intelligence agencies. This is the more so given the history of communal violence in Gujarat. The report of state government itself states:

   'The state of Gujarat has a long history of communal riots. Major riots have been occurring periodically in the state since 1969. Two Commissions of Inquiry viz., the Jagmohan Reddy Commission of Inquiry, 1969, and the Dave Commission of Inquiry, 1985, were constituted to go into the wide spread communal violence that erupted in the state from time to time. Subsequently, major communal incidents all over the state have taken place in 1990 and in 1992-93 following the Babri Masjid episode. In fact, between 1970 and 1992, Gujarat has witnessed 443 major communal incidents. Even minor altercations, over trivial matters like kite flying have led to communal violence.'

   The report adds that the Godhra incident occurred at a time when the environment was already surcharged due to developments in Ayodhya and related events.

   Indeed it has been reported to the Commission that, in intelligence parlance, several places of the state have been classified sensitive or hyper-sensitive and that, in many cities of the state, including Ahmedabad, Vadodara and Godhra, members of both the majority and the minority communities are constantly in a state of preparedness to face the perceived danger of communal violence. In such circumstances, the police are reported to be normally well prepared to handle such dangers and it is reported to be standard practice to alert police stations down the line when situations are likely to develop.

4. Given the above the Commission is constrained to observe that a serious failure of intelligence and action by the

state government marked the events leading to the Godhra tragedy and the subsequent deaths and destruction that occurred. On the face of it, in the light of the history of communal violence in Gujarat, recalled in the report of the state government itself, the question must arise whether the principle of *'res ipsa loquitur'* (the affair speaking for itself) should not apply in this case in assessing the degree of state responsibility in the failure to protect the life, liberty, equality and dignity of the people of Gujarat.

The Commission accordingly requests the response of the Central and State Governments on this matter, it being the primary and inescapable responsibility of the State to protect such rights and to be responsible for the acts not only of its own agents, but also for the acts of non-state players within its jurisdiction and any inaction that may cause or facilitate the violation of human rights. Unless rebutted by the State Government, the adverse inference arising against it would render it accountable. The burden is therefore on the State Government to rebut this presumption.

5. An ancillary question that arises is whether there was adequate anticipation in regard to the measures to be taken, and whether these measures were indeed taken, to ensure that the tragic events in Godhra would not occur and would not lead to serious repercussions elsewhere. The Commission has noted that many instances are recorded in the report of prompt and courageous action by District Collectors, Commissioners and Superintendents of Police and other officers to control the violence and to deal with its consequences through appropriate preventive measures and, thereafter, through rescue, relief and rehabilitation measures.

   The Commission cannot but note, however, that the report itself reveals that while some communally-prone districts succeeded in controlling the violence, other districts – sometimes less prone to such violence – succmbed to it. In the same vein, the report further indicates that while the factors underlining the danger of communal violence spreading were common to all districts, and that, "in the wake of the call for the 'Godhra Bandh' and the possible fall-out of the Godhra incident, the State Government took all possible precautions", some districts withstood the dangers far more firmly than did others.

Such a development clearly points to local factors and players overwhelming the district officers in certain instances, but not in others. Given the widespread reports and allegations of groups of well-organized persons, armed with mobile telephones and addresses, singling out certain homes and properties for death and destruction in certain districts - sometimes within view of police stations and personnel- the further question arises as to what the factors were, and who the players were in the situations that went out of control. The Commission requests the comments of the State Government on these matters.

6. In the light of the fact that numerous allegations have been made both in the media and to the team of the Commission to the effect that FIRs in various instances were being distorted or poorly recorded, and that senior political personalities were seeking to 'influence' the working of police stations by their presence within them, the Commission is constrained to observe that there is a widespread lack of faith in the integrity of the investigating process and the ability of those conducting investigations.

   The Commission notes for instance, that in Ahmedabad, in most cases, looting was "reported in well-to-do localities by relatively rich people". Yet the report does not identify who these people were. The conclusion cannot but be drawn that there is need for greater transparency and integrity to investigate the instances of death and destruction appropriately and to instil confidence in the public mind.

7. The report takes the view that "the major incidents of violence were contained within the first 72 hours." It asserts, however that "on account of widespread reporting both in the visual as well the electronic media, incidents

of violence on a large-scale started occurring in Ahmedabad, Baroda cities and some towns of Panchmahals, Sabarkantha, Mehsana, etc." in spite of "all possible precautions having been taken." The report also adds that various comments attributed to the Chief Minister and Commissioner of Police, Ahmedabad, among others, were torn out of context by the media, are entirely without foundation.

8. As indicated earlier in these proceedings, the Commission considers it would be naive for it to subscribe to the view that the situation was brought under control within the first 72 hours. Violence continues in Gujarat as of the time of writing these proceedings. There was a pervasive sense of insecurity prevailing in the state at the time of the team's visit to Gujarat. This was most acute among the victims of the successive tragedies, but it extended to all segments of society, including to two judges pf the High Court of Gujarat, one sitting and the other retired, who were compelled to leave their own homes because of the vitiated atmosphere. There could be no clearer evidence of the failure to control the situation.

9. The Commission has, however, taken note of the views of the State Government in respect of the media. The Commission firmly believes that it is essential to uphold the right to freedom of speech and expression articulated in Article 19(1)(a) of the Constitution, which finds comparable provision in Article 19 of the Universal Declaration of Human Rights, 1948 and Article 19 of the International Covenant of Civil and Political Rights, 1966. It is therefore, clearly in favour of courageous and investigative role for the media. At the same time, the Commission is of the view that there is need for all concerned to reflect further on possible guidelines that the media should adopt, on a 'self policing basis', to govern its conduct in volatile situations, including those of inter-communal violence, with a view to ensuring that passions are not inflamed and further perpetrated. It has to be noted that the right under Article 19(1)(a) is subject to reasonable restrictions under Article 19(2) of the Constitution.

10. The Commission has noted the contents of the report on two matters that raised serious questions of discriminatory treatment and led to most adverse comments both within the country and abroad. The first related to the announcement of Rs Two lac as compensation to the nexrt-of kin of those who perished in the attack on the Sabarmati Express, and of Rs. 1 lac for those who died in the subsequent violence. The second related to the application of POTO to the first incident, but not to those involved in the subsequent violence.

11. On the question of compensation, the Commission has noted from the report that Rs. 1 lac will be paid in all instances, "thus establishing parity." It has also noted that, according to the report, this decision was taken on 9, March, 2002, after a letter was received by the Chief Minister,"on behalf of the *Kar Sevaks,"* saying "that they would welcome the financial help of Rs. 1 lac instead of Rs. 2 lacs to the breaved families of Godhra massacre".

12. This decision, in the view of the Commission should have been taken on the initiative of the government itself, as the issue raised impinged seriouslly on the provisions of the Constitution contained in Articles 14 and 15, dealing respectively with equality before the law and equal protection of the laws within the territory of India and the prohibition of discrimination on grounds of religion, race, caste, sex or place of birth.

13. The Commission has also noted the contents of the report which state the "no guidelines were given by the Home Department regarding the type of cases in which POTO should or should not be used" and that, subsequent to the initial decision to apply POTO in respect of individual cases in Godhra, government received legal advice to defer "the applicability of POTO till investigation is completed". The Commission intends to monitor this matter, POTO having since been enacted as a law.

14. The Commmission has taken good note of the "rescue, relief and rehabilitation measures" undertaken by the State Government. In many instances strenuous efforts have been made by the collectors and other district

officers, often acting on their own initiative. The Commission was informed, however, during the course of its visit, that many of the largest camps, including Shah-e-Alam in Ahmedabad, had not received visits at a high political or administrative level till the visit of the chairperson of this Commission. This was viewed by the inmates as being indicative of a deeper malaise that was discriminatory in origin and character. Unfortunately, too, numerous complaints were received by the team of the Commission regarding lack of facilities in camps.

15. The Commission has noted the range of activities and measures taken by the State Government to persue the relief and rehabilitation of those who have suffered. It appreciates the positive steps that have been taken and commends those officials and NGOs that have worked to ameliorate the sufferings of the victims. The Commission, however, considers it essential to monitor the on-going implementation of the decisions taken since a great deal still needs to be done. The Commission has already indicated to the chief minister that a follow-up mission will be made on behalf of the Commission at an appropriate time and it appreciates the response of the chief minister that such a visit will be welcome and that every effort will be made to restore complete normalcy expeditiously.

SHILA DAAN PROGRAMME AT AYODHYA

Shila Daan (offering of carved stone) programme was performed on 15-3-2002 at Digamber Akhada, Ayodhya. Sri Shatrughan Singh, Joint Secretary, Ayodhya Cell, Cabinet Secretariat, Government of India was specially flown to Ayodhya from Delhi to receive the *Shila*. Sri Praveen Togadia International General Secretary of V.H.P. expressed satisfaction mentioning that "After the opening of the temple locks in February, 1985, and the *Shila Nyas* ceremony later, this is the first time the Central Government has accepted in principle that the Ram temple will be constructed at the disputed site only and not on the acquired land. Post March 15, they are a satisfied lot, as the acceptance of the Shila by a Central Government representative means a firm commitment by the government to build the temple." Singh's role came under heavy criticism from the opposition parties saying that the bureaucrats have no role in religious matters. *'The Times of India'* reported on March 17, 2002 that "when it comes to hogging the limelight, politicians are forever ready, but for something as controversial as *Shila puja* or *shila daan* it is Attorney Generals and bureaucrats who are called upon to be the sacrificial lamb." Prime Minister Sri Atal Bihari Vajpayee while speaking on 16-3-2002 in Lok Sabha said that Ayodhya issue has to be settled and should not be allowed to develop into a festering wound. Besides creating problems in maintaining communal harmony, it also becomes an election issue though it yields no gains. It was imperative to resolve it either by expediting the court cases or through a negotiated settlement since this matter has become an impediment in maintaining communal harmony.

Orissa Assembly Stormed

On 16-3-2002, the V.H.P. and Bajrang Dal workers were observing a *Dharna* outside the Orissa Assembly in Bhubaneswar protesting the remarks made against V.H.P./Bajrang Dal workers by some of the members of the Legislative Assembly in the House. They ran amuck and stormed the Assembly building, broke the window panes and flower pots etc., ransacked the rooms and corridors including offices of the few ministers. These protesters were wearing saffron bands on their heads and many of them carried *trishuls*. This incident amounted to attack on freedom of speech, more so in the Legislative Assembly. Several newspapers of 18-3-2002 came out with editorials condemning this incident. Prime Minister Sri Atal Bihari Bajpai, while speaking in Parliament on 18-3-2002, said that these people were also shouting slogans of *Atal Bihari Zindabad* and he would prefer to die rather being wished a long life by such hooligans. Demands of banning these outfits were also made by the opposition.

Riots on March 15, 16 & 17, 2002

Following the *Shila Daan* in Ayodhya on 15-3-2002, fierce riots broke out in Ahmedabad, Bharuch, Godhra and other places in Gujarat. In Haryana particularly at Kaithal and Lohari town of Bhiwani shops, houses and establishments of a particular community were the target of arson, loot and attack. Police was also attacked and 2 youths were reportedly injured in police firing. The affected persons had to take shelter in police stations.

Terrorists Attack Akshardham Temple Ahmedabad

On Tuesday, September 24, evening few terrorists stormed the Swaminarain Akshardham temple at Ahmedabad, exploded grenades and fired indiscriminately by sophisticated weapons on devotees, who had collected for prayers. Several innocent persons including men, women, children and infants were killed (about 40) and injured (about 100). Locally available police, para-military forces and Commandoes were pressed into service, who took command of the situation and carried on rescue operations with the help of the local people and temple authorities. Chief Minister Sri Narendra Modi immediately swung into action; held meetings of his cabinet colleagues and officers; appealed to people to maintain peace and not to fall prey to evil designs of the enemy to destabilise Gujarat and the nation. Deputy Prime Minister and Home Minister Sri L.K. Advani ensured necessary arrangements including airlifting of the National Security Guards (NSG) commandoes within a few hours of the incident and subsequently himself left for Ahmedabad that very evening to see that nothing went wrong. Prime Minister Sri Atal Bihari Vajpayee, who was on tour to Maldives, immediately got in touch with New Delhi ; issued necessary instructions and next day cutting short his visit returned to India and straightway went to Ahmedabad to see the things for himself. On the night of September 24/25, the Commando and rescue operations continued and the drama ended on early morning of 25th when two heavily armed terrorists were killed and the temple was freed. Few NSG commandoes and police personnel made supreme sacrifice by laying down their lives in the altar of duty. All political parties and cross sections of people including minorities made repeated appeals for peace in Ahmedabad and Gujarat. Few panic stricken Muslims of Ahmedabad again left their houses and shifted to the refugee camps.

The *'Gujarat Bandh'* call of Congress party on 25-9-2002, given within hours of the terrorists attack in temple remained peaceful. *'Bharat Bandh'* call of V.H.P. (Vishwa Hindu Parishad) and Shiv Sena evoked mixed response as a few incidents of violence took place in Maharashtra, Gujarat, Himachal Pradesh, Bihar, Karnataka, and other States but was free from communal backlash.

The Deputy Prime Minister and Home Minister Sri L.K. Advani, while addressing Non Resident Indians (N.R.Is.) at New Delhi on 10-1-2003 said that Gujarat violence was "an aberration" of which "we are all sad and ashamed" and that India will never be a theocratic state as "theocracy and theocratic state are unacceptable to the Indian tradition, culture and history."

Times of India in its edition dated 21-1-2003 reported that Acharya Giriraj Kishore, senior vice-president of V.H.P. announced on 20-1-2003 at Lucknow that it was making "foolproof" plan to begin the construction of Ram temple once seers announce the date during the *Dharma Sansad,* beginning in New Delhi from February 21. "We have been betrayed once, now we will not go by Prime Minister's false promises." He also said that the outfit would not wait for the court decision once the date for construction is announced. About Gujarat election he said that it was contest between Hindutva and so called secularist forces.

Dharma Sansad at Delhi–February 2003

Dharma Sansad held at Delhi from February 22 to 24 resolved that the V.H.P. would mobilise support from March 5 to 24 for a Ram temple at the very site; gave a call for "Dilli Chalo" and a selected group will arrive in the capital to mount pressure on "Parliament and the government". It was said that "at no stage will we announce a date – but the mobilisation will be such that one day the construction will suddenly begin"

LESSONS FOR MANAGEMENT OF SUCH SITUATIONS

Situations that arose and the problems faced during 1990 and 1992 *Kar Seva* calls, left many lessons for the administration, police and the Security Forces. I have tried to enlist some of them here, as I had been associated with them in one way or the other. Perhaps these tips may be of some help and interest in making arrangements for similar situations in future, not only in Ayodhya but elsewhere too.

(1) Role in Ayodhya/ Faizabad

1. Various calls of Muslim organisations, like 'Ayodhya March' and 'Friday Namaz' etc. be carefully attended to. V.H.P. had been planning various programmes for

Ayodhya during annual fairs and festivals, like *Parikrama* (*Panch Kosi* - (16 Kilometres) and *Chaudah Kosi* -(42 Kilometres) falling in October/November each year, when lakhs of devotees take holy dip in river *Saryu* and march on foot to do *Parikrama* on the traditional routes. These pilgrims, who turn up in large numbers for the occasion, could be used as a ready made Hindu crowd. Anniversary days of important events are also chosen at times to make emotive issues. Advance assessment of the crowd including those coming on calls be done and arrangements be planned and executed in professional manner, which should not be guided by any extraneous consideration except the requirements of the likely law and order problems. Necessary civic arrangements for the people and the security personnel be made separately. All departments of the administration be involved in the management of various anticipated problems arising out of collection of pilgrims/*Kar Sevaks* or any other crowd. Action to ward off terrorist action including suicide squads, be also planned meticulously. Sufficient supply of essential commodities like cooking gas, kerosene oil, fire wood, ration and vegetables etc., which become in great demand, be ensured by the authorities concerned by procuring them in advance as the last minute arrangements may not help. Water supply, sanitation, toilets and other essential needs, should be suitably taken care of.

2. Though disputed structure has been demolished and a make-shift temple has come up, it needs constant vigil as its security, may be jeopardised due to mob attack, sabotage, missile attack or any other way including terrorist actions, which may again send the country to flames.

3. Management of law and order, particularly the security of minorities in Ayodhya and the possibility of outbreak of communal violence in Faizabad should be taken care of every time, particularly when calls are given for outsiders to come to Ayodhya for *Kar Seva* etc. Special care be taken of the vacant houses, shops etc. due to migration of Muslim population. Security of Muslim litigants in Ayodhya dispute be taken care of adequately.

4. Security of Muslims at railway and bus stations at Ayodhya, Faizabad and other places be ensured. Security of Hindus be never forgotten, as episodes, similar to Godhra may take place anywhere.
5. Traffic control including traffic diversions be planned and implemented not only in Ayodhya and Faizabad but also at other feeding points of adjoining Districts of Gonda, Basti, Barabanki, Ambedkarnagar and Sultanpur.
6. Programmes and counter programmes, both for and against, of V.H.P. or BMAC or any other body or individual/s, be carefully attended to so that nothing untoward happens which may aggravate the situation.
7. Taking lessons from 6-12-1992, smooth movement of Security Forces has to be ensured and the things including route, guides and opening of blocked roads be taken care of.
8. Police and magisterial records be updated, maintained regularly and properly so that they are readily available for planning arrangements and also for enquiries, Judicial or otherwise.
9. Security of media persons be adequately attended to so that the attacks like those of 6-12-1992 are not repeated. Advance liaison with them may be of some help.
10. Any other timely action be ensured, which may be warranted by the situation arising at any given point of time.
11. Intelligence and local authorities including police and executive magistrates should draw lessons from the past happenings, collect intelligence and pass it timely to all concerned, assess the situation and take remedial measures in professional manner without fear or favour.

(2) Role Elsewhere

1. During Tension Building

Police including Intelligence machinery must remain extra vigilant on occasions, which are likely to generate tension. Here are some examples of the past few years which caught attention of the people and created serious law and order problems.

1. Tension was gradually generated due to various programmes of competitive communalism arising out of calls and counter calls of Bundhs etc. *Kavi Sammelan* (*Ek Sham - Ram Janam Bhoomi ke Naam*) and Mushiara (*Ek Sham - Babri Masjid ke Naam*) held at Aligarh are the examples of such competitiveness .

2. Following V.H.P. programmes in the past had whipped up communal passions:

   (1) Simultaneous programmes everywhere from house tops at appointed time like beating of *thalis, ghantas, gadiyals*, *shankhs* (counch shells), burning of *mashals* etc.

   (2) Taking out of *'Prabhat Pheris'* where various kinds of slogans including provocative ones were raised exhorting Hindus to unite.

   (3) *Rath Yatras*, marches, *dharnas,* demonstrations, processions and rallies including collective driving on two wheelers to demonstrate unity, solidarity and strength.

   (4) Mass congregations and singing of devotional songs at religious places.

   (5) Mass participation of women and children in various programmes.

   (6) Pasting pamphlets, stickers and writing of provocative slogans/gestures on walls etc. at strategic places, both for and against respective communities.

   (7) Mass display of banners, buntings and flags, Hindus using saffron colour while Muslims using green or black colour.

   (8) Wearing special clothes/dresses/apparels on occasions to display strength and commitment for the cause of the respective community.

   (9) Threats, challenges and provocative public statements of various leaders.

   (10) Programmes of various leaders including politicians and their provocative and suggestive utterances, for and against.

(11) Programmes like *'Ram Shila Poojan'*, *'Charan Paduka Poojan'* and taking out of *'Ashthi Kalash'*.

(12) Speeches and activities from religious places on the occasions of mass congregations like 'Friday *Namaz*' or *'Maha Aarti'*.

(13) Beating of war drums like threat of 'Maha Bharat' for 18 days in Ayodhya from 6-12-1992.

(14) Immediately counteracting of rumours and unearthing the provocative material is of vital importance. Examples of Kanpur and Agra as mentioned in earlier pages could be eye openers.

(15) Security of shrines, not only at Varanasi (Kashi Vishwanath Mandir/Gyanvapi Masjid), Mathura (Sri Krishna Janam Bhumi Mandir/Shahi Masjid), but also elsewhere, should receive utmost attention, as the V.H.P. has been saying that either Muslims should voluntarily give three shrines at Ayodhya, Varanasi and Mathura to Hindus, otherwise they will forcibly occupy 3,000 such shrines/places. Taking lessons from Ayodhya adequate precautions be taken to meet any eventuality from the crowds.

(3) Role Relating to Kar Sevaks

Whenever a call is given for the movement of volunteers of any community or of *Kar Sevaks* to Ayodhya or any other place involving religious sentiments particularly at disputed shrines, following tips based on past experience may be useful while making security and law and order arrangements:

1. Proper and timely assessment of situation, based on open and secret intelligence received from various sources/ channels, be done regularly and suitable advance arrangements be planned and executed, wherever needed.
2. Places of collection and dispersal of such people be attended to properly and regularly, to avoid any untoward incident by and against them.
3. Means of transport, particularly long distance trains and buses for short destinations be taken care of. Problems faced in the past, like manhandling of Muslim passengers, particularly bearded men and women in *burquas* and

forcing them to chant "*Jai Sri Ram*", throwing some of them from running trains (example of 1990 near Jaunpur), mobbing and manhandling of opposition VIPs in trains and at plateforms (example of Lucknow railway station), manhandling and chasing Muslims at railway stations and nearby areas (examples of Rudauli and Barabanki–1992), clashes with rival political groups in trains and plateforms (example of Kanpur Anwarganj Station – 1990) should be taken care of. The lessons of Godhra be never forgotten.

4. Special care be taken of Muslim as well as mixed localities near bus and railway stations, bathing ghats, halts and crossings etc., as problems could arise against or by any group.
5. Problems of confrontation at inter-state boundaries, particularly at B.J.P. and non-B.J.P. ruled States be attended to carefully. Taking lessons from 1990 U.P.-M.P. conflicts at Chitrakoot and Chambal bridge on Etawah-Bhind road, such situations be anticipated and suitable remedial measures taken.
6. Unimaginable problems of logistics including arrests, preparation of arrest warrants, security, transportation, temporary jails, accommodation and food etc. arise during mass arrests as happened in 1990. Adequate advance arrangements be planned and executed as per need.
7. Training of *Kar Sevaks* and volunteers of rival communities, particularly by retired police and defence personnel and their subsequent confrontation with agencies/forces handling law and order should be adequately covered and timely action taken.

(4) Fall Out of the Happenings in Ayodhya

Because of the then prevailing tensions every where in the country and incidents caused by the *Kar Sevaks* in Ayodhya in 1990 and 1992, immediate reaction was witnessed not only in India but also abroad. Certain lessons could be enumerated as:

1. Simultaneous outbreak of serious communal riots at too many places need very heavy deployment of security forces including Para Military forces of the States and the Centre and the Army.

2. Following the demolition of the disputed structure in 1992, mobs attacked and destroyed the religious places not only in India but also in Pakistan, Bangladesh, Dubai, U.A.E., U.K. (London) etc. Such places need to be secured.
3. Security of Embassies and foreign offices and establishments be taken care of, as they could become the target of mob reaction as had happened in Dacca (Bangladesh) where Indian High Commission was attacked in 1992.

(5) Role Related to Political Fallouts

As mentioned earlier, politics plays very important role in such matters. Political parties, their wings and outfits, having different ideologies and at times with conflicting agenda, cause problems for the administrative and police officers. Today one Party may be in power, whose orders are to be obeyed but, due to imposition of President's Rule or due to any other reason, another political party/parties with different ideology and agenda, may suddenly take over the reigns of governance, giving orders which so far had been totally different from those of the previous regime. Such situations were faced in 1990 when Samajwadi Party was in power and immediately thereafter, in 1991 when B.J.P. gained power in U.P. and again in 1992 when same B.J.P. Government remained in power till evening of December 6, and thereafter President's Rule was imposed. Arrests, detentions etc. of the political leaders of different parties create problems, which must be tackled professionally keeping in view the law of the land, their security cover, protocol etc. as today's detenue may be tomorrow's ruler. No disrespect, harshness etc. be shown to them but at the same time, there should be no compromise with the required duties and responsibilities. Sudden dismissal of State Government/s and banning of outfits/organisations cause serious law and order problems but they should be anticipated and suitable legal action taken so that peace is not disturbed and law and order is maintained.

(6) Management of Police and Security Forces

For such occasions and situations, police and security forces be not only trained in advance but their training, discipline, morale and welfare be taken care of by the senior supervisory levels during deployment. Following few tips could be of some use:

1. Forces must be committed to their duties as is required by law and the Indian Constitution and they should perform them faithfully.
2. Professionalism is needed at every level. Forces be trained regularly and equipped properly so that they are always fit to perform.
3. Proper and adequate planning be done to meet various situations – seen and unseen, including those erupting suddenly.
4. Proper care be taken to ward off the attempts by the interested sections in creating psychological impact on Forces. Such examples could be (1) exhortations by the Hindu leaders that Forces will not fire on *Kar Sevaks* as they are also Hindus, (2) some police men putting on '*Tilak*' on fore heads while in uniform, (3) slogans for and against the Forces, (4) complimenting police Forces for showing restraint while shrine was being demolished on 6-12-1992 (as was reported in a section of the press that Sri S.C. Dikshit, former D.G.P., U.P. and the then Vice- President of V.H.P. had done so), (5) special treatment of or contempt towards Forces deployed on duty during communal riots- examples of Hindus providing cots, tea, food, firewood etc. during winters, in their localities and Muslims showing hate and contempt by attacks on and firing at the Magistrates and police forces- In Kanpur, slogans against U.P. Police and P.A.C. were found written on walls in Muslim areas whereas, in Hindu localities they were shown favourable reaction. At places Muslims welcomed the deployment of Army and C.P.M.F. and adversely reacted against the deployment of local police and State Forces.
5. There could be a possibility of confrontation between the State and the Central Forces as such situation had developed in December, 1992 when movement of C.P.M.F. for Ayodhya was resented to by the U.P., B.J.P. Government. Such situations should be avoided by the Governments and the Senior Officers as it could lead to unfortunate results, which may not be in the national interest.

6. Muslims' ire was visible at several places against Police and Para Military Forces for their alleged failure to protect the Babri Masjid. Muslims attacked police parties, police stations and outposts in Bombay and elsewhere too. Care be taken to avoid such situations and to ensure self defence.
7. The oaths of office, administered to ministers at the time of swearing in for upholding the constitutional obligations, doing justice to all without fear or favour, are easily forgotten and narrow interests, of grabbing power even at the cost of blood shed and violence, weigh heavier.
8. I.A.S., I.P.S. officers and other government servants sign statements of allegiance towards Indian Constitution. They should always remember the duties that they owe to the people and the nation. They must rise to the call of duty and should not fail so that they prove that they are still the steel frame Services of the Country, and give no chance to the future generations to assess them otherwise.
9. We should take lessons from the past happenings and prepare for the worst. Professionalism, impartiality and devotion to duty could perhaps help every body and ultimately the Nation.

India is faced with complex problems of internal and external threats. We need to devote ourselves for maintaing everlasting peace and refrain from doing any act which may jeopardise our existance as a nation.

Acknowledgements and References:

1. Gazetteers.
2. Newspapers and Magazines, concerned.
3. White Paper on Ayodhya (Government of India) February 1993.
4. B.J.P.'s White Paper on Ayodhya & The Rama Temple Movement (April, 1993).
5. Magazine 'Communalism Combat' (March-April, 2002)– GENOCIDE Gujarat 2002.
6. Sri Man Mohan Sharma, Photo Journalist, Lucknow.

11

Agra Caste Riots – 1990

Agra which is about 200 kilometers from Delhi had been the seat of power of Mughal Emperors for several centuries and still has an imminent place in Indian history. Fatehpur Sikri was the capital of the country during regime of emperor Akbar, which was later on shifted to Agra. Historical monuments of Taj Mahal, Itmad-ud-Daula, Agra Fort, Sikandara etc. are in Agra city and they attract national and international tourists in very large numbers. Radha Swami Temple is another place which, besides being magnificent, attracts not only tourists but also devotees of Radha Swami faith. With the increasing number of tourists, several posh hotels and other establishments have also come up which immensely contribute to the national economy.

Agra district borders with Mathura and Bharatpur in west, Dholpur of Rajasthan and Morena of Madhya Pradesh in south, Firozabad and Etawah in east and Etah, Aligarh (now Hathras) in north. Ravines of rivers Chambal and Yamuna which extend to Dholpur, Morena, Etawah, Firozabad and Agra had been breeding outlaws and very fertile ground for harbouring notorious gangs of dacoits and kidnappers for ransom. The population of Agra city in 1990 was about ten lacs and Jatavs (*Chamars*–scheduled caste) formed the single largest block (about 35%) of the population, perhaps the only city in India where one single caste has so much dominance. Their main localities are Jagdishpura, Shahganj, Rikabganj and Chakkipat. Jatavs are mainly engaged in leather industry of shoe making and earn lot of foreign exchange by exporting leather goods. Many of them, who are very rich and locally called as 'Seths', own hotels, cinema houses and several other industrial establishments. They are socially, politically and economically very strong and always strongly compete with other sections of the city population. In rural areas too they have a large population but Jats, who are major landholders and progressive farmers, exploit them socially and economically as they are poor landless workers and depend on them for their needs and livelihood. Muslims too have sizeable population in Agra city and they are often accused of spreading communal frenzy, though others too never lag behind. Every year a grand procession on 'Ambedkar Jayanti' (April 14–birth day of Dr. Bhim Rao Ambedkar) is taken out in which weaker sections of society from city and rural areas participate in lakhs. Well decorated *'jhankis'* are taken out through several localities which parade during night also and last for several hours often posing serious law and order problems. There had been serious riots on this occasion in the past necessitating imposition of curfew. Very elaborate administrative and police arrangements are made to ensure peace on this occasion. This occasion has been major contributing factor for their uprising and unity.

After taking over as Inspector General of Police of Kanpur Zone in May, 1990, I went out on 'familiarisation visit' to districts of my Zone. After spending a few days at Agra when I was going to leave for Aligarh, Sri Karamvir Singh, S.S.P. Agra, whispered in my ears, telling that situation in village Panwari was taking serious turn, hence it would be better if I stayed behind at Agra. I called off my proposed visit to Aligarh and decided to camp there only. After briefing me S.S.P. and D.M. (Sri Amal Kumar Varma) immediately left for that village. Sri Suresh Pal Singh, D.I.G. and Sri N.R. Banerji, Divisional Commissioner stayed behind to arrange for extra resources. I too realised the gravity of the situation and arranged for additional resources in addition to what was being done at local level.

Village Panwari is located in west of Agra city near railway station 'Roonakata' – birth place of famous Hindi poet 'Surdas', who enjoys prominent place in Hindi literature because of his popular verses about childhood of Lord Krishna. While going from Agra to this village one has to drive on Delhi-Agra national highway and then take left turn near Roonakata to drive further for about five kilometers. This belt borders Mathura and Bharatpur districts, which have sizable Jat population who consider themselves a superior caste and treat others with contempt, more so the scheduled castes. They could neither think nor tolerate of a lower caste person celebrating social functions, mainly marriages with gaiety. In several villages of Agra, Mathura and Aligarh, they had opposed the taking out of *Barats* (marriage parties) with bands, horses or elephants as they thought that such traditions belonged to them only and if they allow it to the lower castes, their social status will be at stake and lower castes will raise their heads against them. There were some serious incidents in the past, when marriage parties were not only attacked but near relations of the bridegroom were killed and houses of the bride's side burnt. I recollect one such incident of district Aligarh, where I was Probationary Assistant Superintendent of Police in 1965. A marriage party of Jatavs was to be taken out in a village a few a kilometers away from the city, in which bridegroom was to ride the elephant, band was to play music and fireworks to be displayed. Yadavs, another backward caste, did not tolerate this and asked the Jatavs to refrain from such a pomp and show. They approached the district authorities for help, which was provided and senior officers also remained present. When the marriage procession started it was attacked by heavily armed Yadavs, killing about five Jatavs on the spot. After about 25 years of Aligarh incident and 40 years of India becoming a Republic, guaranteeing fundamental rights of equality to all its citizens including abolition of untouchability, similar incidents had happened in districts Mathura and Agra particularly in Fatehpur Sikri and Achhnera, where Jats had opposed such shows by Jatavs. The incident of village Panwari also is to be taken in this background.

A girl (daughter of Chob Singh Jatav) of village Panwari was to be married to a boy Ramvir of *Mohalla* Padma falling under police station Sadar Bazar of Agra city on June 21, 1990. The *barat* (marriage party) was to be taken out with P.A.C. band, (symbol of high status), lights and other pomp and show, which was not acceptable to Jats. The *barat* was to assemble near approach road of the village and then the procession was to go from north side of this village through the Jat locality to south of it where the houses of Jatavs including that of the bride were located. Jats, opposed this move by holding community panchayat and decided that Jatavs will not be allowed to take out their marriage party through their locality and any kind of pomp and show including playing of music by band, fire works etc. were not to be displayed even in Jatav locality. A joint meeting of the two castes could not reach any compromise. When the message of such reaction reached Jagdishpura; Jatavs from bridegroom's side approached the district authorities for help, who assured them of necessary assistance.

A few days before the actual day of marriage, the message that Jatavs had approached the district administration, reached Panwari and Jats not only of that village but also of the entire belt reacted sharply and called a community panchayat. Thousands of Jats from rural areas of districts Agra, Mathura and Bharatpur held a panchayat in Achhnera and decided not to allow the Jatav *Barat* to be solemnised with fanfare, come what may. Jatavs again approached the district authorities to apprise them of the developments and seek suitable assistance, of which they were assured. Having come to know of the developments, Jats again met and finally decided to stick to their guns and if need be to face the district authorities violently. The authorities made necessary arrangements and also stationed police and para-military contingents along with senior officers and Magistrates. This did not deter the Jats and they also made their arrangements to face the police/para-military forces by collecting thousands of caste men, many of whom were to carry lethal weapons including fire arms. The message that Jatavs had sought help of the district authorities, spread like wild fire in the area and Jats as per their community's panchayat decision prepared themselves to face the onslaught. Situation became very tense as Jatavs of Agra City, supported by the Congress and the Bahujan Samaj Party, also got united and decided to take out a rally on marriage day from Jagdishpura to Panwari to press for the enforcement of their constitutional rights. Apprehending breach of peace, the district authorities did not permit the rally. Despite the ban, a Jatav crowd of about four thousand persons, including the bridegroom and *baratis*, collected at Hira Lal Ki Piayu on Mathura Road and pressed for going to Panwari. This crowd was stopped and the *barat* with few influential leaders of the community went to Panwari.

On 21-6-1990, the appointed day of marriage Sri Amal Kumar Varma District Magistrate and Sri Karamvir Singh Senior Superintendent of Police reached Panwari to ensure smooth passage of marriage party on the only route via Jat locality. The *barat* assembled on the outskirts of Panwari and was to proceed under police protection but as soon as the band started playing tunes, Jats who were present in thousands in the houses falling on the route to Jatav locality, started shouting and opposing the Jatav *barat* being taken out with fanfare. Authorities tried to persuade them to see reason and not to disturb the marriage procession on the public thoroughfare but they remained adamant on their decision of not allowing the *barat* to pass through their locality. The authorities asked Jatavs to proceed with their *barat*, but when they had hardly marched a few paces when heavily armed Jats in large numbers accosted them and did not allow to proceed. Police used force and could any how reach the barat to its destination. Jats did not give up and attacked the Jatav locality, set houses on fire, looted their property and also killed and injured several of them. It was a game of might by outnumbering the administrative authorities. Curfew was immediately imposed in Panwari and the ritual of marriage ceremony was any how got completed next morning of 22-6-1990 and then the newly weds were taken to Agra in a police jeep under adequate protection.

The Divisional Commissioner Sri N.R. Banerjee fondly known as Neelu Banerjee, Sri Suresh Pal Singh, Range D.I.G. and I kept on monitoring the situation from Divisional Control Room set up at the camp office-cum-residence of the D.I.G.. On getting information about these serious developments in Panwari, we alerted the Agra city authorities to conserve their maximum resources and remain alert to meet the likely fall out. Other districts of Agra Division having sizable Jat population were also advised to be vigilant.

Some of the *baratis* returned to Agra same night (21/22-6-1990) and narrated horrible experiences of Panwari, causing resentment in Jatav community. Next day remaining *baratis* with bridegroom and bride reached Agra and they too carried horrible tales of atrocities committed by Jats against Jatavs. Local Hindi newspapers too published detailed version with photographs, which further infuriated the Jatavs. Though the city authorities were alert, Jatavs started attacking Jats coming to city for daily business for sale of milk and other agricultural produce. Tension was also generated in neighbouring villages. To check further escalation of such happenings, curfew was clamped on 23-6-1990 in localities of 7 city police stations, mainly those having sizable Jatav population and mixed localities of Jats and Jatavs. Tension kept on mounting in several villages as exaggerated versions of incidents including baseless rumours of molestation and rape of Jat females at the hands of Jatavs in Agra city were spread. As a reaction of this Jatavs were attacked by Jats in several villages, particularly Beri Ka Nagla, Akola etc. where Jatav houses were ransacked and burnt, males attacked causing deaths and injuries and modesty of females outraged. In Agra city Jats too had sleepless nights particularly in Jatav dominated localities. In all these incidents 9 persons were killed and hundreds injured including police personnel. About one thousand persons were arrested. The curfew continued from 23-6-1990 to 3-7-1990 (11 days) and was finally lifted when situation improved. I along with other officers had visited the affected areas and talked to the cross section of people and we were really moved to see the plight of those affected by these conflicts.

Because of the sporadic incidents in city and villages, the two communities developed lot of anger, anguish and hatred for each other. Cutting across the party lines, the political leaders too ganged up in favour of their respective castes, though outwardly they adopted neutral postures. We kept a very close watch on the situation and the district authorities also held peace committee meetings with all the influential leaders of various communities. No leader wanted to antagonise the members of his/her community. In district Agra prominent Jatav leaders were Sarvsri Chhatrapati Ambesh ex-MP Congress, Ramji Lal Suman sitting MP - Janta Dal from Firozabad, Azad Kumar Kardam, ex-M.L.A., Congress and Kishan Gopal sitting M.L.A.-B.J.P. Sri Nihal Singh Jain ex- Congress M.P. was a neutral leader, who commanded respect of all the communities. Prominent Jat leaders were Sarvsri Babu Lal, Block Pramukh, Achhnera, Badan Singh and Vijay Singh Rana, both Janata Dal MsLA. There was Janta Dal government in U.P. with Sri Mulayam Singh Yadav as Chief Minister. These caste riots relating to atrocities by Jats in villages and in reaction by Jatavs in City caused a lot of political embarrassment to U.P. Government. Officers too had several sleepless nights in controlling the situation. It was felt that all leaders of Agra, who were away either to Delhi or Lucknow, be requested to reach Agra to help in restoring the normalcy. M.L.As. were flown in State plane from Lucknow and Sri Ramji Lal Suman MP was asked to reach immediately but he took his own time and avoided facing people as Jats too were his voters. In peace meetings called by the district authorities, these public representatives used to adopt very forbearing attitude but had no courage to tell their respective caste fellows to reconcile and live in peace.

After several days, curfew was lifted when situation gradually improved. The notable aspect was that tourist traffic remained unaffected as there was no curfew in such areas. Looking at the hind sight, one may ponder as to whether Panwari episode was not a denial of constitutional rights of a particular section and why could it not be avoided. Incidents of Agra city too, exhibited violent reaction, which perhaps did not help their cause and their caste fellows had to suffer at the hands of the rival community. It cannot be said that they lived happily thereafter. Such reactions cannot be stopped by administrative actions only but could be minimised by educating the people of legal rights of every citizen and not to make infringements based on preconceived notions or discriminatory traditions. Politicians also need to stop exploiting sentiments of the voters on caste and communal lines and unitedly, exhibit sense of responsibility towards the nation. Let us pray for the best.

12

Varanasi/Chaundauli Caste Violence – 1994

Varanasi about 285 kilometers east of State capital Lucknow is district and Divisional Head quarter. It is a holy place situated on the banks of rivers Varuna and Ganga, which attracts pilgrims and devotees not only from India but all over the world. It has been a seat of learning for classical music and education as three universities namely Banaras Hindu University (B.H.U.), Varanasi Sanskrit Vishwavidhyalaya and Mahatma Gandhi Kashi Vidyapeeth are located here only. Most of the Hindus wish that they should either die here or their ashes be brought for immersion in Ganga so that they find place in heaven. Kashi Vishwanath and other temples attract large number of Hindu devotees, who largely contribute to the economy of the city.

Varanasi used to be one of the biggest districts of U.P. and with its trifurcation two more districts namely Bhadohi (Sant Ravidas Nagar) and Chandauli, its area and population has been reduced. The undivided district was famous for Bhadohi carpets and Varanasi *sarees*. Chandauli, the eastern district of the state which borders Bihar is economically and socially very backward. Majority of the population consists of lower castes, scheduled castes and scheduled tribes, who for centuries and generations have been living in unimaginable poverty as they neither owned any agricultural land nor had other resources of livelihood and were forced to work as bonded labour with upper castes. Many of them still survive on forest produce.

Renowned social reformer Sant Kabir lived in Varanasi and earned his livelihood by weaving cloth. Another great Hindu saint Ravidas, who worked as cobbler belonged to lower caste *Chamar*, but was known for his simplicity and devotion to God. His preachings have been included in holy 'Guru Granth Sahib' of Sikhism. Varanasi had several freedom fighters and some of them later rose as Chief Ministers U.P. and Union Ministers. None of them could do much to ameliorate the plight of these lesser children of God. *Dalit* students because of schooling got the feeling of being equal to all the fellow students, and they started opposing the discrimination meted out to them. The economic and social condition of those, who got government jobs because of reservations, also started improving and they became role model for their class and reacted against their exploitation.

Ghazipur and Azamgarh bordering districts of Varanasi had been electing Sarvsri Jharkhande Rai and Sarju Pandey as members of Lok Sabha and Sri Udal as M.L.A. and all of them belonged to the Communist Party of India, which had been working for the downtrodden and this led to some awakening of these sections of those areas. Although by an Act of Parliament, the bonded labour system was abolished, the land owners never took it sportingly and continued to exploit these people. In the last quarter of twentieth century, leftists known as Naxalites started making inroads with them, tried to awaken their educated youth about injustice at the hands of upper castes and also fought for their cause. Several incidents of attacks on such exploiters occurred which created a cleavage between the 'Haves" and "Have Nots". With the emergence of Bahujan Samaj Party (B.S.P.), new political outfit, scheduled castes and tribes, found a new hope of ameliorating their lot. This party worked hard amongst these sections and created a solid vote bank in its favour. Some of the other backward castes, though were benefited by Mandal Commission recommendations, never identified themselves with the lower castes. Upper castes too did not consider them (OBCs) as equals and developed a feeling that political, economic and social reforms were going against their interests, hence they adopted a hostile attitude towards both the sections. Some of the backward castes supported the B.S.P. and tried to form a formidable block of the SCs/STs and OBCs. Upper castes took it as a major challenge to their political supremacy which was gradually being eroded. Speeches made by the B.S.P. and other supporting party leaders were very hard hitting which further infuriated the upper castes.

In 1993 Vidhan Sabha elections, which were jointly contested by the B.S.P. and the S.P. (Samajvadi Party), several seats were won and they formed the Government with Mr. Mulayam Singh Yadav as chief minister. Sri Dina Nath Bhaskar, a firebrand youth leader of B.S.P., successfully contested from Chandauli seat and became a Minister of State. During elections he made fiery speeches which could not be digested by the interested castes and this further resulted in social disharmony. One Ram Avtar Paswan, the local representative of Sri Bhaskar, who allegedly had links with criminals of Jamania and Bihar, was playing a major role in uniting *Dalits* and was using uncharitable words against upper castes particularly *Thakurs*. This was taken unkindly by the *Thakurs*, and he was ultimately killed by two *Thakur* boys on 4-2-1994 in Chandauli town. Sri Bhaskar while addressing his people at Chanduli allegedly exhorted them to kill at least three persons of upper castes to avenge Paswan's death. Two Thakurs of village Khurhat and one Yadav of neighbouring village Rampur of police circle Dheena were murdered in the following night out side the village while working in fields. The scene of occurrence was a few kilometers away from borders of Ghazipur and Bihar. This led to major incidents of violence in Chandauli town and other areas where poor castes were made the target and it was demanded that criminal cases be registered against State Minister Sri Bhaskar and 3 policemen including station officer of P.S. Dheena, which were subsequently registered and investigated. Police station Chandauli was attacked, roads including busy GT road (National Highway leading to Calcutta) were blocked resulting in complete disruption of traffic. The markets and other establishments remained closed for several days. There was tension all around and the rival castes were after each other's throats but *Dalits* got mortally afraid.

The above incidents led to revival of *Khastriya Maha Sabha* and *Brahmin Maha Sabha* which hitherto had been dormant. The U. P. College Varanasi had been very prestigious institution of Khastriyas and its alumni included many top leaders of the country. Dr. Umrao Singh was also a student and subsequently a teacher of this College before going as Principal of DN College

Tirwa, district Farrukhabad, now Kannauj and I had the privilege of being his student in D.N. College, Tirwa (Kannauj). Students of U.P. College, in retaliation of the killings of *Thakurs* in the villages attacked some students of the college who belonged to the Scheduled Castes and also ransacked the nearby *Dalit* colony resulting in arson, loot, violence and serious breach of peace. The District administration took immediate action to check the escalation of such incidents and clamped curfew in some localities of the city.

As I was looking after the law and order of the state as A.D.G., it was desired by the D.G.P. Sri V.P. Kapur and Chief Minister Sri Mulayam Singh Yadav that I should rush to the affected areas, make personal assessment and take suitable remedial measures to normalise the situation. I reached Varanasi, where D.M./S.S.P. and other officers gave me detailed briefing of the incidents and the prevailing conditions. I, along with local officers reached Chandauli, visited the affected places and held a short meeting at the police station. From there we went to village Khurhat in the afternoon. As it was cold and raining, after visiting the scene of occurrence of the murders, we decided to talk to the villagers. While I was made to sit under a thatch on the outskirts where a *chakki* (floor mill) was installed, other officers went inside the village to talk to the members of every community. While talking to the persons present under the thatch, I was told that it was a fight between the forwards and backwards. I found it difficult to follow certain colloquial Bhojpuri words. I asked one person as to which caste and category he belonged to. With full confidence he said that he was *Nai* (barber) by caste, which was a forward caste, while as per official version *Nais* belonged to other backward communities (OBCs) entitled for reservation. According to him the lower castes were the backwards while all others including OBCs were forwards. There was a complete divide on caste lines and our appeal of peace fell into deaf ears. As adequate police force was posted in villages, further breach of peace was prevented.

As the area was tense and there was possibility of reaction on either side of the border with Bihar, we invited police officers of the neighbouring Bhabhua district for talks. A meeting was held in the Inspection House situated on the banks of river *Karamnasa* which forms boundary between the two states. We returned to Circuit House Varanasi by the evening, where public representatives were present to discuss things for restoring normalcy. Here it was decided that a 'Peace Committee' meeting of important influential persons be held next morning and I should also address them appealing for peace in city and rural areas. Sri Shatrudh Prakash, ex-minister U.P. was of great help. I briefed the D.G.P. about the situation and told him that things were improving but Peace Committee meeting fixed for the next morning will further help. He directed me to immediately rush to Kanpur, as my presence was required there as Kanpur was under curfew following murder of Kala Bachcha a local B.J.P. leader. I left Varanasi in the night itself and was at Kanpur before dawn. Varanasi and Chandauli gradually returned to normalcy.

13

Meerut Caste Conflicts – 1994

The description of Meerut City has already been given under chapter 'Meerut Communal Riots'. The district has sizable population of downtrodden people who are known as Scheduled Castes, majority of whom are Jatavs (*Chamars*), and they are located in thickly populated villages and also in certain *mohallas* of Meerut city, particularly Subhash Nagar and Shergarhi (Shastri Nagar). The majority of them, who are city dwellers, are educated, economically well off and enlightened ones but their exploitation in villages is rampant as land holders employ them as farm labour and pay nominal wages. In villages, whenever they agitate through community panchayats, they are threatened by the land holders not to use their fields for call of nature and taking fodder for animals. Political awakening is gradually raising their morale. In Meerut city, they have maintained neutral posture during communal riots but they and Muslims generally unite during elections. This combination makes them politically very strong and any attempt of their exploitation is resisted.

In 1994, U.P. had a coalition government of Samajvadi Party (S.P.) and Bahujan Samaj Party (B.S.P.) with Sri Mulayam Singh Yadav as Chief Minister. The B.S.P. workers and their supporters were installing statues of Dr. B. R. Ambedkar on open lands all over the State. Some incidents of law and order including conflicts with local authorities had also happened. In this chain, serious conflicts took place between local residents (Scheduled Castes - Jatavs) of *mohalla* Shergarhi, Meerut and the local administration. In mohalla Shergarhi statue of Dr. B.R. Ambedkar was installed on a platform and trench dug all around the local park owned by *'Avas Vikas Parishad'*. Initially the authorities did not take any notice of that, but after a few days they woke up and decided to remove the statue. On the morning of 30-3-1994, a local officer of the *'Avas Vikas Parishad'* informed local police station of PS Medical College that a fully armed crowd of about 150 persons was indulging in digging the park for installing a statue. The Station Officer of PS Medical College with his available force rushed there and found that a crowd of Jatavs, fully armed with *lathis* (canes), *ballams* (spears), firearms etc. was present to meet any eventuality. Senior officers were informed through City Control Room about the seriousness of the situation, who also rushed with whatever extra force was immediately available. The crowd swelled to about 2.000 and continued to guard the park so that the statue of their 'Messiah' Dr. Ambedkar was not forcibly removed by the administration. Officers, including A.D.M. City and Additional Superintendent of Police, City Magistrate and Police Circle Officer tried to pacify the crowd, asked them to see the reason and not to take the law in their hands, but it fell on deaf ears. Assistant Superintendent of Police with women police also reached the scene. The leaders were persuaded to retreat, so that talks could be held in peaceful atmosphere. The crowd retreated upto a place, where brickbats were lying and some of the officers were standing. The mob heavily brick-batted on them, causing serious injuries. Police used force after repeated warnings. The crowd got further infuriated and caused fire arm injuries to a Deputy Superintendent of Police and a few constables and also snatched away the rifle of a constable. Police fired tear gas, lathi charged and finally resorted to firing to disperse the mob. By that time Sri Mohinder Singh, District Magistrate and Sri Birinder Singh Sidhu, S.S.P. had also arrived with extra force. In the operation two rioters were killed and 17 seriously injured who were sent to hospitals for treatment. The Circle Officer Sri Shiv Sagar Singh, station officer and other security personnel numbering about 16 received serious injuries of firearms and sharp edged weapons. They too were treated in hospitals. 29 rioters were arrested. Next day newspapers published several photographs of the riotous crowd armed with *lathis*, firearms etc. and mercilessly beating the policemen.

The situation remained very tense, not only in Shergarhi but also in other localities. The supporters of this cause held several meetings in *mohallas* Brahmpuri, Kamboh Gate, Bhagwatpura, Kalia garhi, Tej garhi, and others, against the use of force and attempt of forcibly removing the statue. Crowds brickbatted on police in Brahm Puri, Jatav Gate and Kamboh Gate areas. A call for taking out processions and Meerut '*bandh*' on 31-3-1994, which was fraught with serious consequences was given. In order to maintain law and order the curfew was clamped in the entire city from early morning of 31-3-1994 which was lifted on 4-4-1994. Extra forces were rushed by us from outside Meerut to assist the local administration. The monetary help of Rs. one lac each to the next of kin of those killed and Rs. 2000 to Rs. 25,000 to the injured were distributed on 1-4-1994 to assuage their feelings.

My Visit to Meerut

Seeing the gravity of the situation I was sent to Meerut. Before leaving I had asked the S.S.P./D.I.G. Meerut about their extra requirements, if any, and whatever they projected, was ordered to reach there at the earliest. In addition to that we moved two P.A.C. Coys to be kept in 6th Bn. P.A.C. Meerut as D.G.P. reserve. I rushed to Meerut, where I got first hand briefing from the local senior officers. I also visited the curfew bound areas of Shergarhi, where the scene of occurrence was, and went to a few houses of the local residents to get their point of view. Later on local influential leaders of this community came to see me, some of whom namely Sri Jhaggar Singh, former M.L.A. and Sri Har Sharan Singh Jatav also former M.L.A., were known to me. They positively responded to my appeal for restoring normalcy and in turn pacified their people. As I was not new to Meerut, people from cross sections saw me to give their views and suggestions for very early restoration of normalcy. Sri Haji Akhlaq Ahmad, local M.L.A. of B.S.P. was of great help. Local media persons, who had covered the incident, and several of whom were my personal friends also gave the unedited version and very useful suggestions. I passed on this information to local officers for their use.

While I was at Meerut, news came at night that Sri Ram Vilas Paswan, a prominent national leader of *Dalit* community was to visit Meerut, who would also go to the affected areas and his visit was fraught with danger of escalating the trouble. The D.M./ S.S.P. decided that they would stop him near Partapur bye-pass and send him back to Delhi. In presence of his senior bosses, S.S.P. Sri Sidhu asked for extra P.A.C. Coys. I told him that sufficient force had already been provided to him and there was no time left for rushing extra force from nearby areas. He insisted that I should arrange for some additional Coys, which he would use only when absolutely necessary. I said that two Coys of D.G.P. reserve were locally present, which would be at his disposal when the situation so demanded. On his insistence I placed both the Coys at his disposal, clearly telling that since there was no force available either at Meerut or in the nearby districts, he would not ask for additional force to which he agreed. Next day when DM / S.S.P. were at Partapur crossing waiting for Sri Paswan's arrival, S.S.P. flashed frantic messages that some crowd had collected there and he immediately needed a few more Coys, which I should provide. I asked the Range D.I.G. to provide the required force from his reserves, upon which he told me that all Range and Zonal reserves were already deployed locally and they had no extra reserves. The S.S.P. flashed a message that he was rushing to see me in this connection. I directed him that instead of rushing to see me he should remain there to tackle the situation with available resources. Sri Paswan was sent back and the city remained undisturbed. Later I felt cheated by the S.S.P. and realised that instead of providing those two Coys to him I should have retained them for emergency as the basic principle for such situations is that officers should always keep some reserves for emergency. Subsequently things normalised and I returned to Lucknow.

14

Uttrakhand Agitation

The eight Districts of Uttar Pradesh, namely, Uttarkashi, Chamoli, Tehri Garhwal, Pauri Garhwal and Dehradun of Garhwal Division and Pithoragarh, Almora and Nainital of Kumaon Division comprised the area of agitation for separate hill State, which had been integral part of Uttar Pradesh since long. It has international borders with Tibet on the north and Nepal in the east. The region was ruled by various kings and dynasties from time to time. Nepal ruled the area twice, firstly from 1223 A.D. to 1248 A.D. and again from 1790 A.D. to 1815 A.D., when British Government annexed it to India who remained in power till 15-8-1947. It contributed 3 Chief Ministers of U.P., namely Pandit Govind Ballabh Pant and Sri Narain Dutt Tiwari, from Kumaon and Sri Hemvati Nandan Bahuguna from Garhwal. They guided the destiny of this State for several decades.

Geography and the People

The geographical area of this region had been 51,224 square kilometers (17.37% of U.P.), 35,000 square kilometers above the altitude of 2,000 meters or more of which 16.5% is snow bound. It had 52.5% forest area and 26% agricultural area. Geographically it has three regions namely, (1) mountainous from where, most of the important rivers originate,(2) *'Bhanwar'* and (3) *'Shivalik'* hills. Till 1991, it had two Divisions, 8 districts, 31 tahsils, 89 Development Blocks, 62 urban areas and 15,128 villages with 6,262 *Gaon Sabhas*. The population was 59,26,146, with 954 females for every 1,000 males. There were 9,89,658 scheduled castes and 2,09,838 Scheduled Tribes people in the area but had negligible population of backward castes. The majority of population is constituted of upper castes, Brahmins and Khastriyas. Majority of Scheduled Castes are known as '*Shilpkars*'(Artisans). All the original residents of Chakrata tahsil of district Dehradun and Dharchula tahsil of district Pithoragarh were declared as Scheduled Tribes. The literacy rate was 51.54%, highest in U.P. The Terai area has sizable population of Sikhs, who are either refugees from Pakistan or are migrants from Punjab and are prosperous farmers..

The region is known as *'Dev Bhoomi'* (land of Gods) because several famous shrines and places of pilgrimage are located in this area. Gangotri, Yamnotri, Badrinath and Kedarnath in Garhwal region are most important of them and are known as '*Dhams*'. Holy rivers Yamuna (Jamuna) and Ganga, which is known as '*Bhagirathi*' here as, according to legend, King Bhagirath an ancestor of Lord Rama, brought it on earth from heavens; originate from Yamnotri and Gangotri respectively of district Uttarkashi. Badrinath Dham is located on river Alaknanda, while Kedarnath is in valley from where Mandakini originates. Five confluences of River Alaknanda are called *Prayags* namely, *Vishnu Prayag* (confluence of Alaknanda and Dhauliganga), *Nand Prayag* (confluence of Alaknanda and Nandakini), *Karna Prayag* (confluence of Alaknanda and Pinderganga), *Rudra Prayag* (confluence of Alaknanda and Mandakini) and *Dev Prayag* (confluence of Alaknanda and Bhagirathi). From Dev Prayag the river is known as Ganga which goes down to Rishikesh and Haridwar (gate way to God) and flowing onwards to Allahabad (*Prayag Raj*–Confluence of *Ganga*, *Yamuna* and invisible *Saraswati*), Varanasi, Patna, Bhagalpur and Farakka. From there it loses its name Ganga and bifurcates into, Padma, flowing to Bangladesh and Bhagirathi flowing in India to Calcutta (now Kolkata) where it is called Hugli. Fortunately I had occasion to visit most of these places. In Kumaon also there are several holy places and tourist resorts. The river Kali mainly makes the boundary between India and Nepal on the east, flows along the route to 'Mansarovar'. Kausani, birthplace of renowned Hindi Poet Sumitra Nandan Pant, is known as 'Switzerland' of India. The hill stations Mussorie in district Dehradun, known as 'Queen of Hills', Nainital head quarters of district Nainital and Kumaon Division, and Ranikhet in district Almora are in this region only. The famous 'Rajaji National Park' and 'Jim Corbett National Park' are in the Terai region. 'Valley of Flowers' and 'Hem Kund Saheb - Sikh Pilgrimage, are on the high altitude in district Chamoli, the trekking route for which is from Govindghat and Pandukeshar.

This area has different cultural and social customs, and altogether different topography affecting economic condition of the people. While plains of U.P. enjoy fertile land, it has hilly tracts of the Himalayas, which contribute to its backwardness with economic and industrial disparities. It is known for its 'Money Order Economy' as most of the money comes from the pensioners or people working outside, particularly as defence personnel and others who work in plains as domestic servants in various cities and towns. Ladies are very hard working, who fetch water from distant rivulets/sources, cook food for their families, work in fields and also bring fodder for the animals. On the whole life is very hard for them. Though, it has maximum forest area but mindless exploitation of forests, mines and minerals and imbalance in developmental planning, created a feeling of discontentment and neglect towards U.P. and Central Governments.

Because of the above-mentioned reasons a demand for separate state, to be named as ' Uttrakhand', gained ground and was raised from time to time. After creation of Himachal Pradesh in 1956 and subsequently of North Eastern States, people of this region also started agitations for separate state to be carved out of U.P. A political outfit namely *'Uttrakhand Kranti Dal'* (U.K.D.) came into being in 1979 and it started taking up the cause forcefully. The U.K.D. also contested elections to U.P. Assembly on some occassions and won a few seats. They also raised their voice very forcefully in U.P. Assembly. Several agitations were also launched from time to time citing following data to justify their demands are given in Table 13.1.

Table 13.1

State	*Population (1981 Census) in lakhs*	*Area in thousand SQ Kms*	*No. of Ms LA*	*MP (Lok Sabha)*	*MP (Rajya) Sabha)*
Sikkim	3.16	7.2	30	1	1
Mizoram	4.94	28.9	30	1	1
Arunachal Pradesh	6.32	38.5	30	2	1
Nagaland	7.75	16.5	60	1	1
Meghalaya	13.56	84.2	60	2	1
Manipur	14.20	22.5	60	2	1
Tripura	20.53	10.4	60	2	1
Himachal Pradesh	42/80	55.7	68	4	1
Uttarakhand	48.35	51.12	19	4	-

MY FOND MEMORIES OF U.P. HILLS

I belong to Gangetic plains and had never seen hills till I reached Mussoorie in 1963 for the foundational course at National Academy of Administration. On way to Dehradun after leaving Haridwar by train, hills could be seen and I got quite excited. We stayed at Mussoorie for about 5 months and there we got several opportunities to visit places of interest. The Tibetan refugee camps, were on our way to Katesar Castle Hostel from main building of our Academy and I learnt a few things about their life style and Budhist culture. From Mussoorie, I went to Mount Abu (Hill station of Rajasthan) for one year's rigorous training of I.P.S. On completion of my district training in Aligarh, I was posted as regular Assistant Superintendent of Police, Bareilly in October 1965. As I was fresher in the district, my S.P. Sri B.N. Nigam, deputed me to Nainital for a fortnight's V.I.P. duty of King Mahendra of Nepal who was visiting with his family members including crown prince Birendra. It was my first exposure of the V.I.P. duty and also of the beautiful hill resort, Nainital. I had occasion to be on duty for fifteen days with the King, and where ever he went, including hill station Ranikhet, I accompanied him as Escort Officer of his convoy and worked under the direction and control of Sri K.P. Agrawal, Superintendent of Police Training and Security, Intelligence Department, U.P. I also enjoyed the beauty of snow clad hills, Naini lake, thick forests and the *terai* belt.

Sri K.S. Tripathi, commandant XXII Battalion P.A.C. (Now III Bn. SSB), Srinagar (Garhwal) went on 35 days' leave and I was deputed to officiate during his leave vacancy. The Bn. had its contingents deployed at various places on hills and I was required to make prescribed inspection visits to these places. Srinagar, is in valley, with the district headquarters at Pauri and I got the opportunity of visiting Rishkesh, Devprayag, Pauri, Rudraprayag, Ookhimath, Satpuli and many other places. It being month of March-April, the climate was enjoyable with flowering of trees and seasonal plants.

In 1981, I was promoted as D.I.G., Security, Intelligence Department, U.P. and immediately after taking over charge, my I.G. Intelligence, Sri SC Dikshit asked me to visit areas of Pauri Lok Sabha constituency, which extended over Pauri and Chamoli Districts. Sri Hemvati Nandan Bahuguna, Ex- Chief Minister, U.P. and then in opposition of ruling Congress Party, was the possible winning candidate, against whom Congress had fielded Sri Chandra Mohan Singh Negi former U.P. Minister and my class - mate in LL.B. at Dayanand College of Law Kanpur. I got the opportunity of visiting Kotdwar, Lansdown, Pauri, Srinagar, Chamoli, Joshimath and Badrinath. It was an enjoyable trip and I got the occasion of freely and frankly interacting with the cross sections of people, as it was my incognito visit.

In May, 1981, I had gone to Internal Security Academy Mount Abu for training and there I read in newspapers that I had been transferred to Nainital as range D.I.G. of Kumaon. On return to Lucknow railway station, when I was going to board the car, a traffic constable congratulated me after smart salute. On my asking as to what for he was congratulating me, he said that I had become D.I.G.. When I told him that I was already a D.I.G., he said that I was going to a Range, supposedly important posting. For lower ranks, side postings, whatever importance they may be having, are of little consequence. As D.I.G. of Kumaon Range with H.Q. at Nainital, I had 3 districts, namely Nainital, Almora and Pithoragarh under my charge. I got several occasions to visit the areas, particularly Champavat, Lohaghat, Pithoragarh, Dharchula, Kaushani, Ranikhet and other places. I would like to share some good and bad experiences of this posting. One day sudden fire broke out on Mall road in Nainital engulfing several posh shops. It being close to my office, I rushed there to supervise the operations. Fire vehicles reached little late and that infuriated the local people, who almost manhandled me. As plenty of water of Naini lake was available, fire was soon put off but not before 2-3 shops had been completely gutted. Sri Dilip Trivedi, young I.P.S. officer, posted there as A.S.P., played a major role in fire fighting, at personal risk. One local correspondent of Hindi daily *'Amar Ujala'* played a key role in having exchange of hot words with me. Police and Fire Brigade, were accused of negligence as most of them belonged to plains and hardly had sympathy for the hill people. Here I came to know about the sentiments of locals, who called themselves as '*Paharis*' and those from plains as '*Deshis*'. *Paharis* had developed lot of hatred for *Deshis* and they used to unite if any *Pahari* was ever ill treated by *Deshis*. A school teacher hailing from plains was murdered because he had scolded one of the *Pahari* students. Government machinery of U.P. was responsible to a great extent for alienating the *Paharis* because every department used to post mostly the tainted, condemned and disgruntled staff on hills. Since they were punishment postings, this staff wanted early return to plains even if they had to pick up quarrels with the *Paharis*. I have great regards for them because they were simple and honest people, unlike those from plains. On my transfer from there, many people were present at Dat near bus station Nainital. the main exit route, to bid me farewell. The *'Amar Ujala'* correspondent profusely apologised for his earlier conduct.

Here I mention a few examples of their honesty and simplicity. Some relatives of Mr. Lumba, District Judge Nainital, who had stayed at night at Inspection House Kausani, on way to Delhi realised that a costly wrist watch was left behind in the bath room there. Mr. Lumba asked me to do something and I in turn asked S.P. Almora to have the Inspection House staff contacted. When the local police went there, the caretaker handed it over to police saying that he was feeling restless and did not know as to how to return it. Really a fine example of honesty. In Nainital my wife went to vegetable market, for purchasing vegetables where she purchased some ladyfingers, and while the seller was putting them in her bag, few pieces fell on the ground. She asked him not to worry, upon which he remarked that why was she paving the way to hell for him as he would be guilty of weighing less. On the occasion of *'Janamashtami'* my son Asim, a young school going boy, went to market for bringing dried coconut. He purchased one and started leaving, upon which the shopkeeper asked him to wait. He took back the coconut, broke it open, found fungus inside, hence took out another piece and repeated the same exercise but found the fungus again. He found the third coconut to his satisfaction, which he gave to my son. Mind it that he did not know that he was the son of a D.I.G.. One evening a coolie, dressed in rags, came to our residence with a few suite cases and bedding, told us that it belonged to a lady passenger, who left bus station after taking his token number and asking him to take it to a house near the residence of D.I.G. He had been searching her for long but could not locate. He asked my staff to take care of it, till he searched that lady. After some time the lady came and started scolding the coolie for not reaching the luggage. I asked her to appreciate his honesty rather than scolding him for no fault of his. These examples are sufficient to prove that they are fine and honest people.

In 1988, new district Haridwar was created by carving out certain areas from main district Shaharanpur and adding a few bordering areas of district Bijnor. As it fell in our jurisdiction,I and Sri V.K. Diwan, Divisional Commissioner were present at the time of inauguration by Sri Narain Dutt Tiwari, Chief Minister, U.P. It was expected that entire *'Kumbh Mela'* area of Haridwar and Rishikesh (District Dehradun) would be included in the new district as it could solve many administrative problems. Every body agreed in principle, but Rishikesh could not be included as hill sentiments were that Haridwar should become part of Pauri Division, instead of Meerut Division. People of Haridwar, particularly of Roorkee objected to it as they would find it difficult to reach Pauri which would involve 5 to 6 hours of hill journey as compared to Meerut which was very nearby and easily approachable by road and train.

In summer of 1989, President R. Venkatraman, was to visit holy shrines of Gangotri and Badrinath. As D.I.G. Pauri found it very difficult to supervise arrangements at both the places, my

Zonal I.G.P. Sri S.K. Mukerji deputed me for Gangotri duty while local Range D.I.G. was deputed for Badrinath. After driving from Rishikesh via Narendranagar and Tehri we reached Uttarkashi, where I met the district authorities and discussed arrangements for V.V.I.P. visit. Next day we went to Gangotri and made night halt, where we learnt that the visit had been called off. We enjoyed the scenic beauty of the hills and river Bhagirathi descending from Gaumukh. The river water was ice cold but transparent. A Sub Inspector from Meerut, who had gone for the V.V.I.P. duty, while taking holy dip in freezing river water started sliding down the current, but was immediately rescued by colleagues. Subsequently he saw me at Meerut and I found him walking on crutches because his feet were badly paralysed due to ice cold water at Gangotri.

After my retirement on 31-7-2000, I, accompanied by my wife, visited Haridwar, Rishikesh, Badrinath and Kedarnath and returned via Adi-Badri, Gairsaind, Ranikhet and Nainital. But for Adi-Badri, Kedarnath and Gairsaind, we had already been to other places earlier. We were looked after very well by the local officers at every place and we really enjoyed the trip.

Agitations and Demands

Known environmentalist Sri Sunder Lal Bahuguna, a non-political person, had launched *'Chipko Andolan'* urging people to save trees from mindless felling. This became a very popular agitation of hill people, particularly women, who clinched the trees by arms whenever contractors came to forests for felling the trees. This became the motivating factor for their unity.

The U.K.D. movement comparatively remained peaceful till 1989 when Government of India passed 'Forest Conservation Act', which was resented to by the hill people. This movement remained some what dormant from 1990 till July, 1994. In August, 1994, U.P. Government led by Sri Mulayam Singh Yadav passed a reservation bill which provided 27% reservation for other backward classes (OBCs) in addition to existing job reservation in favour of the Scheduled Castes (SCs), and the Scheduled Tribes (STs). They had never objected to the reservation for SCs and STs but were deadly opposed to reservation for OBCs as they had negligible population in that area and locals developed a feeling that OBCs from plains would come to Uttarakhand to usurp their jobs. This gave an opportunity to U.K.D. to revive their agitation. It was vehemently opposed by the students, who were also joined by women, children, intellectuals serving and retired employees and ex-servicemen, who are sizable in that region. This became a mass movement and started taking violent turn in August, 1994. Their main demands included:-

1. Formation of Uttarakhand State.
2. Withdrawal of reservation for OBCs and giving reservation to Uttarkhandis under the relevant provisions.
3. Withdrawal of all cases got registered by Forest Department from 1989 onwards.
4. Impending Panchayat elections should not be held till delimitation is completed.

Sri Kashi Singh Airy, M.L.A., U.K.D., launched a scathing attack on U.P. Govt. and sat on hunger strike unto death at Lucknow to demand a separate State, to be called ' Uttrakhand'. As his condition started deteriorating and U.P. Assembly was in session, opposition leaders took up this matter. One day Sri Airy attended the Assembly despite his fading health and made a very emotional appeal in House in favour of their demands and also offered to resign from his seat in case' Uttrakhand' was not created. The capital of this proposed State was to be 'Gairsain', which is equi-distant from most of the places, particularly of hilly regions of Garhwal and Kumaon.

From August to October, 1994, various agitations were launched and hitherto very peaceful people, committed violence at several places with attack on government servants, particularly those hailing from plains. At Mussoorie, a police post was attacked and burnt resulting in injuries to several police personnel including killing of a Deputy Superintendent of Police. Crowds also indulged in looting of police firearms and throwing explosives at them. Roads, the only mode of travel, were blocked by felling trees and placing boulders on them. It became difficult to reach civil supplies and the security personnel on hills. It being *'yatra'* season, tourist traffic was also adversely affected. As it had become a mass movement based on regionalism, all sections of society, including ladies, children, students, old and young,

Sri Kashi Singh Airy

government servants belonging to hills were taking part in processions and strikes which were called very often. Markets could not open due to frequent '*Bandh*' calls. Communication was badly disrupted due to pulling down of telephone poles and wires. Ex-servicemen provided skills of guerilla warfare.

Sri Airy with flag of proposed Uttarakhand State

Seeing the magnitude of the problem, regular monitoring was done at the government level. I being Additional Director General of Police, Law and Order, U.P., had to keep a very close watch on the situation and also rush extra forces and other resources at various places. Various administrative problems were faced in rushing extra help, particularly the men and material. Sri V.P. Kapur, D.G.P., who had the experience of handling the hostile people of Manipur, used to guide us on various matters. The main problems faced were, paucity of sufficient woollens and rain coats, absence of medium vehicles for transporting men as P.A.C. mostly had heavy vehicles, which could not be driven on hills, dearth of hill trained drivers, carrying of sufficient petrol, diesel and lubricants as the same were not easily available locally due to closure of petrol pumps. With experience, we started sending ‘ Road Opening Parties’ (ROPs) with pioneering equipment, saws, axes and ropes for cutting and removing the felled trees. Sufficient dry rations, items of first- aid, torches with cells, kerosene oil etc., were also sent with the police /P.A.C. contingents. We shared our experiences with the field/P.A.C. officers, asked them to give exhaustive briefing about ‘Do’s’ and ‘Don’ts’, accompany and lead their force and as far as possible avoid confrontation with the locals. The security personnel and

Magistrates were advised to refrain from making unnecessary comments about the local people and the ongoing agitation.

Khatima, located in *terai*, of district Nainital, had serious trouble in the last days of August and beginning of September, 1994. During '*Bandh*' call all over region, at Khatima the town crowds got violent, took out processions, attacked police outpost and police station. Unruly crowd which had collected at police station Khatima, attacked the police personnel, fired shots, burnt the official records and personal belongings of the policemen and did not allow the force to move out. The Sub Divisional Magistrate (S.D.M.) and Deputy Superintendent of Police (C.O.) too were not spared. The S.D.M., a young officer had to take shelter in one corner of the P.S. After firing by the police, crowd dispersed and curfew was clamped in Khatima town, which continued for several days. Earlier violent incidents had taken place in Haldwani town which, too was under curfew.

I was ordered to visit Haldwani and Khatima, to have first hand account of the situation. I left in a four seater small U.P. Govt. plane, early in the morning and reached Phoolpur airport, Pantnagar. The senior officers of magistracy and police were present there to receive and brief me. From there we went by road to Haldwani town, which was under curfew. There I found most of the main roads blocked as boulders, readily available on the foothills, telephone poles and tyres were used. Public were not to be seen because of the strict enforcement of curfew. There were two routes for Khatima, one via Sitarganj and the shorter one through forest road *via* Chorgalia. As I was to return to Lucknow the same evening to brief the Chief Minister (Sri Mulayam Singh Yadav) and other senior officers, local officers decided to take me *via* forest road as it was shorter one and had less possibility of road blocks as compared to the other route which had reportedly been blocked at several places and possibility of crowds collecting in towns was there. For a few kilometers, the road was found open and we went unhindered but few kilometers short of Chorgalia, we found the road blocked at several spots as big forest trees had been cut and left on the road. Nearby Chorgalia police outpost was contacted on wireless to rush for help with saws and other equipment, so that road blocks could be removed. It took them some time to clear the road and we left for onward journey to Khatima. On way there were many villages but nobody was willing to talk to us.

On reaching Khatima, I was shown the places of violence including tahsil and police station. With great difficulty, the presence of a few local residents could be procured, with whom I could talk to. They gave me their own version of the violent incidents, squarely blaming the local administration and police for mishandling the situation. Official briefing indicated that crowd had got so violent that they did not listen to reason, advice and warnings and indulged in violent incidents injuring several security personnel and damaging the Govt., property. Having no option left, police firing was resorted to, in which some rioters were killed. Locals also alleged that a few persons were killed far away from this scene and their bodies were left on the railway track. I took round of the curfew bound areas to have the eyewitness account and gave necessary instructions to local officers, advising them to maintain cool so that peace was not disturbed again. On return *via* same route, we found no road blocks. I took off from Pantnagar in evening and reached Lucknow airport by dusk. On way from the airport, I got the wireless message that I should straight way reach the Chief Minister's residence, where he and other senior officers were holding the meeting and were waiting for me. On reaching there I gave the first hand briefing and also my suggestions about handling of this agitation. Later a C.B.I. enquiry was ordered about alleged killings by police at Khatima.

The Civil services probationers of 1994 batch, undergoing foundational course at Lal Bahadur Shastri National Academy of Administration, Mussoorie, were to leave for trekking on higher altitudes. Not that my daughter Rashmi (I.A.S.) and son Asim (I.P.S.), were also undergoing the same course and therefore, I was afraid of their security, I consulted the D.G.P. and the Principal Secretary Home as to whether it was advisable for the Academy to send the probationers for trekking in the wake of ongoing violent agitation. On their advice I sounded the Academy authorities about the prevailing law and order situation in different hill districts, but they decided not to disrupt their scheduled training programme. While going on buses, these trainees were accosted at several places by the hostile crowds, but were allowed to proceed further only when they posed themselves as students going for mountaineering. Had the crowds known that they were officers, perhaps they might have behaved differently.

Rally at Delhi

Dharna and hunger strikes were carried out at Delhi to impress on the Central Govt. to take an early decision as U.P. Assembly had earlier passed three resolutions recommending the formation of a new State. A call for holding a huge rally at Delhi on Mahatma Gandhi's birth day on October 2, 1994 was given and to make it a grand success. Men, women, children and old persons were mobilised from all the hill districts and they were asked to travel in buses, medium and light vehicles and secretly carry firearms and explosives. The U.P. administration also made preparations to meet the challenges of traffic bottlenecks and other law and order problems likely to be created in plains. While most of the traffic from Kumaon was to come *via* Rudrapur, Rampur and Moradabad, the traffic of Garhwal was to come *via* Haridwar, Roorkee, Muzaffarnagar and Meerut. Some vehicles from Kotdwar side were to go *via* Bijnor and Meerut. Traffic from all these places was to converge in district Ghaziabad, gate way to Delhi. Those coming from various sides were asked to form convoys at appointed places and from there they were to proceed in groups. Police barricading and road barriers were put up on concerned roads and sufficient police and P.A.C. was deployed for traffic and crowd management. Protesters left hills by road and started reaching the appointed spots by the evening of 1-10-1994. Situation reports from most of the districts indicated that agitators were in belligerent mood and were prepared to meet the police in case they were stopped. Heavy movement started creating problems on both the national highways i.e., Delhi-Moradabad and Delhi Haridwar and persuasions by administration calling them to behave fell on deaf ears. Local authorities of each district managed the affairs according to the need of the hour. At few places, buses broke the traffic barriers and proceeded ahead. D.G.P.'s Control Room was flooded with such messages and from here, messages were passed to concerned districts, to remain ready to meet the situation but avoid confrontation, as far as possible. Traffic from Moradabad and Bijnor went ahead but serious law and order problems were created between Roorkee and Muzaffarnagar. At Narsan, district Haridwar, they went ahead after, breaking open the barriers, refusing to be searched, burning two roadways buses, brickbatting on police and also snatching of two service rifles.

The rowdies were very agitated and were prepared to meet any challenge of the administration. They were stopped at a place called Rampur tiraha, on the outskirts of Muzaffarnagar city. Serious confrontation took place on 2-10-1994 around dawn and later on during day. Police/P.A.C. personnel were attacked, rounds fired at them and attempts were made to snatch their weapons. While dispersing, rioters used to take shelter in nearby sugar cane fields and then resurface to confront the security forces. Police had to resort to use of force including firing in which about half a dozen protestors were killed and about three dozen wounded, who were taken to nearby hospitals for treatment. Several cases, including under Arms Act, were registered. Later very serious allegations, including rape of women participants, were made. A CBI enquiry resulted in chargesheeting of several police men and government servants. This proved to be turning point for this agitation. In Delhi rally, Government of India was urged to carve out a new state named as 'Uttrakhand' at the earliest.

(Source: Map- Road Atlas –Welcome India Series, TTK HEALTH CARE LIMITED- PRINTING DIVISION, 2003)

New State Formed

The new State named " Uttaranchal" was formed on 9-11-2000 along with "Jharkhand" and "Chhatisgarh". Two districts of plains namely Haridwar and Udham Singh Nagar wanted to remain with U.P. but despite agitations they finally went to Uttaranchal. The agitation was launched for" Uttarakhand" but the then Union Govt. led by B.J.P. named the State as "Uttaranchal". There was agitation about having capital at Dehradun instead of Gairsaind but ultimately Dehradun was made the temporary capital of "Uttaranchal". A separate Legislative Assembly was constituted and those sitting legislators of U.P., who hailed from Uttranchal automatically became its members. As majority of the legislators belonged to B.J.P., the first government of 'Uttaranchal' was of B.J.P.. The Congress came to power in next elections. Sri Kashi Singh Airy, who spearheaded this agitation could not win many seats and his wish of Gairsaind becoming the Capital is still a dream. The women had played a key role for this State but they too did not feel happy as they neither got sufficient representation in State Legislature nor the due recognition. Now we wish all the best for "Uttaranchal" people.

15

Preserve Peace to Preserve India

Till nineteenth century, Indians lived in peace and no noticeable riots, violence or conflicts came to notice. The first quarter of the twentieth century, but for a few isolated incidents of violence, by and large, remained free from serious riots. There was a visible increase in communal riots as India struggled for freedom. The riots of Noakhali (now in Bangladesh) shook Mahatma Gandhi and our freedom movement received a set back. Several cities in the country witnessed serious communal and sectarian riots. The communal divide and disharmony between two major communities, Hindus and Muslims, ultimately resulted in partition of our motherland in 1947. The two nation theory did not last long and East Pakistan (now Bangladesh) ceded from West Pakistan in 1971. Immediately after independence in 1947 and creation of two Pakistans, East and West, mass exodus of population took place. While majority of Sikhs and Hindus had to migrate from Pakistan to India, a small section of Muslims from India left for West Pakistan. The migration of Hindus and Muslims from either side of East Pakistan and India, was generally smooth but the western front witnessed unprecedented violence, killings, arson, loot and unimaginable torture and misbehavior with womenfolk. Several trains, carrying migrants to and fro, were attacked on either side and mass scale killings shook the humanity. Hindus and Sikhs from Pakistan, who were called 'refugees' in India, were rehabilitated on war footing and they soon joined the mainstream. The Muslim migrants from India to Pakistan, mostly from central and western parts, were welcome there for the time being but later on they came to be known as "*Muhajirs*" and met with unwelcome behavior resulting in serious riots. *Muttahida Quami Movement* (MQM) is still continuing. Muslims migrating to East Pakistan were mainly from eastern U.P., Bihar and West Bengal, and were called as "Bihari Muslims", whose credentials were suspected as they sided with Pakistani Forces during 1971 war. Hindu migrants from East Pakistan soon became part of the Indian milieu and were never subjected to any discrimination. In 1971 war, huge Muslim population took refuge in India and many of them did not go back even after victory and creation of new nation 'Bangladesh'. From 1971 onwards, Bangladeshis have been crossing over to India and finding refuge in various bordering States and big cities of India where they work as rag pickers and menials. These illegal settlers are unwelcome and their presence is resented to by some political and religious outfits.

The British policy of 'divide and rule' had sown seeds of discord between the communities, who indulged in serious skirmishes posing threat to the security and very existence of the nation. Before independence, all were Indians, but after partition Muslims became a minority in India while Hindus and Sikhs were reduced to minority in Pakistan. India became a secular, socialist and democratic republic, whereas Pakistan chose to be a theocratic country. Allegations of persecution of minorities in both the countries had been made from time to time. In India a section of Muslims tried to put up a joint front against their alleged discrimination and persecution. Those seeds of mistrust and disharmony have gradually taken shape of big trees and communal termite is slowly eating into the age-old roots of our peace.

Soon after our independence, serious communal riots broke out in many parts of the country but western India including U.P. was worst hit. Such riots in Rohilkhand (seven districts namely Bijnor, Moradabad, Rampur, Budaun, Bareilly, Pilibhit and Shajehanpur of undivided Rohilkhand Division - with Bareilly as Head Quarters) had spread to villages, towns and cities. I remained Superintendent of Police, Budaun, then a district of Rohelkhand Division, in 1970-71 i.e. 23 years after India's Independence but horrible tales of riots of 1950, were still fresh in the minds of the eye witnesses. Sri J.D. Shukla, I.C.S., Chairman Board of Revenue, U.P., who was District Magistrate then, visited our district and shared many of his first hand experiences of those riots. The assassination of Mahatma Gandhi, Father of the Nation, on 30-1-1948, was another blow to the country. The unhappy legacy of the partition related violence continues even now and we face riots every now and then in most parts of India on some pretext or the other.

The decade between 1951 to 1960 was comparatively peaceful as no major riots took place. From 1960 onwards sentiments of the people were aroused by various interested sections including political parties on several counts, particularly caste and communal considerations, cow protection, opposition to Hindi as the official language of the country and for Urdu to be accorded the status of second official language in some states, labour, agrarian agitations etc. Meerut communal riots of 1968 and Bhiwandi riots of Maharashtra 1969 were the bloodiest till then. More and more riots occurred between 1971 to 1976. On the eve of 1971 Lok Sabha elections, serious communal riots broke out in Aligarh following which D.M. and S.S.P. were placed under suspension. During Emergency days in 1975-76 people, particularly the poorer sections cutting across the caste and communal barriers, got mortally afraid of the forced family planning measures. A section of the Muslims termed it to be unislamic and incited their community to oppose any such move, which led to riots at a few places in U.P., particularly in villages of Sultanpur and Muslim dominated locality of Khalapar in Muzaffarnagar city where curfew was imposed to control the situation. These incidents were aimed mainly against government officials because family planning measures were being implemented against the wishes of the people. An interested section of the Hindus started blaming lower Hindu castes in general and Muslims in particular for not falling in line with the national policy of population control, which according to their perception, would upset the population equations disadvantaging those whose number becomes less. It is noteworthy that in 1977 Lok Sabha elections, the Congress party could not win even a single seat out of 85 in U.P., and number game in other States of

Hindi belt was no better. The main reason for this electoral debacle of Smt. Indira Gandhi was attributed to the coercive family planning methods besides 'Emergency' excesses.

Last 20 years of twentieth century were full of sound and fury of serious caste and communal frenzy, which was caused on some pretext or the other. Serious riots of Moradabad in 1980 on the eve of *Id-ul-Fitr*, led to confrontation between Muslims and local administration as allegedly Police failed to check the entry of pigs at the place where *Namaz* was being held. Later on it became a Muslim-Hindu riot and U.P. Police was squarely blamed for committing atrocities on Muslims, though police outpost in *Mohalla* Galshahid was attacked, policemen killed and their belongings burnt and looted by the Muslim crowd of that locality. On the intervention of Government of India, the U.P. P.A.C., paramilitary force of the State, was withdrawn from this city and the C.R.P.F. was deployed. This was the starting of accusations against the police in general and the P.A.C. in particular and in subsequent years P.A.C. was not deployed there, and a section of Hindus termed it as 'appeasement policy' of the Government.

The unprecedented violence, particularly at Dehi, Jamshedpur and Kanpur, against Sikhs in 1984 following the assassination of Prime Minister Indira Gandhi, later gave rise to Sikh militancy and the country had to pay a very heavy price in tackling the demand for a separate '*Khalistan*' nation for Sikhs. A call by the Vishwa Hindu Parishad (V.H.P.) for construction of a magnificent temple at the disputed site at Ayodhya and various programmes launched to mobilise the Hindus resulted in unprecedented serious riots simultaneously all over India, particularly following the *'Kar Sewa'* calls of 1990 and 1992. Since then several Muslim militant organisations like S.I.M.I. (Student Islamic Movement of India) etc. have launched their campaign to mobilise the Muslims against the security forces and Hindus. Attack on P.A.C. pickets resulting in deaths of *Jawans* in Meerut and Kanpur and clashes with the police and killing of the Additional District Magistrate Pathak in Kanpur, are some of the examples. Hindu militants too have united against minorities in general and Muslims in particular in various parts of the country. The unprecedented violence in Gujarat following ghastly and reprehensible incidents at Godhra of burning alive train passengers of Sabarmati Express, mostly *'Kar Sevaks'*, returning from Ayodhya, shook the right thinking people of our country. Allegations of partisan attitude and commissions and omissions on the part of Gujarat Government, the state bureaucracy, the district administration and the state police have been taken note of very seriously by the National Human Rights Commission and the Supreme Court of India and they are intervening to ensure justice. The then Prime Minister Sri Atal Bihari Vajpaee, had to advise Chief Minister Sri Modi to follow *'Rajdharama'*.

Riots and violence have been caused by various factors, some of which could be enumerated here. Historically speaking India was invaded several times by the foreign Muslims who ruled this country for centuries, converted a section of the Hindus to Islam and some of them also indulged in destruction of the Hindu shrines, converting them into mosques. Hindus could not do much to defend their shrines and conversions at that point of time, but with the passage of time and India becoming independent, a section of the staunch Hindus have started demanding restoration of their destroyed shrines, particularly at Ayodhya, Kashi (Varanasi) and Mathura. They had been appealing to Muslims to voluntarily give these 3 shrines to Hindus failing which 3,000 such places will be taken over forcibly all over the country. Whereas a small section of the Muslims has been telling their community to voluntarily and peacefully pass on these three shrines to Hindus, but another section, which controls the Muslim psyche, had been vehemently opposing any such move. This and several other factors have gradually resulted in emergence of rabid communal outfits, who have been continuously indulging in sowing seeds of discord by poisoning the minds of their respective communities. Whereas a section of the Muslims had assertively been demanding that there should be no interference in their Personal Laws, Urdu be accorded status of second official language and Muslims be given proportionate reservation in government jobs, a section of the Hindus had been vehemently opposing it and any government or political party speaking in favour of the Muslim cause has been dubbed as pseudo-seculars.

Revival of Fundamentalism

The last two decades of 20th century witnessed emergence of fundamentalism in all sections of our society. Prominent display of the religious signs and slogans on vehicles and other public places, like 786 (*Bismillah-o-Rahman-e-Rahim*), *Jai Shri Ram*, *Jai Shri Krishna*, *Jai Mata di*, etc. have caught up rapidly and at the same time official slogans and symbols of our national unity have remained confined to public transport vehicles (trucks, taxis and three wheelers) only, because permits would neither be issued nor renewed unless these symbols and slogans are painted on such vehicles. Private vehicles rarely display such symbols/slogans urging for national unity. Hindu devotees in large numbers have started visiting various religious places from one corner of the country to the other. Lakhs of Shiva devotees, popularly called as '*Kanvariyas*' go to Haridwar in Uttranchal and Deoghar in Bihar every year in the month of *Shravan* (July/ August) to take holy Ganges water from Haridwar, march on foot to long distances covering hundreds of kilometers and offer to deities of Lord Shiva in temples, particularly at Pura Mahadev (Meerut rural area) and Kali Paltan temple of Meerut City in U.P. and Baij Nath Dham in Jharkhand. This practice is gradually increasing and the educated and wellplaced persons too are participating in large numbers. Muslims too have started hiring buses for taking parties to various religious places like Ajmer Sharief etc., for '*Ziyarat*' (pilgrimage). Sikhs are also not lagging behind as they have started visiting their places of pilgrimages in large numbers. This is not to say that people did not go on such pilgrimages earlier but the increasing participation is an indicator of the rise of religious fundamentalism even amongst the educated classes. Almost all the communities, besides taking out customary processions, have been insisting on taking out new processions and that too through non-conventional and disputed routes leading to violence. There is a greater stress on taking out new religious processions like *Barawafat*, *Moharrum Chehallum*, *Durga Pooja* and *Ganesh Chaturthi* etc. where stress is being laid on increasing the number of participants, display of fire works and illumination of buildings. Besides collecting voluntary contributions, the organisers forcibly stop trucks and other road transport to collect money and do not allow them to proceed till they pay. If some body refuses to pay, these self-proclaimed volunteers indulge in rowdyism and create serious law and order problems. Increasingly greater stress is being laid on collecting crowds on roads on the occasions of religious congregations, fairs and festivals. Spilling over of *Namazis* on roads in front of mosques and conducting *Maha Aartis* on roads are some of the examples.

Of late stress is also being laid on the construction of new buildings and the renovation of old, dilapidated and abandoned religious places, which has been resented to by the opposite communities at many places on several occasions. Gods are being used as tools for grabbing and encroaching upon public land and mushroom growth of roadside temples and *mazars* (graves) and collection of devotees there on given days/dates are the examples. Cremation and burial places too are not being spared. Ever increasing use of loud speakers fitted on the tops of temples, gurudwaras and mosques, besides causing noise pollution and public nuisance, also create disharmony at times. Attempts by the administration to restrict such activities are termed as anti-religious.

Another noticeable feature is exploiting the sentiments of the respective communities in furtherance of their agenda by undertaking mass mobilisation programmes such as '*Yatras*' (*Pad*-Foot and *Rath*-vehicular chariots) taken out by known outfits and personalities and the counter calls for 'long marches' etc.; calls and counter calls of '*Bandhs*' for some cause or the other; hoisting of black, green or saffron flags and buntings on shops, houses and other buildings, wearing of identifying scarves of respective outfits/groups, holding of '*Kavi Sammelans*' named as "*Ek Sham Ram Janam Bhumi ke Naam*" and counter '*Mushiaras*' known as "*Ek Sham Babri Masjid ke Naam*" on Ayodhya issue. All such programmes add to the hardening of attitudes, mutual bitterness, intolerance and aggression towards each other. The emergence of *Senas* and various other communal and caste outfits for defending the cause of the respective communities is another pointer for alienating the Security Forces. Security Forces including the state police, Para-Military Forces of the States and the Centre and the magistracy are being targeted by physical attacks on them and also by creating hatred or friendship towards them. Whereas the U.P. P.A.C. was criticised by the Muslims in U.P., the same Force was welcomed by Muslims as their saviours in Assam during Bodo agitation. The C.R.P.F. is targeted in Jammu and Kashmir but is welcomed in U.P. and other states. The Muslims welcome Army and other C.P.M.F. during riots but ignore the State Forces. Some Hindus not only welcome the State Forces but also take care of their little comforts during deployments in riot-affected areas. These are really unwelcome signs for any civilised and harmonious society.

Earlier Congress remained the Party in power, both at the Centre and in various States, but gradually their vote-bank was eroded as various efforts were successfully made to divide the voters on communal, caste and regional considerations. These developments, though suited certain groups and parties, have not been yielding fruitful results in building a harmonious society. The politicians with their eyes on Panchayat, State Legislatures and Parliament elections, first think of their votes-banks and thus act to win the favours of their respective communities. They fully exploit the caste, communal and religious considerations of the people and seek their votes on these lines. Unfortunately the spread of education has not made any significant dent on the thought process of our people and the caste and community are their prime considerations in the electoral process. In curfew situations they go to their respective localities for distributing aids in the form of rations etc., which again creates a wedge. During Muzaffarnagar riots of 1988, the experiment of not allowing interested individuals or groups to go to localities of their community for distributing aid either in cash or in kind, paid rich dividends as donors were asked to deposit the aid items in Collectorate, which were mixed and distributed to the riot victims by the district administration. This went a long way as nobody knew the source or name of the donor, who in turn could not derive any sectarian or political mileage.

Immediate causes of the sparking of violence and outbreaks of riots could be categorised as (1) taking out processions through unconventional and non permitted routes, (2) throwing of colour, '*gulal*' etc. on persons who resent it, (3) objection to playing of music in front of mosques and other religious places, (4) presence of objectionable animals at the time of prayers – as happened in Moradabad in 1980, (5) marriages, eve-teasing and sexual relations between members of the opposite groups, (6) reaction and repercussion of riots of other places, examples being of 1977 Shia-Sunni riots of Kanpur in reaction to Lucknow sectarian riots and Delhi communal riots of 1987 as a fall out of Meerut riots, (7) cow slaughter and throwing of flesh of objectionable animals at religious places, (8) reaction to religious conversions, (9) intolerance during fairs and festivals, (10) mischievous media reporting, (11) vulgar display of religious fervour on the localities specially at the places inhabited by the members of the other community, etc. The prime indicators of recent riots are, (1) continued efforts to innovate methods including rumours to generate communal hatred and tension, (2) due to better communication and visual displays, more and more places are getting affected simultaneously as happened during *'Ayodhya Kar Sewa'* movements of 1990, 1992 and carnage at Godhra incidents that spread in Gujarat and other places in India (3) recurrence of riots with greater severity, (4) hitherto peaceful towns and villages on the outskirts of riot prone areas have been affected, (5) shaking of age old social bonds, (6) increasing violence resulting in greater loss of life and limbs, destruction of property affecting trade and employment, (7) organised group confrontations, (8) increasing intolerance and hardening of attitudes, (9) ever increasing aggressiveness aimed at rival communities and also armed attacks on and confrontation with the Security Forces, (10) organized advance preparations to foment troubles, (11) efforts to win favours and subvert the loyalties of the administration and the 'Security Forces' by playing upon their sentiments, resulting in demands for proportionate representation in police and paramilitary forces, (12) temporary migration of the minorities to safer areas, selling and buying of property including houses located in the areas of the other community and settling amongst their own groups.

Caste Conflicts and Atrocities

Through ages, it has been the prerogative of certain castes and communities to exploit certain lowly born persons in India. Before independence of our country, some social reformers did try to ameliorate their lot but they could not make noticeable impact. During freedom struggle, Mahatma Gandhi and Dr. B.R. Ambedkar fought for the cause of depressed classes and as a consequence certain constitutional provisions were made for their emancipation. The preamble of Indian Constitution resolves to secure to all its citizens: Justice, social, economic and political; equality of status and opportunity; and to promote among them all; fraternity assuring the dignity of the individual and the unity and integrity of the Nation. In furtherance of this, stringent provisions were made guaranteeing certain fundamental rights to all the citizens including abolition of untouchablity. Under Articles 341 and 342 of the Constitution, certain castes and tribes were categorised and termed as Scheduled Castes and Scheduled Tribes respectively and provisions of reservations in government services and seats in State Assemblies and Lok Sabha were made. Several laws were enacted by Parliament and State Legislatures to safeguard their interests. Serious efforts were made for implementing these laws and rules framed there under and various schemes were also launched to ensure their social and economic upliftment. Spread of education and job opportunities have helped them in realising that their future lies in breaking the age old shackles of bondage and exploitation at the hands of vested interests of upper classes. Perhaps about half a century, since our freedom, could not arouse the 'Haves' to take care of the interests of 'Have-nots', instead they are still indulging in their exploitation by committing various kinds of atrocities. These deprived classes have become aware of their rights and are no longer willing to undergo age-old exploitation and they want their amelioration at the earliest by stricter enforcement of laws. Their attempts to seek their constitutional rights have been vehemently opposed at certain places as is clearly made out from Agra and Varanasi/Chandauli caste riots.

Appeal

It is said that in a certain meeting called for maintaining harmony, when one speaker, appealed to the audience to maintain "*Bhaichara*" (Brotherhood), the other speaker retorted by saying that whereas we consider you as "*Bhais*" (brothers), you consider us as "*Chara*" (fodder). The need of the hour is to combat the divisive forces with all the powers, constitutional, legal, administrative, social and economic etc., at our command. There appears to be a dearth of universally accepted leaders, whose appeals could make the rabid communalists and exploiters to shun violence and rise above the petty considerations. We need to create a "Think Tank" involving intellectuals, social reformers, even rabid casteists and communalists, who in turn should keep on meeting during peace and riot situations to devise ways and means for permanent peace in the country. Public opinion need to be mobilised in right direction by holding peace marches, frequent seminars and *sammelans*, where common sharing of platforms be ensured, teaching the student community about maintaining harmony all the times and under all circumstances, avoid spreading the caste and communal poison and stopping of all divisive programmes and propaganda.

Mr. S.T. Hollins, the then U.P. Police chief (I.G.P.) in his annual report for year 1934 sent to U.P. Government, wrote, "there were no less than 60 communal riots during the year as compared with 9 during 1933. The immense increase in riots of this nature gives much food for thought. In my opinion communal tension is much more acute now than it was when I first joined the service in 1902. I think the finest service the leaders of the present day can render to their country is to persuade their co-religionists to adopt a more conciliatory and forbearing attitude towards those who are not of the same religious persuation as themselves." What shall we say now after holocaust of 1990 and 1992 riots. Taslima Nasrin's "*Lajja*" written after bloody reaction in Bangladesh following Ayodhya riots in India was proscribed and she is in exile. Is this the price one has to pay for being humane?

In 1904, in his unique tribute to India (undivided), famous poet Sir Allama Iqbal expressed:-

"मजहब नहीं सिखाता, आपस में बैर रखना।
हिन्दी हैं हम, वतन हैं हिन्दोस्ताँ हमारा"।।

" Religion does not teach nurturing of mutual hatred; we are Indians and India is our motherland."

Why are we negating our own Indian philosophy of "बसुधैव कुटुम्बकम्" (the whole universe is one family)? During my service, particularly while dealing with riots, I have seen the sufferings of innocent men, women and children of all sections, with no water, food or milk during riots and curfew, no shelter above their heads because their dwellings were burnt and destroyed, no survivors in families as they were killed and no takers of dead bodies for last rites, no body to take care of the injured, neighbours willing to help but forced to desist from doing so. Will this lead us to a united, prosperous and secular India so that we become a world power? Certainly not. Let us not forget the disintegration of India, Pakistan and Ugoslavia on ethnic and other grounds. My appeal to all my fellow country men/ women will be to maintain everlasting peace because, our Nation is precious and let us defend it by shunning violence and riots. Remember, "who dies if India lives and who lives if India dies?" Let us preserve peace to preserve India.

INDEX

T

U

V